✓ S0-CCE-355

# How to Succeed in Law School

## Second Edition

**Gary A. Munneke, J.D.**
**Pace University School of Law**

**BARRON'S**

Copyright © 1994 by Barron's Educational Series, Inc.
Prior edition copyright © 1989

All rights reserved.
No part of this book may be reproduced in any form,
by photostat, microfilm, xerography, or any other means,
or incorporated into any information retrieval system,
electronic or mechanical, without the written permission
of the copyright owner.

*All inquiries should be addressed to:*
Barron's Educational Series, Inc.
250 Wireless Boulevard
Hauppauge, New York 11788

International Standard Book No. 0-8120-1449-9

Library of Congress Catalog Card No. 94-71804

PRINTED IN THE UNITED STATES OF AMERICA

7   8800   987654

# Acknowledgments

I wish to thank law students beyond count who have contributed their insights to my perspective on law school, but especially Sharon, Terry, and Ann. I also want to thank my former colleague Kathy Turezyn, who worked with me to develop many of the sample exam questions. I thank Betty Donovan and Jennifer Chin for their work in typing this manuscript. Finally, I acknowledge the thinking of Brian Siegel, whose thoughts have been incorporated in this edition.

—Gary A. Munneke, J.D.

**The author gratefully acknowledges the following sources:**

*Legalines; Torts, Adaptable to Materials by Prosser.* Copyright © 1988 by Harcourt Brace Legal & Professional Publications, Inc. Reprinted with permission of the publisher.

*Gilbert Law Summaries: Torts* by Marc A. Franklin, Twentieth Edition. Copyright © 1993 by Harcourt Brace Legal & Professional Publications, Inc. Reprinted with permission of the publisher.

*Torts in a Nutshell: Injuries to Persons and Property,* 1977 by Edward J. Kionka. Reprinted with permission of the West Publishing Company, St. Paul, Minnesota.

"Intentional Interference with the Person," reprinted from *Prosser & Keeton on Torts,* Fifth edition, 1984, with permission of the West Publishing Company, St. Paul, Minnesota.

*Cases and Materials on Torts,* 8th Edition, by William L. Prosser, John W. Wade, and Victor E. Schwartz. Foundation Press, New York, 1988.

Sample Multiple Choice Exam Questions reprinted with permission of Professor Richard Walck, Williamsburg, Virginia.

*Restatement of the Law, 2nd, Torts,* copyright © 1964 by the American Law Institute. Reprinted with the permission of The American Law Institute.

# Table of Contents

# About the Author

Gary A. Munneke is a professor at Pace University School of Law in White Plains, New York. He is the author of numerous books and articles on the legal profession and legal education, including the areas of career planning and placement, as well as lawyer recruitment and training. These publications include: *The Legal Career Guide, Careers in Law, Opportunities in Law Careers, Your New Lawyer, Non-Legal Careers for Lawyers,* and *Materials and Cases on Law Practice Management.* He has spoken at numerous programs for lawyers, law students, and prelaw students, and conducts specialized training for entering law students on how to succeed in law school.

Professor Munneke is a member of the Texas and Pennsylvania bars, and is active in the American Bar Association where he serves as chair of the Law Practice Management Publishing Board. He has served on the editorial boards of *Legal Economics* and *Barrister* magazines, as a member of the Task Force on the Role of the Lawyer in the 1980s, and as president and research chair of the National Association for Law Placement. He has been recognized as a fellow of the American Bar Foundation, and by *Who's Who in American Law.* Before coming to Pace, where he teaches Torts, Professional Responsibility and Law Practice Management, Professor Munneke was a member of the faculty at Widener University School of Law and assistant dean at the University of Texas School of Law where he received his J.D. in 1973.

# CHAPTER 1
# What Is Success?

## A. Introduction

Because this book is about how to succeed in law school, a good starting point might be to try to define success. How you define that elusive term may well determine whether or not you achieve it in law school, in your career, and in life. Whereas much of this book addresses the nuts and bolts of maximizing your potential in the legal education process, before you take the time to look at the specifics, consider briefly the bigger picture.

In 1994, over 800,000 people in the United States call themselves lawyers. Of these, slightly over half are engaged in the private practice of law. They provide legal services for individual and institutional clients. All the rest work in a wide variety of roles in corporations, government agencies, education, private associations, the military, and entrepreneurial activities. Their work is as varied as human endeavor itself. While the lawyer population is concentrated most heavily in large urban and metropolitan areas, lawyers live and work almost everywhere.

Most readers will have heard or read that the United States today has more lawyers than any society in history. Many will have heard somewhere that all these lawyers represent a colossal waste of intellectual talent, or that our country is "overlawyered" already. Such views ignore the reality that the institutions of a complex, pluralistic, rights-oriented society require lawyers in order to function. Whether or not society benefits from so many lawyers, those who enter the legal profession cannot escape the consequences of these numbers. Law practice is extremely competitive, and many lawyers at some point in their careers will not practice law. For someone just starting law school, the range of opportunities after graduation is heavily influenced by law school performance.

## B. How You Define Success

Take a few minutes to create a fantasy of your perfect job. Imagine yourself at that point in your career where you have achieved all the goals you have set for yourself by undertaking a legal education. What kind of work will you be doing? For whom will you work? What services will you provide? In what kind of organization will you work? What will be your role? Where will you be? What will your lifestyle be like? When you look back over your life, what will you tell people were your accomplishments? When you die, what will they say at your funeral?

Although you may not be able to know with certainty where life's crooked road will take you, you can and should imagine where you would like it to go. Store your fantasy in a pocket in your mind. Pull it out when times get tough. Change it when times change. Run with it when time flies. Implicit in this fantasy should be your own definition of success. That definition will determine your perception of success in law school as well as life. There are several predominant views on law school success, and it may help you to look at those now.

Will you consider yourself a success in law school if you graduate at the top of your class? If this is the criterion, then there is little hope for most entering law students. With 175 law schools there can be only 175 valedictorians. If there are 40,000 annual law school graduates, only 4,000 can graduate in the top 10 percent of their class. Many people who choose to go to law school are competitive by nature. For them it is the race that counts. Like an Olympic gold medalist, there is no point in aspiring to attain second place. These students often have pursued life as a series of competitions with winning as the ultimate objective. They will pursue their careers with the same ardor, seeking victory in every case, and defining success as a win-loss record.

If you must win every battle in every war to consider yourself successful, the chances are good that you will be doomed to failure, in law as well as life. In this profession, victory is seldom total or defeat ultimate. You will win some, lose some, and settle some on the courthouse steps. Your competitive nature can help you if you maintain some perspective.

Do you define success as finishing law school? Perhaps you are just thankful to have been accepted. Maybe school has always been a struggle for you, and you have fought and clawed every step of the way against formidable odds and slim probabilities. You might be the first in your family to attend law school, or even college. English may be a second language for you. Your resources may be so limited that you have had to work and scrape to put yourself through school. You may have personal or family problems that get in the way of accomplishing what you might without these impediments. For you, simply graduating may be the end of your dream.

If you define success as this sort of uphill battle, you should remember not to set your sights too low. You cannot let your problems become your excuse. And you cannot let graduation become the culmination of your search for success.

Do you define success as getting the job you want when law school is over? Frequently, people in this group place too much of their identity on one outcome. They set themselves up for failure by establishing goals based on vague, ill-considered perceptions of what lawyers do or how much money they make. Sometimes these students are seeking shortcuts to material goals; sometimes their interests are defined by a political, social, or moral agenda for which law is a vehicle.

These students need to keep an open mind. They need to realize that opportunities other than those they perceived when they entered law school may ultimately serve them better. They need to have alternatives if their first choices fail to materialize.

Do you define success as learning? In many respects, this is a sensible approach to law school because it places success in the context of developing the professional skills and obtaining the legal knowledge to become a competent lawyer. Here, too, lie pitfalls for the unwary.

In the most extreme form, you may adopt learning itself as your goal and become a professional student. If you are lucky, you will get a job as a law professor and be paid for your study. If you are unlucky, you simply may be considered a dilettante by friends and colleagues. In the less extreme form, you may find practice frustrating, never having time to fully research any subject or keep up with changes in the law or reflect about what the law ought to be. If you define success in this way, you will need to let your pragmatic side out from time to time.

Do you define success in terms of personal happiness? Perhaps law school and a legal career are vehicles for financing or creating the lifestyle you want. It is clear that a career in law can provide a vehicle for attaining a good lifestyle, and that it can afford in the long run great personal and professional satisfaction.

Although in one sense all of us want to be happy, some people confuse long-term satisfaction with short-term gratification. For them, happiness means having fun. Unfortunately, some people never learn to delay gratification. They want the best of everything; they want it all; they want it now. They forget that law school is not always fun, and practice is frequently not easy. Having a good time can stand in the way of doing what you have to do. On the other end of the spectrum are those individuals who seek happiness but forestall satisfaction forever. For these puritans, the good life is always just around the corner.

Do you define success in terms of recognition? You may have relied upon pats on the back and the encouragement of friends and loved ones to let you know that you have done a good job. Your wall may be covered with certificates and awards that demonstrate your success. Your quest for such tangible acknowledgments of your efforts may have become the dominant, motivating force in your life.

Unfortunately, in law school the pats on the back are all too few. And after graduation, you may find that fame is frequently fickle and elusive. In the practice of law, you may labor long in the vineyards without being recognized for the quality of your wine.

## C. Everyone Is Unique

You can help yourself in law school by defining success in a way that is consistent with your goals in life, flexible enough to bend with the winds of change, and realistic enough to let you feel good about yourself for what you accomplish.

The purpose of presenting these scenarios is not to discourage or depress. It is rather to demonstrate that there are many ways to define success, and that each has inherent dangers. Author Adele Scheele, in a 1979 book, *Skills for Success,* suggested that successful people possess a battery of skills that help them achieve their goals. Scheele's research on lawyers found that many of the individuals who were described by their peers as "successful" referred to their good fortune as "being in the right place at the right time." Scheele hypothesized that it was more than luck, and that being in the right place at the right time represented a set of quantifiable skills. This book proceeds on the assumption that success is not a matter of fate, but a complex and imprecise commodity involving specific skills that can be taught. Whereas it is ultimately subjective, and never total, success can be achieved if you know how to go about it.

This book contains eight chapters. Chapter 2 discusses important considerations in choosing a law school. Chapter 3 provides an overview of the law school experience. It will help you to know what to expect and how to cope. Chapter 4 deals with the study of law. It will help you to manage the learning process. Chapter 5 addresses the examination process, including both studying and taking tests. It will help you to maximize your performance on these instruments. Chapter 6 covers law school after the first year. It will help you to derive all the benefit you can from your legal education. Chapter 7 offers some specific advice to women, students of color, and physically challenged students, who represent student populations with unique concerns. Chapter 8 examines legal education after the first year, and offers insights into ways to maximize success in the upper class years. If these problems apply to you, the chapter will include suggestions on how to overcome them. Chapter 9 looks beyond law school to your career as a lawyer. It will return again to the issue of success, and offer some parting thoughts to abide you on your journey. Throughout the text, you will find specific examples and hints to help you to deal with the practicalities and uncertainties of law school.

## D. Something Different

The very fact that you have picked up this book suggests that you are entering law school with at least a mild degree of trepidation. You probably have been inundated with horror stories from family, friends, prelaw advisors, and newspaper articles. You may have been warned that law school is "unlike anything you have ever done before." This unsettling pronouncement implies that a law school is like some impenetrable swamp, pocked with quicksand and populated by vile creatures lying in wait to devour the hapless traveler.

Remember: 40,000 of us every year come out alive and well on the other side. It may help to look back on some of the other barriers in your educational life.

When your mom bundled you off to kindergarten, she admonished you, "This is school. It's different from anything you have ever done before." And when you left elementary school to go to junior high, she reminded you, "This year you have to change classes every period. It's going to be different from anything you have ever done before." Then you went away to college, and if you can think back to that eventful day, your car was packed to capacity with all your earthly belongings and whatever else you could sneak out of the house. Remember mom and dad on the porch waving, as they told you once again, "You're on your own now, Sandra. Nobody to tell you what to do; nobody to wake you up. This is different from anything you have ever done before." Surprisingly, miraculously, you survived all those previous transitions. Those of you who have worked, gone to graduate school, served in the military, or gotten married could cite other experiences different from anything you have ever done before.

The point of all this is that you survived those other transitions in life, and you can survive this one. In fact, one of the reasons you will succeed in law school is that you have learned how to handle things you have never done before. You bring with you to law school a unique set of skills and abilities that have helped you to succeed before. When you understand how law school works and what you need to do, you can succeed here, too.

# CHAPTER 2
# Choosing a Law School

## A. The Right School for You

It is axiomatic to say that every law school applicant should strive to choose the best possible law school for him or her. Many readers will have spent much of the past year applying to law schools and trying to make the "right" decision. Even casual reflection should confirm the obvious—there is no single best choice for every person. As individuals we are diverse and heterogeneous, and our needs vary considerably.

Many applicants do not stop to think that success in law school starts long before they actually enroll; success may be influenced dramatically by their choice of school. Some, perhaps on the assumption that law schools are basically interchangeable, simply select the most prestigious school (based on some magazine survey). The quality of the educational program and the reputation of the institution are definitely factors to consider, but they are not the only factors. Even among superficially similar law schools, a closer look will indicate that each has its own personality. If you have ever spent time around identical twins, you probably learned that they are not all that identical. It is the same with law schools.

Your decision about which law school to attend should focus on your own unique needs as a student. If you can find a good fit for your personality, study habits, competitiveness, interests, and values, you will be a happier law student. And if you are a happy law student, you will probably be a good law student.

How many unhappy law students are dissatisfied with law school itself, and how many are dissatisfied with the law school they attend? Who knows? It is very likely, however, that at least some of the discontented students would have fared better in a different environment.

If you discover that you are not satisfied with your choice of law schools, think about changing schools before changing careers. Almost all schools accept a small number of transfer students after their first year; many schools accept visiting students (who graduate from their "home" school) for up to one year of study. A few schools offer foreign study programs (see p. 149) that could provide respite from an uncomfortable situation.

Competition for transfer seats is generally intense. Since law schools usually admit no more transfer students than the number they have lost from the previous year's first year class, and since the number of applicants is often much greater than the number of available seats, academic excellence is often a prerequisite for acceptance as a transfer student.

The downside of transferring is that transfer students walk into a situation where friendships among classmates have been made, law reviews and moot court teams have been selected, and adjustment to law school has been completed. Transfer students may feel isolated; they may lose academic credit; they may have difficulty explaining the change when they go to job interviews. This is not a decision to be made lightly, but for some students transferring or visiting at another school may be a viable option. It is undoubtedly easier to make a choice you can live with at the outset than to undo a bad choice later. Analogies to marriage immediately come to mind.

## B. Your Law School

What factors contribute to making your law school unique? Although it is easy to make generalizations about the law school experience, based upon similarities in legal education throughout the United States, there are some important differences among law schools also. Your law school may have special traditions, rules, and other elements that make it different from the prototypical law school described here.

One issue that tends to have a disparate impact on law schools is prestige. Sometimes these differences in prestige are articulated euphemistically as "national," "regional," and "local." These distinctions are basically meaningless, and usually confusing. There are between 10 and 15 genuinely "elite" law schools that are widely recognized as most prestigious. There are probably 20 to 30 other law schools that think of themselves as, and are considered in some circles to be, comparable to those in the first group.

A third group of one hundred or more schools have not attained or do not aspire to the inner circle. These include many newer schools, state law schools whose primary mission is serving the population of their state, established law schools whose resources limit their objectives, and law schools where internal considerations (e.g., disputes with a central university administration, faculty infighting) have held back the school's development.

In many larger cities, there are two or more law schools. Within the area, there is probably a pecking order of prestige, influencing each school's ability to attract students. New schools, and older schools with checkered histories in the legal community, may not receive the recognition that the quality of their educational programs merit .

A few schools comprise a fourth group whose institutions provide a minimal quality of education. They lack adequate resources to do more than train lawyers for a purely local practice. These schools barely meet American Bar Association accreditation standards and, sometimes exist under the cloud of losing ABA approval. Fortunately, only a handful of accredited schools fall into this category.

A fifth group of schools includes those that lack national ABA accreditation and are approved only in the state where they operate. The graduates of these schools usually can sit for the bar examination only in the state where they went to school. These institutions tend to be the least prestigious in the law school world.

Prestige generally is not a matter of discrete categories, but rather a fuzzy continuum that varies considerably depending upon the source. The relative prestige of the school, as perceived by those within the law school itself, has an impact on perceptions and attitudes within the law school community. Students at the most elite law schools may be rather smug; all others carry with them inferiority complexes of varying degrees. Your success in law school will depend in part upon your ability to maintain a positive attitude about yourself and your school, regardless of where you might be.

## C . Setting

Another differentiating characteristic among law schools is the law school setting. As stated previously, the nation's largest metropolitan areas have several law schools, and these law schools vary from purely urban settings to suburban ones. Other law schools may be found in smaller cities, including many state capitals. Still other schools are located in small towns outside any major population center. These differences in environment have significant impact on the individual school's culture. For instance, urban campuses tend to attract more diverse student bodies than do suburban schools. The availability of legal employers to provide part-time jobs for law students may vary considerably. For instance, law schools located in seats of government will have access to more employment positions in the public sector.

## D. Day Versus Evening School

A final differentiation is between schools that have part-time or evening programs and those that do not. Part-time students usually work during the day at full-time jobs and go to law school at night. Evening students fall into two basic groups: those who must work full-time in order to attend school, and older students returning to school as part of a mid-career adjustment. The backgrounds, interests, needs, and attitudes of evening students differ from their full-time counterparts. Thus, law schools with day and evening programs possess two distinct subcultures.

There may be other differences in law schools as well. Is your school state supported or private? Does the school have special course concentrations or programs? Does the faculty view the school's mission as a broad educational one, preparing its graduates for the practice of law, or teaching students enough law to pass the bar exam? Although legal education may be similar wherever you are, every institution is unique.

In order to succeed in law school, you should understand the unique setting of your particular school. Take some time to learn its strengths, weaknesses, and educational eccentricities. Find out what you need to do to benefit personally from your school's educational program.

CHAPTER **3**

# Understanding the Law School Experience

## A. The Law School Calendar

No two people are the same. A key to your success will be your ability to channel the skills you already have into a new educational program, while building new skills that will serve you in the future as a lawyer. It may help you to understand what is happening during the first year of law school by looking at the law school calendar. Although every law school is slightly different from all the others, in many respects they are all much the same. Virtually every law school in the United States models its curriculum, particularly in the first year, after the Socratic system promulgated at Harvard Law School in the 1870s. Although legal education has evolved in the past century, the general comments in this chapter will be substantially descriptive of your law school experience regardless of where you go to school.

### 1. Orientation

Law school starts with orientation. Orientation is designed to introduce you to the law school community (and some would say to lull you into a false sense of security about the upcoming ten months). The first step is check-in. Check-in is run by the Admissions Office, and you will be greeted by the smiling countenance of the admissions officer who recruited you or dealt with you during the admissions process. The Admissions Office will want to make sure that you have paid your tuition, that your financial aid is in order, and that your registration is complete. Depending on how check-in is organized, you may or may not have to wait in a long line. If the line is long, it generally portends three to four years of the same thing.

After checking in, and grabbing a cup of hot coffee, you will proceed to an auditorium where you will be subjected to a series of speeches you will not remember. You will hear from the dean, some associate deans, assistant deans, the financial aid officer, placement director, student bar president, law review editor, moot court board chair, head of security, and other administrators and students too numerous to name. They will all tell you how glad they are to see you, how talented you all are, and how their doors will always be open. You will never see most of them again. While most schools have abandoned the tactic, a few of them may still use the old "Look to the right of you; look to the left of you; one of you won't be here next August." The truth is, the 90–95 percent of those who enter law school eventually will graduate.

After this convocation, you may be given a tour of the facilities, including the law library, by engaging upperclass students just dying to tell you what law school is "really like." You also may be solicited by various student organizations; they will all be around and still anxious for your membership after the first year.

One of your first lessons in law school will be to separate the wheat from the chaff. Find out where the assignments are posted. Find out how you can sign up for a locker. Learn to recognize The Dean by sight. (There are many deans, but only one Dean.)

At many schools, class assignments for the first day are posted prior to orientation. An assignment sheet for each class will also tell you what books to buy for the course so you can go to the law school bookstore and pick up your books before the crowds arrive. Don't wait until school has started to obtain your books and start reading. For a checklist of what to do orientation day, see Orientation Checklist on page 13.

### 2. First Classes

Unlike in undergraduate school, the first classes in law school are generally real classes. The professor may simply walk in and call on a student for the first case. She may give a short speech on what will be expected of you in her course before turning to the cases. Or she may provide a background lecture for most of the first hour. It is likely that the professor will not simply say, "Hello, I'm Professor Jones.

## Orientation Checklist

_____ Admissions

     _____ College transcripts (if needed)

     _____ Identification

_____ Financial aid (if applicable)

_____ Registrar — class schedule

_____ Bursar — bring checkbook if not prepaid

_____ Course assignments

_____ Bookstore

_____ Parking sticker

_____ Locker

_____ ID photo

_____ Law school tour

_____ Find out who is "The Dean"

_____ Nearby food

_____ Library carrel (if available)


Notes:

Your assignment for Tuesday will be to read the first 30 pages in the book. I'll see you Tuesday." During the first class, the professor may present certain special rules such as the maximum number of class cuts you are allowed, the number of times you may be unprepared before being dropped from the course, what the final exam will be like, what her office hours will be, what outside materials (hornbooks, treatises, etc.) you should read. Such information is important to know.

Such works as *One L* and *The Paper Chase* probably have instilled a sense of fear in the minds of many beginning law students. In reality, not all law professors are as foreboding and intimidating as Professor Kingsfield, although the terror and alienation described there is very accurate.

You will find yourself in a lecture hall with roughly one hundred more or less equally frightened souls. Your sense of anonymity and privacy will be invaded by the seemingly all-knowing professor armed with a seating chart and an uncanny ability to identify the least prepared student in the class to discuss the case at hand.

During the first week of classes, you will learn the ground rules. Let there be no doubt about it: this is the lions versus the Christians, and regardless of your religious affiliation, you and your classmates are the Christians.

Also, during the first week, you will be introduced to the subject matter to be covered in each course, the professor's unique philosophy of legal education, a new language called legalese, and those ponderous, pictureless tomes called casebooks.

You will also begin to get acquainted with your fellow law students. You may meet a few individuals whom you come to know as real people. Most of your classmates will fall into one of two groups: the nameless faces who fill the classroom and the ones who, by virtue of having been called on or volunteered to speak in class, are identified by name (as in "Mr. Simon, who sits in the first row in Torts"). Custom dictates that you use last names to identify students (as in "Ms. Miller" or "Mr. Musser") and you refer to the teacher as "Professor" or "Dean" as appropriate.

You may encounter some upperclass students who offer with a certain patronizing smugness to teach you the tricks of the trade. A healthy sense of skepticism about the value or motives of such advice is a good sign that you will eventually become a successful lawyer.

### 3. Routine

After the first week of classes, you will begin to establish a pattern in each course, and a timetable for your entire life. The reading will average between 10 and 30 pages per night, per class. You may find that the progress in some of the classes is painfully slow, with the professor covering only a portion of the assigned reading each time. Some classes may move along at an almost military clip of three to four cases per class, no matter what. During the first few weeks, you will find yourself spending an inordinate amount of time "briefing" cases (see Chapter 4), attempting to fathom the classroom discussion, and wondering secretly if someone in the admissions office hadn't screwed up sending you an acceptance letter. You will wonder with increasing frequency whether you screwed up in deciding to come to law school. During this phase of school, you may wonder why everyone else in the class but you seems to know what is going on.

When I was in law school, there was a guy named Holtzman, and although Holtzman was only 3 or 4 years older than most of the rest of us, it seemed that in every class he had some personal experience relating to the case. If the case involved shoes, he had been in the shoe business; if the case involved clothes, he had been in the clothing business; if the case involved doctors, he had been in the medical business.

Other students will amaze you with their seeming ability to converse freely with the professor in legalese, whereas you find yourself stuck at the "Bonjour, Jean" stage. But you will derive hope from the fact that some students' comments will seem totally inane to you, reassuring you that you must be smarter than *someone* in the class. And you will find a wicked satisfaction in seeing a handful of students whose hands are always in the air given their comeuppance by the professor. In every class, there will be at least one individual who, no matter how bloodied by the fray, will keep coming back for more. A pack psychology will come to dominate the class and seek to drive out the weak or the deviant. By mid-semester, the fear of embarrassment in front of the class will inhibit all but the most fearless souls from making rash statements. This mentality is typified by graffito on a bathroom stall at one law school: "After the sixth week of class, if you don't know who the class jerk is, it's you."

These pressures to conform may dissuade some students from ever participating in class discussions unless specifically required to do so by the professor. By laughing at a fellow student, you help to create an environment where one day others may laugh at you.

As the semester wears on, the professor comes to be viewed not so much as a god, but as a common enemy. You learn that the classroom routine is a game the teacher always wins. You learn that the stupidest answers have some value, and you begin to recognize that even the most articulate students really don't know much more than you do. When you come to this realization, you will have reached another milestone in your law school journey.

### 4. The Wall

Somewhere between the tenth and twelfth week of classes you will "hit the wall." It is during this period that some students actually drop out of school; virtually every student at least contemplates that possibility. By this time in the semester, your work is piling up, final exams are just around the corner, and you still don't have a clue what you need to know. At this point, when your psychological and physical resources are drained, you will wonder if you can possibly survive for two and a half or three and a half more years. It is critical when you "hit the wall" to press on. It may help during this period to talk to a sympathetic professor, mentor, or counselor. Family and loved ones, who up until now have been totally supportive, will seem to become part of the problem. Prelaw school friends may find that you have changed, and you may find yourself increasingly irritated that they never "see the issue."

### 5. Panic

By about the thirteenth week of the semester, you will have no time to worry about such self-indulgent psychological concerns, because finals will be upon you. Some professors, in what is variously perceived as a last-minute attempt to catch up with the syllabus or a final effort to break your backs, will increase the reading assignments to two or three times what they were at the beginning of the semester. A full-scale panic attack may threaten to debilitate you before the first test. Somehow, you will survive.

### *6. First Semester Finals*

At last, final examinations will arrive. As a rule, law school exams average one hour of exam for each credit hour of class. The amount of material you will have to study will be immense (see Chapter 5). Whole parts of some courses may be incomprehensible when you go back to review them. When you walk out of these exams, your head will feel like Evander Holyfield used it as a punching bag. You will have no idea how well you did, but if you thought the test was easy, you probably missed something really big.

### *7. Semester Break*

Semester break is the time when you regroup. Immediately after your last exam, your impulse will be to engage in the most hedonistic activity possible. Many will actually succumb to this impulse. Next, you will sleep for two days. Then, you will engage in mindless activity such as watching soap operas or football games, reading trashy novels, attending holiday parties, or "vegging out" with your family. If you are an evening student, you may not have the luxury of all of this R & R. However, to the extent possible, you should try to get away from both school and work for a while.

Toward the end of semester break, you will begin to think about law school again. You may do some reading for class. You may reflect about how you will avoid making the same mistakes you did the first semester. You will rush madly to clear up loose ends in your personal life, in order to give yourself time to devote your full attention to law school.

### *8. Renewed Hope*

The second semester is better in some ways, and worse in others, than the first semester. It is better in that you now know the ropes. You have a better picture of what to expect. You have a clearer idea of what it will take to succeed. On the other hand, the work load will pick up even more. The professors will take off at the same pace they ended the previous semester. In addition, at many schools a required moot court problem will swallow the bulk of your free time.

### *9. The January Blues*

During January (and sometimes February or March) first semester grades will be posted. The wait for grades may be agonizing. The actual knowledge of your grades may be worse. Most students are disappointed in some or all of their marks. You learn how fast the track really is. Unfortunately, many students do not handle this experience well. They go into a depression they do not escape until after the bar exam. Although there is no grade for it, your grade point average may depend on your ability to bounce back psychologically and to learn from this experience.

### *10. Falling Behind*

In all but the warmest climates, the arrival of spring will bring the last great temptation of the school year. When the flowers begin to bloom, and warm winds touch the land, sitting in a law school classroom will not be your first choice of activities. Spring break may help, but chances are good that you will fall behind in your reading and studying. If you are not careful you could find yourself in the proverbial hot water.

### *11. The Mad Rush*

As March dissolves into April, you will once again find yourself staring at final exams. If you have been diligent you will simply experience anxiety about finishing the year on a high note; if you find yourself hopelessly behind your schedule, you will be working feverishly to catch up. The last weeks of school will pass quickly, and your first year will be almost over.

### *12. Finals Again*

Final exams in the spring probably will not seem as daunting. The experience will be the same as in the fall, but this time you will be more prepared for it mentally. The amount of work you cover in these exams will be more prodigious than in the fall. But the skills you have developed during the course of the year will make the load seem more manageable. This time, when finals are over, you will just go home, have dinner with friends, and go on about your business.

Over a period of 36 weeks, more or less, you will have been transformed from an ordinary person into a budding lawyer. Whether you want it or not, like it or not, or need it or not, you will never be the same again. The process is in some ways like marine boot camp, taking apart whatever you were before you arrived and rebuilding it into a new person.

Whatever other criticisms of law school one might make, it certainly cannot be said that the program does not work. The purpose of this book is not to debate the merits of our system of legal education. It is to help you to deal with the process as it exists.

## B. Law School Courses

The curriculum at most American law schools is similar. In fact, the first year law school curriculum has not changed appreciably in the past one hundred years. At the same time, there are minor variations in course offerings from school to school, reflecting differences in educational philosophy and institutional tradition.

Most law school courses are offered as 2-, 3-, or 4-semester-hour courses. Full-time first year students take 5 or 6 courses for a total of 15–16 credit hours; part-time students generally take 1 or 2 fewer courses and 10–11 hours. At some schools, grades are based on an entire year's work for 4- to 6-hour courses. You will study some, if not all, of the courses described below during the first year of law school. Some schools will defer certain courses until the second year or not require them at all.

### 1. Torts

The word tort comes from an old French term meaning wrong. Torts as a law school subject area refers to a series of legal actions and remedies against wrongdoers for injuries sustained. Torts fall into three broad groups: *intentional torts* where an actor intends conduct that causes injury to another; *negligent torts* where an actor owing a duty to act with reasonable care toward another breaches that duty and causes injury resulting in damages; and *strict liability torts* where an actor causes injury to another without fault or intent but is held liable for policy reasons. You will study a number of distinct tort actions, including assault, battery, false imprisonment, and intentional infliction of emotional distress; negligence actions; misrepresentation; defamation; products liability; and privacy. Most of the examples presented in this book are taken from tort cases.

### 2. Property

The Property course deals with the rights associated with the ownership of property. In the beginning of the course you will probably discuss the origins of property rights in Anglo-American law. You will study such tantalizing questions as who owns the rights to the meteorite: the farmer in whose field it fell or the guy walking down the road who saw it fall? Some of us are still trying to figure that one out. A small portion of the course is devoted to the law of personal property, but the bulk of the year will involve issues relating to real property, or land. In the first semester, you will devote considerable time to basic concepts such as estates in land, transferability of land, and title. Some time during the year you will learn about future interests, those medieval devices for controlling the ownership of land beyond the life of the owner. In the second semester, you will deal with more modern concepts such as easements, zoning, and land use planning.

### 3. Contracts

Contracts involves the study of the body of law governing the making and breaking of agreements. You will learn what it takes to create a binding contract with another party. You will spend considerable time discussing what happens when one of the parties breaks its promises, or breaches the contract. You will learn about liquidated damages, specific performance, express and implied warranties, and unilateral contracts. Much of the course will deal with the development of contracts in the commercial setting, including the "battle of forms" and substitution of statutory law in the form of the Uniform Commercial Code for the common law in many situations.

### 4. Civil Procedure

Civil Procedure refers to the rules by which the civil courts operate. Most Civ Pro instructors utilize the Federal Rules of Civil Procedure in teaching their courses. Some of the course may touch upon historical material, such as the evolution of the English forms of action into the rules of procedure of today. Most of your time will be spent looking at such concepts as jurisdiction (including subject matter, personal, and diversity), standing, discovery, pleading, appeal, summary judgments, and numerous other provisions of the Rules. A substantial part of the course will address the "Erie problem." The case of *Erie Railroad v. Tompkins* held that the federal courts, while applying federal procedural rules, must apply the substantive common law of the state. The ripples from this seemingly simple rule have extended far beyond the original case and have engrossed generations of judges, law professors, legal writers, and students (perhaps "engrossed" is too strong a word for the student response).

### 5. Constitutional Law

Many law schools require Constitutional Law during the first year. As the name suggests, Con Law deals with the enforcement of rights and duties established under the United States Constitution. Because there are so many constitutional issues, no two professors will emphasize exactly the same topics. You will look at some fundamental problems such as jurisdiction and standing, separation of powers, the commerce clause, and the privileges and immunities clause. You will deal with cases arising under the first, fifth and fourteenth amendments, as well as others. Perhaps most importantly, you will study the decision-making process in the United States Supreme Court from Chief Justice Marshall's power grab of judicial review in *Marbury v. Madison* to Chief Justice Rehnquist's reshaping the direction of the Court in the 1980s.

### 6. Criminal Law

Criminal Law is the law of crimes. For a good portion of this course, you will grapple with concepts such as intent, mens rea, and lesser included offenses. You will learn the basic elements of crimes you have known about all your life, and a few you have never heard of before. You will study such issues as the right to trial by jury, double jeopardy, the state's burden of proof, and conspiracy.

### 7. Professional Responsibility

Although most law schools offer Professional Responsibility during the last year of law school, some require it during the second year, and a few the first. Professional Responsibility deals with the ethical obligations of the lawyer in representing clients. A few of the subjects you will cover in this course are: lawyer/client confidentiality, conflicts of interest, legal fees, advertising and solicitation of business, fitness to practice law, lawyer discipline, and candor to the tribunal. In a broader sense, however, professional responsibility addresses the role of the legal profession in society. What is a lawyer anyway? Are there limits on his or her conduct? Is law a business, a profession, or both? What is the role of the bar association? Can one be a good lawyer and a good person at the same time?

### 8. Legal Writing

At every law school, there is a course known by a variety of names, but with a general aim of teaching you how to conduct legal research, draft legal briefs and memoranda, prepare and make oral arguments, and gain an understanding of a legal system. These courses are often much maligned by first year students, but revered by lawyers who come to know the value of the skills they learned in that course. Legal Writing frequently requires a time commitment out of proportion with the amount of credit received. An important consideration during the course of the school year will be your ability to allocate time to Legal Writing in accordance with its relative importance and credit weight, and not to set aside work in other classes for research, writing, and advocacy projects.

## C. The Professors

Law students develop a special relationship with their first year teachers. It is not uncommon to experience a love/hate relationship with these professors. Later in law school you will wonder how you placed some of these individuals on such high pedestals. During the first semester of law school they will be like gods: not necessarily in their perfection of appearance, but in their seeming knowledge and omnipotence.

Many of those who become law teachers attained their positions by having done very well academically in law school. Additionally, many of them enter the profession after having served as judicial clerks for the United States Supreme Court or other prestigious tribunals. Increasingly, today, law teachers have some experience in the practice of law. They come from large law firms, corporations, and government agencies. All of them have made an affirmative decision to pursue a career in education, rather than one in a traditional area of law practice. Professors who worked in large law firms or possess more than a few years of experience probably have taken a considerable cut in pay to enter the teaching field. Although law professors as a group have a higher median income than the average of all lawyers, they probably could make more money doing something else.

Law professors come in all sizes and shapes. It is difficult and somewhat risky to generalize about any diverse group of individuals. However, anyone who has attended law school will recognize the following few basic types:

*Old School*—The Old School professor believes in applying the Socratic method the way Dean Langdell must have intended. This professor thinks the only thing unrealistic about Professor Kingsfield in *The Paper Chase* is that Kingsfield was just too soft. My own Contracts professor was from the Old School. The only affirmative statement he made the entire year was, "Hello, my name is Professor Loisieux." He genuinely believed that it is necessary to reduce you to a quivering mound of jelly in order to strip away the last vestiges of non-legal thinking before inculcating that elusive commodity, the ability to "think like a lawyer."

*The Sadist*—This variation of the Old School professor reduces you to a blithering idiot because it's fun. Having been beaten up by neighborhood bullies as a child, the Sadist now wreaks revenge on unsuspecting law students by brutalizing them into submission. It may be difficult to distinguish between these two professors while you are in school, but, in later years, Old School will turn out to be a truly nice person.

*Your Buddy*—This professor wants to be everybody's friend. She doesn't want to be on a pedestal, but to party with you, hang out with you, and talk law with you. It is easy to forget that Your Buddy will not be sitting in the exam room with you, sweating out grades with you, or going through job interviews with you.

*The Crit*—At some schools, you may encounter adherents of the critical legal studies movement. The Crits didn't care for law school when they were there, and now that they are teachers, they want to do a better job. Underlying the views of many of these teachers is a

Marxist or at least a leftist philosophy that the legal education system is geared to furthering the economic interests of the rich and powerful in society. Their approach to education is likely to involve questioning the underlying values expressed in court decisions and the judicial system.

*The Legal Economist*—The law and economics movement has evolved on the right just as the Crits evolved on the left. The Economist approaches a case by analyzing the relative economic costs of different solutions to the problem in reaching a decision.

*The Philosopher*—Although most of your professors will be grounded somewhere in reality, occasionally you may encounter an instructor who talks more about Camus and Kant than he does Cardozo and Learned Hand. The philosopher will seem to float in and out of touch with the class as his cerebral meanderings take him to increasingly sophisticated strata of understanding. Unless you were a philosophy major, you quickly will conclude either that you are stupid or the prof is nuts.

*The Novice*—You may be given the rare treat of a law professor in his first effort in teaching. Teaching in a law school requires skill that is developed over a period of years, and it may be said of your Novice that no matter how enthusiastic, his or her best years are still in the future.

*The Writing Professor*—In most schools, special instructors are retained to teach the Legal Writing course. These teachers are often young lawyers who aspire to enter the teaching profession, practicing lawyers who are interested in dabbling in education, or graduate law students at your school. In many schools, the Writing Professor is not accorded the same status as regular faculty members, despite the demands of the job. The grades, however, count the same on your transcript.

## D. The Students

### 1. Classmates

Your classmates can be allies as well as foes during your struggle to master the first year of law school. They can help you to cope in a number of different ways. First, they can help you with assignments. If you happen to miss a class, you need to find someone whose notes you can review. If your own notes have gaps, you may be able to fill them with the help of someone else. If reading assignments or case citations are unclear, you should identify one or more people to call. Even though law school is a competitive environment, most students are willing to help out in this way, as long as their generosity is not abused.

You may study with one or more other students from time to time. Formal study groups will be covered more thoroughly in Chapter 4; informal small group discussions are common even among students who do not organize formal study groups. In law school, a great amount of learning takes place outside the classroom, and to the extent that your out-of-class conversations are discussions begun during class, the learning process will continue.

If you have ever been to the zoo, you may recall watching a pride of lions or other large cats. The young ones will tussle and play endlessly. Sometimes Mom or Dad will play too, letting the kittens attack and snarl and slap. You know that the older cat can send the kittens flying with a flick of the paw, but they play along until they get bored. You know that the kittens are learning skills they will need as adults in the wild, and the big cats are helping in the process. You also know that the kittens learn from their mock battles with each other just as they do from Mom and Dad. In law school, the professors take on the role of the big cats, and you as kittens should learn from them. However, you should remember that you learn from the rest of the litter as well.

Your classmates can provide an outlet from the pressures of law school. Whether it involves coffee in the morning, eating lunch or dinner, exercising or working out, or partying, you need to socialize from time to time. Those of you who are married to people unconnected with the legal profession and those who have jobs in nonlegal settings may find it less difficult to break away from law school psychologically. On the other hand, it may be more difficult to find the time to get to know your classmates socially. If you don't want your families and coworkers to despise you because you talk about law all the time, you should try to make some time to get to know your fellow law students in a social setting.

There is an insidious downside to developing relationships with your classmates. Several caveats are in order. Law school is very competitive. Some students will help no one. Some students will promise help, but fail to deliver. Some will take far more than they give. Always remember that the admissions committee did not pick the first year class on the basis of integrity. Although you will meet some of the most honest and honorable people you could hope to know, you may also encounter others who would stoop to any depth to get ahead and use any means to reach a desired end. Most of you will conclude that you are unwilling to lie, cheat, and steal in order to succeed in law school. Do not be so naive as to believe that everyone feels the same. Beware of the snakes in the grass, and pick your friends carefully.

Your classmates can exert considerable pressure not to succeed. A collective striving for mediocrity may seem to be the norm. Those who study too much, talk too often in class, or don't get into the law school social scene may be branded as outsiders. You have had to deal with similar peer pressure since grade school. The point here is that the pressure to conform does not end in law school. You may have seen the gopher game at the boardwalk or midway. In this game, the gopher pops his head out of one of the number of round holes while the player, wielding a mallet, tries to knock him back into the hole again. If you imagine that the class is the midway player ready to knock down any gopher who has the audacity to stick his head up above the crowd, you get the picture.

One way the group may push you toward mediocrity is by encouraging you to socialize. Although occasional social activity is beneficial, too much can be the kiss of death. When study sessions deteriorate into bull sessions like you had when you were a freshman in college, when quick lunches extend into afternoon shopping trips, when an occasional class party becomes an evening ritual, then you will know you have exceeded the bounds of moderation.

Some semblance of self-discipline in the area of time management is absolutely essential. Time management will be covered in more detail in Chapter 6; at this time you should note that you must decide how much time you are willing to devote to personal and social activities, and live with that decision.

Socializing with other students can take on a more serious note: emotional involvement through love and dependency. Guess what? Law students fall in love. They fall in love with each other and with nonlaw students. It would be futile to say: "Don't fall in love." However, if you do, you will find yourself in turmoil. When you fall in love, your lover tends to become (at least during early stages of infatuation) all-important in your life. Unfortunately, so does law school. Justice Holmes once remarked that the law is a jealous mistress. This conflict appears in the novel *Phantom of the Opera*. Christine, the heroine, is torn between her physical relationship with the Viscompte de Chegny and her passion to excel in her career represented by her relationship with the Phantom. It is interesting to note that the author of the book, Gaston Laroux, was himself a lawyer, and may have understood the conflict in terms of the law.

A second dangerous emotional involvement is to buy into someone else's problems to the detriment of your own studies. Law students are not immune from the vagaries of life. Some of your friends will have serious problems while they are in school. The stress of law school may compound their anxiety. Some may turn to you to serve as an emotional crutch. In fact, some students are like magnets for those with problems. Lest your friend's difficulties drag you down, the best thing you can do is to get them to go to someone who can really help.

### 2. Upperclass Students

When you arrive at law school, you will find a place already populated by students who have gone before you. These upperclass students will be ready and willing to regale you with tales of their own experiences in the first year, to give you the inside scoop on all the profs, and to share the definitive answers on what you need to do to get ahead. Some of them will want you to join their organizations, come to their parties, or buy their old books. They may seem like the smug but grizzled veterans joined in the field by some new recruits in the standard war movie: "Don't worry, kid; I'll show you what you need to do to get out of this place alive." Of course, in the movies, the guy who says that always seems to get killed.

The lesson to learn is to take everything you hear with a grain of salt. You will find out information that is useful. Every law school has a grapevine, and the news, if not always accurate, is at least entertaining. Some of your sources may prove better than others. So use what you can and discard the rest.

Consider the motivation of the upperclass student who offers advice. Is this someone who just likes being a big shot? Someone who needs reaffirmation for his or her own decisions in law school (even if those choices have produced a record of mediocrity)? Someone who would like to ask you out? (Yes, this goes on in law school like everywhere else!) Someone who wants to sell you something (bar reviews, books, bar association memberships)? You do not have to shun all these people, just remember that they want something in return for their information. (In the words of Hannibal Lecter from *The Silence of the Lambs*, "Quid quo pro, Clarice.")

While casual advice should be approached with skepticism, it might be valuable to look for an upperclass mentor. Such a person might well be someone who has similar interests, career aspirations, problems, or background. For example, a first year student with young children at home might encounter an upperclass student who has gone through the same experience and survived. A mentor might be someone you happen to meet and become friendly with during the course of the year. Some schools even offer programs that assign upperclass mentors to first year students. However it occurs that a true mentoring relationship develops, take advantage of it.

A mentor can help to guide you through the law school maze, talk to you when you are down, share your joy when you are flush with success, and set an example for you to follow. Mentoring relationships are built upon a foundation of common interest, molded by walls of trust, and covered by a protective roof of the experience of the mentor for the student. Mentoring relationships are common in the legal profession, not only in law school but in practice as well. To the extent that you find a good mentor, you will discover that the law school experience is a more palatable one.

### E. The Law School Culture

#### 1. Rules and Procedures

Law school culture is unique, created in part by the intense experience of those involved, and in part by the insular setting of the law school itself. Because most law students did not attend undergraduate school at the university where they attend law school, they tend to have limited interaction with the university community generally. The law school on many campuses is set apart on the edge of campus or on a separate campus altogether. Some law schools are not connected with an undergraduate university at all. There are advantages and disadvantages to attending an "independent" law school. Such a school can devote all its resources to the law students, but may lack the rich culture of a university setting.

There may be other differences about the physical location or layout of the law building(s) that make the law school environment unique. Does the law school share its campus with undergrads or graduate students? Does the law school share space with other departments? Are law school facilities located in one building or several? The presence or absence of a nonlegal academic community affects not only the type and extent of extracurricular programs and activities, but also the sense of the law school as an insular institution.

In one sense, every law school is different (see Chapter 2), but in another sense, every law school is the same. Regardless of the idiosyncrasies of different law schools, the process of legal education is similar everywhere. In this environment, a distinct law school culture has evolved. Law schools have their own student government (the Student Bar Association, or SBA), activities, social events, intramurals, and newspapers. Some law schools even have their own yearbooks. At many law schools, the students put on an annual comedy show, generally making fun of the faculty in a singular effort to even the score for a year's worth of abuse.

Within the law school culture, there are several common elements worth noting. First, rules and procedures take on a distinctly legal flavor. Announcements and information may be posted by the registrar, the Dean's Office, or teachers. You will be deemed to know what is in these notices by virtue of the doctrine of constructive notice. The upshot of this concept is that you have to watch out for announcements that pertain to you. The first example of constructive notice during your law school tenure will be the posting of class assignments on a wall or bulletin board prior to the beginning of classes. You will find very little hand-holding by law school teachers and administrators. Students who graduated from small intimate colleges may find this somewhat of a shock.

A second concept that permeates the rules and procedures is the notion of due process. Lawyers, more than those who are not trained in the law, tend to be aware of individual rights to hearings, representation, confrontation of accusers, and appeal. Most law schools operate under some code of conduct for dealing with academic dishonesty, as well as a code of academic standards to cover issues involving academic performance. Both sets of rules tend to focus heavily on due process and protection of the individual.

Another aspect of the law school culture is that it is a small world. The largest law school in the country has around 2,000 students; at most law schools the enrollment is no more than several hundred. The small size of the student body, combined with the nature of the educational process, means that students know much more about each other, law school affairs, and their professors than they did in all but the smallest undergraduate schools. Unlike your high school or college acquaintances, you will tend to maintain contact with many of your law school classmates throughout your career. At every law school there is a student grapevine, laden with information about everything from what courses to take, which firms to interview, to who is sleeping with whom. The old adage, "Believe a tenth of what you hear and half of what you see," is apropos.

## 2. Socializing and Breaks

You will find an abundance of opportunities for escape from law school studies in the form of parties and school-sponsored social events. During the year, there will be several receptions, mixers, and even a dance or two sponsored by the SBA. Many student organizations offer periodic social events for their members. And informal groups of students organize their own parties as a break from the grind of law school or meet at a local bar for drinks after class.

In fact, if you are interested, you can find a party almost every night. Unfortunately, partying leads you down a certain path of self-destruction in law school. Everyone needs an occasional break from study; however, the occasional break can easily become a regular habit. The party scene can become an escape from law school pressures generally, and may shift your values away from learning.

If you were a party animal in college, it may be difficult to break out of old patterns. Unfortunately, most of us cannot get by with the same antics we did in undergraduate school. In law school, one all-nighter will not save a semester of neglect. For additional thoughts on this topic, see Chapter 6, which deals with time management and related subjects.

Law school provides abundant breaks between and during semesters. You will probably have two weeks or more between the end of first semester exams and the start of spring semester classes. Most schools provide a spring break midway through the second semester. And, of course, summers are open.

Students usually use breaks during the year either to get away for a vacation or to get ahead in their work. Sometimes you may not have a choice. If you decide to vacation, leave your guilt at home. If you take your books with you, plan and make time to study. If you have no time to study, do not make a pretense of it by surrounding yourself with symbols of law school while doing nothing to further your cause.

Summer vacation is another matter. Here are 12 to 14 weeks that you can utilize in a variety of different ways. How you choose to spend your summer vacation will have an impact, one way or the other, on your legal education.

A large percentage of law students work for legal employers during the summer. Although it is harder for them to find positions, many first year students take this option, even if they have to work for free. For some students, it is necessary to work in high paying nonlegal jobs in order to earn enough to come back to school the next year.

Many students go to summer school, at their institution, or abroad (see Chapter 8, page 149). You may find, however, that you are so burned out that you simply want to relax. And some students do just that after the first year. If you want to travel, this might be the time to do it, before you take your first job.

### 3. Competition

A final note about the law school culture is that it is competitive. Entrance to law school was competitive; law school itself competitive; and law practice by its nature is competitive. Your relationships with other students will be colored by competition. Ironically, many students try to deny the competitive nature of the process. They will say to each other that grades don't matter. They will ostracize fellow students who appear too competitive. They may deny to other students that they study as much as they do. On the other hand, competitiveness can go too far. In all likelihood, before you graduate from law school, you will hear about at least one cheating incident at your school. You will see other examples, such as library books being mis-shelved by unscrupulous students. If you should be tempted, it's not worth it. In the 1988 presidential campaign, a law school indiscretion may have cost one candidate nomination for the presidency of the United States.

# CHAPTER **4**
# Studying the Law

## A. The Classroom Experience

The most memorable part of the upcoming year will be the time you spend in class. Assuming that you spend 15 hours per week in class over the next 30 weeks, you can plan on 450 or more classroom hours of instruction during your first year of law school. Whereas other parts in this book deal with subjects such as outlining, synthesizing, and exam taking, this section deals with succeeding in the classroom. Maximizing the amount you can learn should be your fundamental objective, and a measure of your success. This section is subdivided into a number of discrete topics: preparation, class discussions, note taking, and follow-up.

One preliminary suggestion is that you attend class. Some professors permit a certain number of absences; others say they do not care about attendance at all. There are students who seem to consider it a moral obligation to take the maximum number of cuts allowed. My experience is that there is a high correlation between class attendance and first year grades. If you had a job, you wouldn't plan to miss the maximum number of allowable sick days and personal days just because your employer permitted it. To maintain a professional approach to law school, you will want to attend class without fail, stay up with your reading, and put in the same number of hours as a student that you plan to devote to your work as an attorney.

### 1. Class Preparation

You just cannot succeed in law school by going to class and showing up for the exams. Apocryphal stories abound in law school lore about students who never go to class, read someone's outline once before the exam, and invariably get the highest grade in the class.

Even if such a stellar performance is possible, the chances are incredibly great that you will not be the performer. The truth is that you will work your tail off just trying to stay even. At most law schools, virtually everyone has a comparable history of academic success, but you undoubtedly will encounter some individuals who appear to run on different octane from everyone else. In most cases, these students simply work harder and more efficiently than their classmates. Thus, even if you are at the top of your class intellectually, the best assurance of academic success is hard work. Much of the effort occurs before class through reading and briefing the cases assigned.

To begin with, you must know how to read cases and other legal material. Your prior educational experience will have given you the fundamental skills, but those need to be adapted to the educational demands of law school.

In order to help you become familiar with the process of reading and briefing cases, we are going to examine a case from first year Torts involving one of the most memorable characters you will encounter: little Brian Dailey. The case, *Garratt v. Dailey,* appears in several first year casebooks.

Although we will be using this particular case as an example, the methodology can (and will) be applied countless more times throughout law school in all your classes, and, indeed, throughout your legal career. It will be well worth your time to think through the approach to dissecting this case, and thereafter to practice the technique until you master it, the sooner the better.

During the first weeks of law school you will find the case method to be cumbersome, time consuming, and confusing. You may feel that you are not studying efficiently, that your education would proceed much more smoothly if someone would just give you the answers and not expect you to decipher them from the hieroglyphic-like readings of appellate cases. The more cases you read, the more facile you will become with the format, the language, the analysis, and the style. The more cases you brief, the more quickly you will be able to do it. So, just do it.

To read the case critically, skim it to get an idea of what it is about. Note that this case appears in the contents of the casebook under the topic "Intent." A threshold question is: Why did the authors include this case? A quick overview of the *Garratt* case might bring to your attention some basic information.

## 1. INTENT

### GARRATT v. DAILEY

Supreme Court of Washington, 1955.
46 Wash.2d 197, 279 P.2d 1091.

HILL, Justice. The liability of an infant for an alleged battery is presented to this court for the first time. Brian Dailey (age five years, nine months) was visiting with Naomi Garratt, an adult and a sister of the plaintiff, Ruth Garratt, likewise an adult, in the back yard of the plaintiff's home, on July 16, 1951. It is plaintiff's contention that she came out into the back yard to talk with Naomi and that, as she started to sit down in a wood and canvas lawn chair, Brian deliberately pulled it out from under her. The only one of the three present so testifying was Naomi Garratt. (Ruth Garratt, the plaintiff did not testify as to how or why she fell.) The trial court, unwilling to accept this testimony, adopted instead Brian Dailey's version of what happened, and made the following findings:

"III.  *  *  *  that while Naomi Garratt and Brian Dailey were in the back yard the plaintiff, Ruth Garratt, came out of her house into the back yard. Some time subsequent thereto defendant, Brian Dailey, picked up a lightly built wood and canvas lawn chair which was then and there located in the back yard of the above described premises, moved it sideways a few feet and seated himself therein, at which time he discovered the plaintiff, Ruth Garratt, about to sit down at the place where the lawn chair had formerly been, at which time he hurriedly got up from the chair and attempted to move it toward Ruth Garratt to aid her in sitting down in the chair; that. due to the defendant's small size and lack of dexterity he was unable to get the lawn chair under the plaintiff in time to prevent her from falling to the ground. That plaintiff fell to the ground and sustained a fracture of her hip, and other injuries and damages as hereinafter set forth.

"IV.   That the preponderance of the evidence in this case establishes that when the defendant, Brian Dailey moved the chair in question *he did not have any wilful or unlawful purpose* in doing so; that *he did not have any intent to injure the plaintiff, or any intent to bring about any unauthorized or offensive contact with her person or* any objects appurtenant thereto; that the circumstances which immediately preceded the fall of the plaintiff established that the defendant, *Brian Dailey, did not have purpose, intent or design to perform a prank or to effect an assault and battery upon the person of the plaintiff.*" (Italics ours, for a purpose hereinafter indicated.)

It is conceded that Ruth Garratt's fall resulted in a fractured hip and other painful and serious injuries. To obviate the necessity of a retrial in the event this court determines that she was entitled to a judgment against Brian Dailey, the amount of her damage was found to be $11,000. Plaintiff appeals from a judgment dismissing the action and asks for the entry of a judgment in that amount or a new trial.

The authorities generally, but with certain notable exceptions, [citation] state that when a minor has committed a tort with force he is liable to be proceeded against as any other person would be.
* * *

In our analysis of the applicable law, we start with the basic premise that Brian, whether five or fifty-five, must have committed some wrongful act before he could be liable for appellant's injuries.
* * *

It is urged that Brian's action in moving the chair constituted a battery. A definition (not all-inclusive but sufficient for our purpose) of a battery is the intentional infliction of a harmful bodily contact upon another. * * *

We have in this case no question of consent or privilege. We therefore proceed to an immediate consideration of intent and its place in the law of battery. In the comment on clause (a) of § 13, the Restatement says:

*"Character of Actor's Intention.* In order that an act may be done with the intention of bringing about a harmful or offensive contact or an apprehension thereof to a particular person, either the other or a third person, the act must be done for the purpose of causing the contact or apprehension or with knowledge on the part of the actor that such contact or apprehension is substantially certain to be produced." [Citation]

We have here the conceded volitional act of Brian, i.e., the moving of a chair. Had the plaintiff proved to the satisfaction of the trial court that Brian moved the chair while she was in the act of sitting down, Brian's action would patently have been for the purpose or with the intent of causing the plaintiff's bodily contact with the ground, and she would be entitled to a judgment against him for the resulting damages. [Citations]

The plaintiff based her case on that theory, and the trial court held that she failed in her proof and accepted Brian's version of the facts rather than that given by the eyewitness who testified for the plaintiff. After the trial court determined that the plaintiff had not established her theory of a battery (i.e., that Brian had pulled the chair out from under the plaintiff while she was in the act of sitting down), it then became concerned with whether a battery was established under the facts as it found them to be.

In this connection, we quote another portion of the comment on the "Character of actor's intention," relating to clause (a) of the rule from [1 Restatement, Torts, 29, § 13]:

"It is not enough that the act itself is intentionally done and this, even though the actor realizes or should realize that it contains a very grave risk of bringing about the contact or apprehension. Such realization may make the actor's conduct negligent or even reckless but unless he realizes that to a substantial certainty, the contact or apprehension will result, the actor has not that intention which is necessary to make him liable under the rule stated in this section."

A battery would be established if, in addition to plaintiff's fall, it was proved that, when Brian moved the chair, he knew with substantial certainty that the plaintiff would attempt to sit down where the chair had been. If Brian had any of the intents which the trial court found, in the italicized portions of the findings of fact quoted above, that he did not have, he would of course have had the knowledge to which we have referred. The mere absence of any intent to injure the plaintiff or to play a prank on her or to embarrass her, or to commit an assault and battery on her would not absolve him from liability if in fact he had such knowledge. [Citation] Without such knowledge, there would be nothing wrongful about Brian's act in moving the chair and, there being no wrongful act, there would be no liability.

While a finding that Brian had no such knowledge can be inferred from the findings made, we believe that before the plaintiff's action in such a case should be dismissed there should be no question but that the trial court had passed upon that issue; hence, the case should be remanded for clarification of the findings to specifically cover the question of Brian's knowledge, because intent could be inferred therefrom. If the court finds that he had such knowledge the necessary intent will be established and the plaintiff will be entitled to recover, even though there was no purpose to injure or embarrass the plaintiff. [Citation] If Brian did not have such knowledge, there was no wrongful act by him and the basic premise of liability on the theory of a battery was not established.

It will be noted that the law of battery as we have discussed it is the law applicable to adults, and no significance has been attached to the fact that Brian was a child less than six years of age when the alleged battery occurred. The only circumstance where Brian's age is of any consequence is in determining what he knew, and there his experience, capacity, and understanding are of course material.

From what has been said, it is clear that we find no merit in plaintiff's contention that we can direct the entry of a judgment for $11,000 in her favor on the record now before us.

Nor do we find any error in the record that warrants a new trial. * * *

The cause is remanded for clarification, with instructions to make definite findings on the issue of whether Brian Dailey knew with substantial certainty that the plaintiff would attempt to sit down where the chair which he moved had been, and to change the judgment if the findings warrant it. * * *

Remanded for clarification.

[On remand, the trial judge concluded that it was necessary for him to consider carefully the time sequence, as he had not done before; and this resulted in his finding "that the arthritic woman had begun the slow process of being seated when the defendant quickly removed the chair and seated himself upon it, and that he knew, with substantial certainty, at that time that she would attempt to sit in the place where the chair had been." He entered judgment for the plaintiff in the amount of $11,000, which was affirmed on a second appeal in Garratt v. Dailey (1956) 49 Wash.2d 499, 304 P.2d 681.]

------

1.  Can a child five years and nine months old have an intent to do harm to another? And if so, how can that intent be "fault"? Suppose that a boy of seven, playing with a bow and arrow, aims at a girl of five and hits her, and she is injured. Is he liable? Weisbart v. Flohr (1968) 260 Cal.App.2d 281, 67 Cal.Rptr. 114. See Weisiger, Tort Liability of Minors and Incompetents, 1951 U.Ill.L.F. 227.

What did you get out of this overview? First, you probably noticed the caption, which tells us about the judicial history and citation of the case. Here, we are looking at a 1955 decision of the Supreme Court of Washington (the state, not D.C.). Different casebooks will utilize slightly different formats, but they will all provide similar information about the case. Next, you must have noticed "HILL, Justice." This tells us who wrote the opinion. Some names appear again and again in the casebooks, so the fact that a certain name, such as Cardozo, appears may provide insights into the court's reasoning.

Right after Hill's name is a statement of the facts. Basically, five-year-old Brian Dailey pulled a chair out from under Ruth Garratt, causing her to fall and fracture her hip. Garratt sued Dailey, and the trial court held that the kid did not intend to injure the victim. Now on appeal, we get to the real nut of the case: what exactly does "intent to do something" mean?

At this point, you probably are curious about the outcome, so you flip to the end where you discover the case was "Remanded for clarification." It was sent back to the trial court, but it was not affirmed or reversed. A note from the casebook editors in brackets says that upon reflection and using the appellate court's definition of intent, "knowledge with substantial certainty," the trial judge found for the plaintiff Garratt to the tune of $11,000, which was affirmed on a second appeal.

A question following the case asks, can a five-year-old intend to harm another? Based on the outcome of this case the answer must be yes. Then the editor sneaks in the question, "how can that intent be 'fault'?" That can lead to an interesting classroom discussion about whether fault and liability are necessarily co-extensive, and whether the standard ought to be the same for intentional torts and negligence torts.

By now you have a pretty good idea of what is going on, but to understand the court's decision, you have to tackle the heart of the opinion. The best way to do this is to go back to the start and read the case through one time without stopping, to see if you understand it. Some cases will seem clear to you after one careful reading. Many cases will include language, terms, or concepts that are confusing. You may finish reading some cases and have no idea what you read.

You cannot read a case, in which every word is important, as you would a trashy novel. Speed-reading will not help you to dissect the words in a case. Distractions may cause you to lose totally your train of thought. With a little discipline, however, you will pick up the main ideas of the case.

During your first reading of the case you should not write anything. Before going further, take the time to define terminology that is new to you, using both a regular dictionary and a law dictionary. During your second reading, highlight or underline key phrases and make notes in the margin. One reason not to buy used books in law school is the burden of following the previous owner's notations.

A more careful reading of the case leads to several observations. After summarizing the facts, Justice Hill quotes salient factual findings of the trial court AND italicizes certain words, to the effect that Brian did not intend to harm the arthritic lady or to play a prank. Generations of law students and, perhaps Justice Hill, may have suspected otherwise. The problem is that the Supreme Court can't overturn the trial court's findings of fact, only its application of the law.

After quickly dispensing with the preliminary issue of whether a minor who commits a tort with force can be held liable (he can), the court turns to a statement of the law on intent. First, the court cites the Restatement of Torts. Although persuasive and not binding, restatements are often cited by courts because they are clear and well thought-out. In other cases, the court might turn to statutory provisions or prior cases in the jurisdiction or elsewhere. As in *Garratt*, at some point in the case—most often after the statement of facts—there will be an explication of the relevant legal principles.

To be found liable, the court says, Brian "must have committed some wrongful act...," and that a battery would constitute such an act. A battery is defined in the opinion as "the intentional infliction of a harmful bodily contact upon another," and the question boils down to intent. Notice how the court narrows its consideration from wrong to battery to intent, which it defines as an "act...done for the purpose of causing the contact or...with knowledge...that such contact...is substantially certain to be produced."

Thus armed with the law, the court proceeds to apply the law to the facts in this case. This deductive process is repeated in some form in virtually all legal reasoning. Logically, the statement of the law is the major premise, the critical facts present a minor premise, and the conclusion follows by applying the former to the latter.

In this case, after looking at the positions of both plaintiff and defendant, and acknowledging that the lower court found no intention to harm, the court concluded that the decision was not dispositive on the key issue of whether Brian knew to a substantial certainty that if he pulled the chair out from under Ruth Garratt, the consequence of contact with the ground was substantially certain to follow. Now we know that if the court had found in the trial court opinion facts to support an inference or legal conclusion that Brian had such knowledge, it would have reversed; as it is, the case must be remanded.

The decision or holding is the part of the case that articulates the court's conclusion. Sometimes the court will telegraph the holding by saying, "We hold…" or "It is our decision…" Often, as here, the holding is not set off in any obvious way. Can you find the holding here? Look six paragraphs up from where the court remands the case, to the paragraph beginning, "A battery would be established if…." In the following paragraph the appellate court directs the lower court how to apply the law on remand.

In the end, the student takes away an understanding of intent that is different from the concept of the term she brought with her to law school. The class in which *Garratt* is discussed (and perhaps the final exam) will present other fact situations applying the definition of intent as knowledge with substantial certainty that a consequence will follow an act.

If the case is fairly straightforward and/or comprehensible to you at this time, you may be able to prepare your brief (see page 45). Frequently, you will have to reread the case a third or fourth time to fully appreciate what it is all about. The process is a painstaking and time-consuming one. At the beginning of the year, the process will take much longer, and you will often miss the issue, salient facts, or aspects of the court's reasoning. By approaching case preparation as suggested here, however, you can significantly improve your chances of understanding the cases.

When you think you understand the case, you will want to reflect critically about how the case fits into the course material. The notes at the end of the case contain questions for further consideration. Sometimes these questions are designed to help you understand the case or think about the legal principle involved. Sometimes they raise policy issues or question the court's position. The notes will contain short excerpts of other cases. Although you probably will not have time to look up all these note cases, it would be a mistake to ignore them. The note cases often suggest contrary results and ask you to distinguish them from the principal case. Sometimes these distinctions will be based on factual differences or on differences in law among jurisdictions; sometimes the conflicts will seem to defy explanation.

Class preparation entails reading thoroughly, thinking about issues, and attempting to come to grips with thorny problems. You will find it helpful to develop your own hypotheses about the cases you read and test these theories in class.

Now that you know how to read an appellate case, it may be useful to try another one on your own. Remember to skim the case quickly to garner key information that will help you work your way through a more in-depth reading. Beginning law students often get bogged down in the verbiage or sidetracked by what turns out to be the court's digression from the central issue. After skimming the case, read it carefully, noting important facts, statements about the applicable law, and the analysis applying the law to the facts in the case. Do not be afraid to highlight or underline passages or to make notes in the margin. Read the case again until you feel you comprehend not only the result but also the reasons for the result.

The following case is taken from the same section of the casebook as the *Garratt* case:

## McGUIRE v. ALMY
Supreme Judicial Court of Massachusetts, 1937.
297 Mass. 323, 8 N.E.2d 760.

QUA, JUSTICE. This is an action of tort for assault and battery. The only question of law reported is whether the judge should have directed a verdict for the defendant.

The following facts are established by the plaintiff's own evidence: In August, 1930, the plaintiff was employed to take care of the defendant. The plaintiff was a registered nurse and was a graduate of a training school for nurses. The defendant was an insane person. Before the plaintiff was hired she learned that the defendant was a "mental case and was in good physical condition," and that for some time two nurses had been taking care of her. The plaintiff was on "24 hour duty." The plaintiff slept in the room next to the defendant's room. Except when the plaintiff was with the defendant, the plaintiff kept the defendant locked in the defendant's room. ＊ ＊ ＊

On April 19, 1932, the defendant, while locked in her room, had a violent attack. The plaintiff heard a crashing of furniture and then knew that the defendant was ugly, violent and dangerous. The defendant told the plaintiff and a Miss Maroney, "the maid," who was with the plaintiff in the adjoining room, that if they came into the defendant's room, she would kill them. The plaintiff and Miss Maroney looked into the defendant's room, "saw what the defendant had done," and "thought it best to take the broken stuff away before she did any harm to herself with it." They sent for a Mr. Emerton, the defendant's brother-in-law. When he arrived the defendant was in the middle of her room about ten feet from the door, holding upraised the leg of a low-boy as if she were going to strike. The plaintiff stepped into the room and walked toward the defendant, while Mr. Emerton and Miss Maroney remained in the doorway. As the plaintiff approached the defendant and tried to take hold of the defendant's hand which held the leg, the defendant struck the plaintiff's head with it, causing the injuries for which the action was brought.

The extent to which an insane person is liable for torts has not been fully defined in this Commonwealth. * * *

Turning to authorities elsewhere, we find that courts in this country almost invariably say in the broadest terms that an insane person is liable for his torts. As a rule no distinction is made between those torts which would ordinarily be classed as intentional and those which would ordinarily be classed as negligent, nor do the courts discuss the effect of different kinds of insanity or of varying degrees of capacity as bearing upon the ability of the defendant to understand the particular act in question or to make a reasoned decision with respect to it, although it is sometimes said that an insane person is not liable for torts requiring malice of which he is incapable. Defamation and malicious prosecution are the torts more commonly mentioned in this connection. * * * These decisions are rested more upon grounds of public policy and upon what might be called a popular view of the requirements of essential justice than upon any attempt to apply logically the underlying principles of civil liability to the special instance of the mentally deranged. Thus it is said that a rule imposing liability tends to make more watchful those persons who have charge of the defendant and who may be supposed to have some interest in preserving his property; that as an insane person must pay for his support, if he is financially able, so he ought also to pay for the damage which he does; that an insane person with abundant wealth ought not to continue in unimpaired enjoyment of the comfort which it brings while his victim bears the burden unaided; and there is also a suggestion that courts are loath to introduce into the great body of civil litigation the difficulties in determining mental capacity which it has been found impossible to avoid in the criminal field.

The rule established in these cases has been criticized severely by certain eminent text writers both in this country and in England, principally on the ground that it is an archaic survival of the rigid and formal mediaeval conception of liability for acts done, without regard to fault, as opposed to what is said to be the general modern theory that liability in tort should rest upon fault. Notwithstanding these criticisms, we think, that as a practical matter, there is strong force in the reasons underlying these decisions. They are consistent with the general statements found in the cases dealing with the liability of infants for torts, [cc] including a few cases in which the child was so young as to render his capacity for fault comparable to that of many insane persons, [cc]. Fault is by no means at the present day a universal prerequisite to liability, and the theory that it should be such has been obliged very recently to yield at several points to what have been thought to be paramount considerations of public good. Finally, it would be difficult not to recognize the persuasive weight of so much authority so widely extended.

But the present occasion does not require us either to accept or to reject the prevailing doctrine in its entirety. For this case it is enough to say that where an insane person by his act does intentional damage to the person or property of another he is liable for that damage in the same circumstances in which a normal person would be liable. This means that in so far as a particular intent would be necessary in order to render a normal person liable, the insane person, in order to be liable, must have been capable of entertaining that same intent and must have entertained it in fact. But the law will not inquire further into his peculiar mental condition with a view to excusing him if it should appear that delusion or other consequence of his affliction has caused him to entertain that intent or that a normal person would not have entertained it. * * *

Coming now to the application of the rule to the facts of this case, it is apparent that the jury could find that the defendant was capable of entertaining and that she did entertain an intent to strike and to injure the plaintiff and that she acted upon that intent. See American Law Institute Restatement, Torts, §§ 13, 14. We think this was enough. * * *

[The rest of the opinion holds that whether the plaintiff consented to the attack or assumed the risk of it is an issue to be left to the jury. There was no evidence that the defendant had previously attacked any one or made any serious threat to do so. The plaintiff had taken care of the defendant for fourteen months without being attacked. When the plaintiff entered the room the defendant was breaking up the furniture, and it could be found that the plaintiff reasonably feared that the defendant would do harm to herself. Under such circumstances it cannot be ruled as a matter of law that the plaintiff assumed the risk.]

Judgment for the plaintiff on the verdict.

———

1. Can an insane person have an intent to do harm to another? And if so, how can such an intent be "fault"? How does the lunatic differ from the

automobile driver who suffers a heart attack, in Cohen v. Petty, supra, page 11?

2. The American decisions are unanimous in their agreement with the principal case. The result has, however, been much criticized. See, e.g., Bohlen, Liability in Tort of Infants and Insane Persons, 23 Mich.L.Rev. 9 (1924); Curran, Tort Liability of the Mentally Ill and Mentally Deficient, 21 Ohio St. L.J. 52 (1960). Good, recent discussions of the whole problem include Fridman, Mental Incompetency, 79 Law Q.Rev. 502 (1963), 80 Law Q.Rev. 84 (1964); and Note, Insanity as a Defense, 54 Marq.L.Rev. 245 (1971).

3. It has been held, however, that the insanity may prevent the specific kind of intent necessary for certain torts, such as deceit, when the defendant is to be held liable only if he knows that he is not speaking the truth. See Irvine v. Gibson, 117 Ky. 306, 77 S.W. 1106 (1904); Chaddock v. Chaddock, 130 Misc. 900, 226 N.Y.S. 152 (1927); Beaubeauf v. Reed, 4 La.App. 344 (1926).

4. Even if an insane person lacks the ability to form the intent to commit a tort, an action may lie against persons responsible for controlling the insane person, based on negligent supervision. See Rausch v. McVeigh, 105 Misc.2d 163, 431 N.Y.S.2d 887 (1980).

## 2. Briefing Cases

In law school, you are asked to read and brief legal cases. The basic action in your classes is a question and answer dialogue led by the professor. Briefing is a mechanism that helps you play the game.

There is nothing mystical about briefing cases. The technique simply permits lawyers and law students to get a thumbnail sketch of a sometimes long appellate opinion. It should tell you quickly and accurately what you need to remember about the case.

In private practice, the busy partner may ask an associate to brief several cases. A judge may ask her law clerk to brief cases relating to an upcoming decision. Your law professors ask you to brief cases for a variety of reasons. The first reason is to teach you an approach to legal analysis that will in time become second nature to you. The second reason is to provide focus for classroom discussions. A third reason is to teach you a skill that you will always be able to utilize.

Whatever reasons there may be for the seeming drudgery of briefing cases, accept the fact that this activity will take up a substantial part of your time for the next three to four years, and beyond. So it makes sense to learn to do it well as soon as possible.

There are shortcuts to be sure. These shortcuts have certain risks that you should know when you consider whether or not to employ them. The first shortcut is the canned brief. For many of the more popular law school casebooks, you may buy a book that contains briefs of all the cases in the book. Your professors will inveigh, some vociferously, against the use of canned briefs. You will have to weigh the risks. The simple truth is that learning the law involves learning how to attack legal questions. When you brief a case, you develop the analytical skill you need as a lawyer; when you read a brief written by someone else, you learn only information, and that really doesn't help you to understand the case.

A brief should be utilized contextually. The brief for your senior partner is prepared with an eye toward its ultimate use in an appellate argument, a trial, a speech for the bar association, and so on. The brief is a shorthand statement of what the case means in a particular setting, rather than an objective statement of facts and law for all times. In classroom terms, this means that your brief should be a device to help you understand the case in light of your professor's approach to the subject matter and your own comprehension of the material.

Who among us has not relied on a canned brief occasionally? There are times: you stayed out too late the night before; you didn't hear the assignment until fifteen minutes before class; your mother died and you just didn't feel right about reading Contracts at the funeral. Canned briefs can be useful occasionally to compare to your actual briefs. However, these applications for canned briefs should be for extraordinary situations rather than everyday practice. You will not understand *Garratt v. Dailey* by using canned briefs any better than you did *Moby Dick* by reading Cliff Notes in high school.

A second shortcut is to split up the briefing duties among several people in the study group, photocopying and passing out the work product to all. This system, although less expensive than buying commercial briefs, suffers from all the same drawbacks of canned briefs with the added disadvantage that the quality is no better than the students in the group. Assuming that you are not the dullest person in your study group, this means that some or all of the briefs you get will be inferior to the ones you would produce yourself.

A third shortcut is the technique of book briefing. With a highlighter to mark major points in a case and a pen to make notations and comments in the margin, you can avoid a lot of writing. After you have become experienced in reading and dissecting cases, you may find book briefing to be a useful tool. During the first year of law school, however, you need the discipline of going through the drill. I remember playing basketball in high school, and spending what seemed to me needless hours on what the coach called "fundamentals." Looking back on both basketball and law school, learning the fundamentals was necessary to success.

Let's look at the briefing process. The first thing to remember is that the operative word is "brief." At least early in your first year of law school, you may notice that your briefs are longer than some of the cases. In your compulsion to cover everything and your inability to discern what to include, you can defeat the purpose of doing the brief. You must learn to distinguish what is important and what is not. In one sense, this is complicated by the fact that most cases have been edited for inclusion in the casebook, meaning that almost everything can be important, especially if the professor chooses to make it so. Some students have an instinct for what is important; others must learn by trial and error. One way you can test your briefing skills is to listen when other students are called to recite in class. When someone else states the issue exactly as you did and gets shot down immediately, there is a message. When someone sees the case completely differently than you, you should think again about your analysis.

First of all, there is no one way to prepare a brief. Ultimately, the brief is a tool for you to use. If it accomplishes that objective, it is a good brief. Every professor will have his or her own thoughts on how to write a brief, and if you look at your classmates, you will see almost as many styles as there are people.

Generally, briefs include the following elements:

*Case Description*—This includes the name of the case, the court and date, and a general statement of the procedure posture (e.g., Who is suing whom, and why? How did the case get to where it is?). This information is usually quite straightforward, although in the early months of law school you might have some difficulty tracing the history of a particular case. One reason for this is that all courts do not use the same designations for the parties. You may see the terms petitioner and respondent, plaintiff and defendant, appellant and appellee, as well as other terms. To make matters worse, sometimes the names of the parties are reversed from trial to appeal (e.g., *Smith v. Jones* becomes *Jones v. Smith* if Jones is the party appealing). Despite the tediousness of figuring out these relationships, your understanding of the cases will be immensely aided if you comprehend this background information.

*The Facts*—One of the tricks of briefing is to learn which facts are important and which are not. Professors sometimes seem to take the position that every fact is equally important. This may move you to write statements of the facts as long as those in the casebook. This obviously doesn't work. You need to learn how to recognize the important facts. Draft a single sentence that includes as many factual points as possible. Include all those facts that the court will need in order to make its decision. After distilling these salient facts, supplement your first sentence with other information you think the court will need to know. If you read a book, a friend might ask you what the book was about. You could answer the question by retelling the story, but then your friend wouldn't have to read the book. You could say: "The book was about a mad sea captain named Ahab and his obsessive desire to kill a great white whale named Moby Dick. After some time at sea, and much whaling, the confrontation between Ahab and the whale ends in the destruction of the ship and its crew."

Another way to look at the facts in your brief is to think of them as a shorthand reminder about the more detailed facts you have read. In other words, if the words you write can trigger your memory as to other facts in the case, you don't have to write out all the information.

*The Issue*—As difficult as distilling the facts may be, identifying the issue in a case can be much more difficult. A good bit of the first semester in law school is spent developing the skills of spotting and articulating issues. To start with, there are usually many ways to view the issue. The parties may see the issue differently. It may be stated broadly or narrowly, depending on whether the author wants it to cover the facts in the particular case or not. Normally, however, the issue is stated as a question that can be answered yes or no.

The issue as stated should contain enough information to articulate the difference between the positions of the parties. When looking for the issue, ask yourself why these parties are in court. Because this is probably an appellate case, there is some reason the parties couldn't settle it before. What are they fighting about? What is the gulf between them? Another useful question sometimes to ask is why did the author use this particular case in the casebook?

*The Holding*—The holding is usually a one-sentence statement of the legal principle upon which the court's decision rests. The holding answers the question raised by the issue. It is a statement of law that you can read standing alone or in the context of the case. In some cases, the holding can be lifted verbatim from the case; in others, you will have to rephrase the words in the opinion. For purposes of later study do not state the issue by simply noting "yes" or "no" in answer to the question asked in the issue. Some complex cases may contain multiple issues requiring more than one statement of holding. But usually you can distill the court's decision into one sentence.

*The Rationale*—This step outlines the logical steps in the court's reasoning process. The purpose of this part of the brief is to help you understand how the court reached its decision (as opposed to what it decided). Judicial decisions are based on rational arguments. Depending on the case, these arguments may be simple or complex. You should read the case critically, to see if the court's reasoning is faulty or if you agree with the assumptions. Remember that the brief contains a summary of the court's reasoning, not a restatement of the opinion.

*The Disposition*—Although many brief formats do not include this item, it makes sense to mention somewhere in your brief who actually won or lost, and what will happen to the case after this decision. Sometimes the disposition is clear from reading the case, whereas sometimes it is not.

*Concurring and/or Dissenting Opinions*—Sometimes the case will include concurring opinions where one of the judges on the bench agrees with the disposition of the case, but disagrees in part with the reasoning of the majority. In a dissenting opinion, the judge disagrees with the outcome of the case. When the casebook includes these opinions, the authors usually want to demonstrate that there are different ways to look at the problem. You may find that you agree with the majority opinion after reading it, and then find yourself persuaded by the dissent as well. Depending on the case, you can either summarize the reasoning of the concurring or dissenting opinion as you did in the rationale above, or you can summarize the critical differences between the reasoning in these opinions and the majority.

There is no magic in the format for preparing a written case brief. Everyone eventually settles on an organization that makes sense to them. It is important, however, to prepare each brief the same way; the same information should appear in the same place in every brief. This permits easy access to the information when you need it quickly, for example, when you are called on during class.

The format on page 51 is one that you can use or modify. You will note that there is general information about the case at the top, followed by the facts, issue(s), holding, and reasoning, as well as dissenting and/or concurring opinions at the end.

This format also leaves considerable space in the lefthand margin for class notes; many students leave space following the case for notes. It may be easier to follow the class discussion if you are working from one notebook instead of two. Sometimes class notes will require more space than you have provided next to the brief, so you may also want to allow extra space for them. One possibility is to leave the back of every page blank for overflow notes. (Hint: use the page facing the case you are discussing, that is, the back of the previous case, for overflow notes.) The topic of note taking is discussed more fully in a later section in this chapter. Before turning to that subject, let's try to do a few briefs utilizing the cases presented earlier in this chapter.

It should be apparent to you that the information you gleaned from these cases fits neatly into the brief format described above. Looking at the *Garratt* case, you recall that you identified basic information about the jurisdictional history and procedural setting of the case, the salient facts, the law on intent, the court's reasoning, and the disposition of the case. In fact, the brief is practically written for us. Transcribing this information to paper using the brief format just given, the result might look something like the brief that appears on page 53.

Now, you try your hand at briefing, using the *McGuire* case that you read. Remember: the key is to be brief. Your brief should be a shorthand guide to the opinion, and not simply a condensed version of it.

As your first year of law school progresses, you will build a greater facility for reading and dissecting cases. You will learn to recognize facts, identify issues, and appreciate legal reasoning. You will analyze cases in a fraction of the time it takes you now. Since you will always use this skill, the investment of time and energy now is worthwhile in the end.

### 3. Classroom Routine

During the first year of law school most classes will be run by the professor using some form of Socratic dialogue. Despite the wide variation in teaching styles, the Socratic method operates on a few

## Model Brief Format

```
Notes                    [Name of case]

                         [Court (date)]

                         [Procedural setting]


                         [Facts]















                         [Issue(s)]

                         [Holding]

                         [Analysis]



                         [Disposition]

                         [Dissent]
```

basic principles. The first and most obvious is that the professor asks the questions and you give the answers. Some students may fake participation by posing questions to the professor. These students may find the tables turned against them when the professor says, "That's an interesting question, Mr. Jones. You've obviously thought about it. What do you think the answer is?" Or they may find their question twisted into one even more bizarre hypothetical and lobbed back into their court.

The second rule is that the professor is always in control. Because he controls all the questions, he also controls the course of the discussion. This situation is compounded by the fact that the professor knows the law and you don't. The scene is reminiscent of the old county fair where the professional boxer takes on all local comers with the prize going to anyone who can last a round. Needless to say, few of the amateurs win the prize. Perhaps an even better illustration would be the chess grand master who simultaneously plays 50 amateurs in a local tournament. The master, who locks horns intellectually with each contestant, ultimately prevails against all of them.

The third rule is that the student never wins. Even if it were a fair fight, you wouldn't win. But it's not, because the professor is both contestant and referee. Whatever you say is wrong, or at least questionable. If you say a case is correctly decided, the professor suggests that maybe a case with a contradictory result is better law. Or maybe the facts in the case should be distinguished from the rule of law you cited. If the rule is right, the policy may be bad. Or if you say the case is wrong, the professor may say the case is right. It may seem like a perpetual shell game. You have to pick which one of three shells is hiding the pea, and no matter which one you pick, the pea is always under a different shell.

The purpose of this drill is basically twofold: first, it aims to teach you to take a position and defend it logically, even in the face of hostile questioning; second, it forces you to question your own thinking. It attempts to demonstrate that there are different sides to almost any question. In time, you learn that given any set of assumptions, you can construct a logical argument to support the position. And you learn to hold your ground. In the classroom, it is more honorable to defend a position that is ultimately wrong (although few positions are truly, ultimately wrong) than to waffle at the professor's first probing question. By picking apart the flaws in your logic, while simultane-

Notes:

Garratt v Dailey
SC Wash 1955
Appeal of J for D

F: Dailey - 5- pulled chair out
from under Garratt-elderly-
causing broken hip. G sues D.
D says he intended no
harm - couldn't get chair
back when G started to sit
Tr. Ct. finds damages = $11,000

I: Did Dailey intend the act
which caused Garratt's injury?
(Can a 5-yr. old have intent?)

H: Intent may be defined as
knowledge with substantial
certainty that consequences
will follow, and if lower
ct finds such intent, D is liable

A: If child understand his act
may bring about a particular
consequence, he may be liable.
Different from intent to harm.

D: On remand, Ct. holds for P (G)

ously forcing you to question and defend your position, the professor helps you to approach problems analytically, which is an important part of the learning process.

Many of us react badly to this criticism. We come to law school with an intellectual smugness, brought about in part by past educational successes, and in part by a deep-seated need to avoid being proven wrong in public. Some students experience terrible anxiety concerning classroom participation; a few become obsessed with the fear of being called upon in class. Some students become so traumatized by their perceived humiliation at the hands of the professor that they literally never recover, and throughout law school barely speak in class when spoken to. Some students withdraw from class itself by talking, doing other things in class, cracking jokes, or not reading class assignments. By doing these things the student, in effect, rejects the validity of the classroom experience. If the Socratic method has no worth, then their self-confidence is not undermined, because they haven't succeeded at something worth succeeding.

The truth is that the Socratic method does teach you valuable skills. You will reconfigure the way you approach and solve problems. No matter what you do after this, you will always "think like a lawyer." How then do you succeed in class? You must accept from the start that this is a learning experience. Whatever doubts you may have, keep in mind that you can learn from everything that goes on around you; from the professor's jibes, classmates' quips, and your own foibles. Don't worry if you don't look good. Everyone has a day in the spotlight, and almost everyone leaves feeling more or less inadequate. Your success here does not depend on performance at all.

Your classmates and professor don't hold up cards like judges in the Olympics: "Very good, Mr. Jones. That's about a 9.4; excellent technique. That answer would have scored higher but the difficulty level of the question was low." "Ms. Smith is really going to have to come up with a perfect answer here in order to stay even with the Germans."

There is nothing wrong with joining the fray; you learn by participating. The more you talk, the easier it is, and the better you get at making arguments. Although you can learn the skill by observing others, you can't beat experience as a teacher.

When I was in law school, there was one fellow who answered all the time. And the professors literally brutalized him. At a party, some of us asked our Torts professor how this guy could get knocked down so much and keep coming back for more. The professor said, "He's learning." And sure enough, at the end of the year, this guy was right up at the top of the class. Remember that your grades are based upon what you assimilate, not what you say in class. (Some schools, though, allow professors to adjust the grades upward or downward for outstanding classroom participation.)

The key to learning in the classroom is preparation. When you have read and briefed the cases, and considered the issues before-hand, you have a better chance to grasp what is going on in the class-room discussion. If you read the cases for each day's class before you go to class, you have won half the battle (see pages 33–34).

In order to get a flavor of the classroom experience, take a look at another case on intent. Read it and brief it as you did the other two cases in this chapter. Think about how the three cases might fit together in a discussion of intent. Look at the note cases and ques-tions following the case to get a sense of where the classroom dis-cussion might be going. These notes sometimes, but not always, offer a preview of the professor's game plan. This case involves a 1970s look at a very 1990s issue: sexual harassment.

### SPIVEY v. BATTAGLIA
Supreme Court of Florida, 1972.
258 So.2d 815.

DEKLE, JUSTICE. \* \* \* Petitioner (plaintiff in the trial court) and respondent (defendant) were employees of Battaglia Fruit Co. on Janua-ry 21, 1965. During the lunch hour several employees of Battaglia Fruit Co., including petitioner and respondent, were seated on a work table in the plant of the company. Respondent, in an effort to tease petitioner, whom he knew to be shy, intentionally put his arm around petitioner and pulled her head toward him. Immediately after this "friendly unsolicited hug," petitioner suffered a sharp pain in the back of her neck and ear, and sharp pains into the base of her skull. As a result, petitioner was paralyzed on the left side of her face and mouth.

An action was commenced in the Circuit Court of Orange County, Florida, wherein the petitioners, Mr. and Mrs. Spivey, brought suit against respondent for, (1) negligence, and (2) assault and battery. Respondent, Mr. Battaglia, filed his answer raising as a defense the claim that his "friendly unsolicited hug" was an assault and battery as a matter of law and was barred by the running of the two-year statute of limitations on assault and battery. Respondent's motion for summary judgment was granted by the trial court on this basis. The district court affirmed on the authority of McDonald v. Ford, [223 So.2d 553 (Fla.App.1969)].

The question presented for our determination is whether petitioner's action could be maintained on the negligence count, or whether respondent's conduct amounted to an assault and battery as a matter of law, which would bar the suit under the two-year statute (which had run).

In *McDonald* the incident complained of occurred in the early morning hours in a home owned by the defendant. While the plaintiff was looking through some records, the defendant came up behind her, laughingly embraced her and, though she resisted, kissed her hard. As the defendant was hurting the plaintiff physically by his embrace, the plaintiff continued to struggle violently and the defendant continued to laugh and pursue his love-making attempts. In the process, plaintiff struck her face hard upon an object that she was unable to identify specifically. With those facts before it, the district court held that what actually occurred was an assault and battery, and not negligence. The court quoted with approval from the Court of Appeals of Ohio in Williams v. Pressman, 113 N.E.2d 395, at 396 (Ohio App.1953):

" * * * an assault and battery is not negligence, for such action is intentional, while negligence connotes an unintentional act."

The intent with which such a tort liability as assault is concerned is not necessarily a hostile intent, or a desire to do harm. Where a reasonable man would believe that a particular result was *substantially certain* to follow, he will be held in the eyes of the law as though he had intended it. It would thus be an assault (intentional). However, the knowledge and appreciation of a *risk,* short of substantial certainty, is not the equivalent of intent. Thus, the distinction between intent and negligence boils down to a matter of degree. "Apparently the line has been drawn by the courts at the point where the known danger ceases to be only a foreseeable risk which a reasonable man would avoid (negligence), and becomes a substantial certainty." In the latter case, the intent is legally implied and becomes an assault rather than unintentional negligence.

The distinction between the unsolicited kisses in *McDonald,* supra, and the unsolicited hug in the present case turns upon this question of intent. In *McDonald,* the court, finding an assault and battery, necessarily had to find initially that the results of the defendant's acts were "intentional." This is a rational conclusion in view of the struggling involved there. In the instant case, the DCA must have found the same intent. But we cannot agree with that finding in these circumstances. It cannot be said that a reasonable man in this defendant's position would believe that the bizarre results herein were "substantially certain" to follow. This is an unreasonable conclusion and is a misapplication of the rule in *McDonald*. This does not mean that he does not become liable for such unanticipated results, however. The settled law is that a defendant becomes liable for reasonably foreseeable consequences, though the exact results and damages were not contemplated.

Acts that might be considered prudent in one case might be negligent in another. Negligence is a relative term and its existence must depend in each case upon the particular circumstances which surrounded the parties at the time and place of the events upon which the controversy is based.

The trial judge committed error when he granted summary final judgment in favor of the defendant. The cause should have been submitted to the jury with appropriate instructions regarding the elements of negligence. Accordingly, certiorari is granted; the decision of the district court is hereby quashed and the cause is remanded with directions to reverse the summary final judgment.

It is so ordered.

---

1. Distinguish:

A. The intent to do an act. The defendant fires a rifle, or drives an automobile in excess of the speed limit.

B. The intent to bring about the consequences—the bullet, or the car, hits a man. It is this that is always important in determining whether there is an intentional tort. See Etcher v. Blitch, 381 So.2d 1119 (Fla.App.1979), cert. denied, 386 So.2d 636 (1980).

2. Distinguish:

A. The defendant does not act. He is carried onto plaintiff's land against his will. Smith v. Stone, Style 65, 82 Eng.Rep. 533 (1647).

B. He acts intentionally, but under fear or threats. Twelve armed men compel him to enter plaintiff's land and steal a horse. Gilbert v. Stone, Style 72, 82 Eng.Rep. 539 (1648).

C. He acts intentionally, but without any desire to affect the plaintiff, or any certainty that he will do so. He rides a horse, which runs away with him and runs the plaintiff down. Gibbons v. Pepper, 1 Ld.Raym. 38, 91 Eng.Rep. 922 (1695).

D.  He acts with the desire to affect the plaintiff, but for an entirely permissible or laudable purpose. He shoots the plaintiff in self-defense, or as a soldier defending his country.

In which of these is there an intent to do harm?

3.  In some cases it may not seem important to distinguish between negligent and intentionally wrongful conduct: the defendant will be held liable in either situation. Nevertheless, the distinction may be legally significant. Thus:

A.  Will defendant be liable for punitive damages? See infra, Chapter 10, Section 3.

B.  Will the defense of contributory negligence be available to defendant? See infra page 569, note 10.

C.  Will defendant's employer be liable under the doctrine of *respondeat superior*? See infra page 649.

D.  How far will the law trace the consequences of defendants' wrongful act? See Tate v. Canonica, 180 Cal.App.2d 898, 5 Cal.Rptr. 28 (1960) (liability for causing suicide).

E.  Will the defendant be protected under a liability insurance policy? See Allstate Ins. Co. v. Hiseley, 465 F.2d 1243 (10th Cir.1972). Cloud v. Shelby Mut. Ins. Co., 248 So.2d 217 (Fla.App.1971).

F.  Has the state statute of limitations run? See the principal case.

G.  Will an employer be subject to liability to an employee in spite of a general worker compensation immunity shield?

An exception is sometimes permitted for intentional wrongdoing. Does an employer's intentional failure to train an employee to perform a dangerous task supply the requisite intent to injure under the workers' compensation intentional injury exception? See Reed Tool Co. v. Copelin, 689 S.W.2d 404 (Tex. 1985). What about an employer's deliberate exposure of employees to dangerous products? See Millison v. E.I. du Pont de Nemours & Co., 101 N.J. 161, 501 A.2d 505 (1985). In Blankenship v. Cincinnati Milacron Chemicals, Inc., 69 Ohio St.2d 608, 433 N.E.2d 572 (1982), cert. denied, 459 U.S. 857 (1982), the court held that the relevant workers' compensation statute did not expressly prohibit lawsuits based on intentional torts and harm caused by an employer's intentional conduct was not an injury arising out of the "normal course" of employment. Note, however, that not all jurisdictions hearing suits for intentional torts have gone as far as Ohio in broadening their concept of "intentional." But compare Bardere v. Zafir, 102 A.D.2d 422, 477 N.Y.S.2d 131 (1984), aff'd, 63 N.Y.2d 850, 472 N.E.2d 37, 482 N.Y.S.2d 261 (1984), holding that in the absence of a showing of "specific acts [by the employer] directed at causing harm to particular employees" the doctrine will not apply.

4.  Does this mean that a court's characterization of a defendant's conduct as "negligent" or "intentional" is influenced by the legal effect of its finding? Cf. Lambertson v. United States, 528 F.2d 441 (2d Cir.1976), cert. denied, 426 U.S. 921 (1976).

Imagine that you are sitting in Torts class, and the professor says, "Let's talk about the *Spivey* case." He pauses to look at the seating chart or to make a dramatic effect. His eyes scan the room methodically, stopping at you. "What happened in this case?" You look at your brief and your casebook, and you try to explain how the plaintiff was hugged by the defendant, causing her injuries. "Did he hug her hard? Is that what caused the harm?" You explain that you don't know how hard the hug was, but you do know that the harm was unforeseeable. "What is unforeseeable?" You mumble something about knowledge of the risk, but before you are finished, the professor has shot back, "How would you say that this knowledge of a risk is different from knowledge that consequences are certain to follow?" The former, you say, has to do with negligence, the latter, with intent. "Is there some line that divides intent from knowledge about a risk?" Before you can answer, the professor is asking you hypotheticals, some you recall vaguely from the notes, and others whose source you wouldn't begin to guess.

The hypothetical game works like this: if you answer five times that the plaintiff wins and the sixth time that the defendant wins, the professor wants to know why the defendant wins in the last case but not the others. If you answer that the plaintiff wins all six times, the professor will want to know what the defendant needs to do to win one. In other words, no matter what you say, there is always another question.

After the professor has grilled you for a while, other students may raise their hands to talk. The professor may or may not acknowledge the volunteers. At some point, the professor will try to coax from you the legal principle involved in the case: "What do you think we ought to get out of this case?" And you might respond that intent is a state of mind where knowledge that consequences are substantially, not absolutely, but substantially certain to follow, and anything short of this must be negligence. "Whose mind?" Excuse me? "Whose mind do we look at to determine knowledge—the defendant's?" Well, the case says a reasonable person. "So you're telling me that it's not what the defendant actually knew but what some abstract, fictitious 'reasonable' person knew that counts?"

Here, the discussion might dwell briefly on the difference between a subjective standard, looking at the defendant's own state of mind, and an objective reasonable person standard. "*Garratt* didn't mention anything about reasonableness did it?" The last case, you think to yourself. He's asking about the last case. "You do remember the last case don't you?" Yes, of course, you reply, having used the instant to flip back to your *Garratt* brief. The Restatement doesn't mention reasonableness. "Did the judge here just make this stuff up, or what?" The one thing you don't want to say is, I don't know, but you don't, so you do. Smiling that gotcha smile, the professor suggests, "You might want to check that out after class."

The professor might have asked you why the defendant was arguing that his conduct was intentional. You were ready for that one. The statute of limitations had passed, so if defendant's conduct was an assault and battery, the plaintiff could not recover. It was pretty slick of the plaintiff's lawyer, you note, to transform this case into a negligence action.

### 4. Note Taking

Another skill critical to success in the classroom is effective note taking. You have to find a note taking system that works for you. Here is one formula: brief your cases in a separate notebook for each class. If you use the kind that has a vertical line down the center of the page, you can brief cases on the right and take notes on the left. It may also prove helpful to use different colored pens for professor's comments, classmates' thoughts, and your own notes. Thus, you can segregate the professor's ideas for later study purposes. Student comments may or may not prove valuable. Your own notes represent a synthesis of what you have heard and what you have read. Remember, also, that you tend to stop listening when you write. Some students find it more productive to just listen in class, then take notes immediately afterwards. Most people don't have enough confidence in themselves as listeners to be able to do this. However, if you manage to cut down your writing time and increase listening time, you will learn more in class, particularly if after class is over you immediately reread your notes and fill in the gaps.

Another helpful hint is that the professor's questions are as important as the answers. Ask yourself what question the professor is posing, particularly when the professor raises questions that are never answered or leaves you with a question at the end of class. Also, listen carefully for phrases and statements by the professor that recur with enough regularity to be considered themes. Try to think about common threads that tie large blocks of material together. Look beyond the individual cases, and try to get a feel for what the course is all about, especially as seen through the eyes of the professor.

Develop a set of shorthand symbols that you use consistently in all classes to save writing time in briefs and notes. A list of commonly used symbols is found on page 62. You will undoubtedly make your own additions to this list as time passes.

Modern technology offers additional help with note taking. Cassette recorders permit you to make tapes of classes that you can replay later. Some students listen to their tapes in the car while commuting; others use the recordings to go back and clarify their recollections and fill in gaps in their written notes. Beware: some professors object to the use of tape recorders in class, so find out in advance if the practice is permitted.

An increasing number of students are bringing laptop personal computers to class. Not only can these students type their notes directly to a disk, but they can access their briefs electronically as well. Unfortunately, some old-fashioned professors may fail to see the benefit of classroom computing, just as some oppose tape recording. The times are changing, however, and the computer illiterate eventually will give way to the technologically savvy. The computer and the tape recorder are just two tools for the use of law students and lawyers. If you possess the technology, you should use it. See page 74 for additional thoughts on the application of technology in the law school setting.

## B. After Class

### 1. After Class Review

For many students, when class is over, it is on to the next assignment. They may discuss what transpired in class with a few other students, but for the most part the rule of the day is: never look back.

If you assume that learning takes place in the classroom setting, and that you may lose 50 percent or more of what you learned within 24 hours after leaving class, you might conclude that it would be worthwhile to take steps to retain as much as possible of what you have learned while it is still fresh on your mind.

# Note-Taking Symbols

| | |
|---|---|
| P or ⲦⲄ | Plaintiff |
| D or Δ | Defendant |
| TP or Θ | Third Party |
| CA | Cause of Action |
| Q or ? | Question |
| H | Holding |
| BP | Burden of Proof |
| K | Contract |
| T | Tort |
| IT | Intentional Tort |
| N | Negligence |
| SL | Strict Liability |
| Df | Defense |
| CN | Contributory Negligence |
| AR | Assumption of Risk |
| 4C | Foresee |
| PF | Prima facie |
| DM | Damages |
| BR | Breach |
| Du | Duty |
| BFP | Bona fide purchaser |
| PUN | Punitive |
| STD | Standard |
| RIL | Res ipsa loquitur |
| NPS | Negligence per se |
| ORPP | Ordinary Reasonably Prudent Person |
| L | Lawyer |
| W/ | With |
| W/O | Without |
| & | And |
| v. | Versus |
| Aff | Affirmed |
| Rem | Remanded |
| Rev | Reversed |
| Ct | Court |
| J | Judge |
| Jmt | Judgment |
| RS | Restatement |
| ∅ | Not |
| ∴ | Therefore |
| Be | Because |
| EX | Except/Exception |
| EV | Evidence |
| INF | Infer/Inference |
| Prof | Professor says |
| s/be | should be |
| = | Same as, equal to |
| ≠ | Not the same as, equal to |
| SoL | Statute of Limitations |

A simple technique requiring 15 minutes or less per class will allow you to maximize your retention. As soon as possible after class, go to a quiet place such as the library and read through your notes. Fill in any blanks you find. Two months from now you will not remember what any of your half-completed sentences or chicken scratchings mean. Highlight questions and comments that you consider particularly important. Add your own personal ideas, particularly answers to the professor's questions. Reformulate your statements of the issues and holdings in the cases if classroom discussion suggested that changes are in order. Highlight case holdings, either your original or revised version. By doing this simple daily review, you should be amazed how much simpler your later study efforts become.

## 2. Talking to Professors

Many professors talk informally to their students after class is over. Frequently, they will provide insights into the material that were not clear in class. Even if you do not have any questions to pose, it may be fruitful to go down and listen.

If you have specific questions, or if you are unusually confused, your professors will be available to talk with you. Some students are reluctant to interrupt their professor or to appear to their classmates to be currying favor. These fears are generally groundless. Your professors, however, are not likely to respond favorably if they feel you are using them simply as a substitute for doing your own thinking. Professors who are unwilling to spoon-feed you the answer (if there is such a thing) during class will be unwilling to spoon-feed you after class also. If you go to see a professor about a question, you should have taken the time to think about it, formulate your own statement of the problem, and consider possible answers. You should have reviewed any cases on the subject. The question, "Excuse me, professor, but what did you say the holding in *Spivey v. Battaglia* was?" will probably be met with icy silence. On the other hand, the following approach is likely to produce a more favorable response: "I was troubled by our discussion in class on the *Spivey* case. Don't you think that women should have a legal remedy against unwanted advances? The court basically ignores the real issue here by talking about intent." "When was this case decided, Ms. Jones? 1971? Were courts back then—in Florida—likely to be responsive to sexual harassment claims?" "Yes, but we have to start somewhere." "Maybe we did. What happened in this case that was unusual?" "Well, for one thing the plaintiff's lawyer gets around the statute of limitations problem by arguing negligence." "Right. So by letting Spivey go forward on the negligence theory, the judge is giving her a remedy, or at least a shot at it. Was the defendant's conduct intentional? Probably, by the Restatement definition. When he put out his arms to hug her, he knew with substantial certainty that offensive if not harmful contact would result. Is the court wrong in *Spivey*?" "Maybe, but I'm glad she can argue negligence, even though she ought to sue the bastard for sexual harassment." "And today, Ms. Jones, she would."

In short, when you see a professor privately, you can expect the same kind of exchange that you would get in class, although it may seem that the professor is much more willing to provide answers (or at least opinions) than during class. As in class, however, you have to meet the professor halfway for the dialogue to work. Most students who take the time to talk to their professors outside of class are surprised by the professors' openness and candor.

### 3. Outside Reading

Professors will often cite cases, articles, and hornbooks not included in the casebook. These references should be checked out. I remember Professor Loisieux in Contracts, who used to say periodically at the end of class, "See what the UCC has to say about that." Now we didn't open the UCC all year long. We studied common law contracts. But, guess what? The final exam was all UCC.

In college, everything you needed to know in American History was contained in your American History book, or the professor's lectures. In law school, your casebook and classroom discussions are but two tools to help you understand the subject matter. There are many others. One resource is hornbooks, such as Prosser and Keeton on Torts (see Appendix B, pages 159–163). Hornbooks are annotated discussions of the law in a particular subject area. Another resource can be found in the restatements, such as the Restatement (Second) of Torts (see Appendix B, page 164). Restatements are summaries of the law in a field synthesized by leading authorities on the subject. Other aides include nutshells (see Appendix B, pages 165–171), short (150 pages) overviews of the law in a given area, and commercial outlines (see Appendix B, pages 172 and 175). You will note that the resources referred to in Appendix B all address the same issue of intent raised in *Garratt*, *McGuire*, and *Spivey*. The resources all offer additional insights to help you understand the concept.

Although all your professors told you to avoid commercial outlines, almost all students buy and use them. These comments are offered on the assumption that you will not be deterred from your reliance on these products. First, you do not need to buy every commercial outline on the market. The leading outlines are Gilbert's, Legalines, Emanuel's, West's Black Letter Law Series, and multistate bar review outlines (produced by several vendors). At some schools, you can purchase outlines specific to courses and instructors at that school. Find a series that is easy for you to follow. The professor, when pressed, may even begrudgingly acknowledge her personal favorite for her subject area.

The commercial outline can only be used effectively as a supplement to your own outline and study materials. As will be suggested later in this chapter (see page 67), the process of outlining itself is integral to the learning process. If you are merely taking someone else's work product, whether it is that of another student or the professor who did the job for Gilbert's, you will not force yourself to organize and conceptualize the principles in your own mind. You will be memorizing a bunch of rules.

A second important caveat if you use commercial outlines is to study the course you actually took, not the course as seen through the eyes of the outline's author. Different professors organize the material differently, view the cases differently, and emphasize different areas to a greater or lesser degree. So, unless your professor is actually the author of that commercial outline, remember that the author will not be grading your exam. With these warnings in the back of your mind, you may find these outlines extremely helpful to clarify your own thoughts, provide concrete examples, and give you some reasonable basis for reviewing your own work product.

Because there is so much review material, it is important to know when to stop. When you practice law for a living, you can always find another case or law review article to read. But because your client is paying the bill, you must decide at some point that your research is sufficient. In law school, it is impossible to leave "no" stone unturned;

you simply have to turn over enough stones to get the job done. The skills of knowing when to say enough and learning not to follow time-consuming dead-end trails are critical. Many students actually hurt their performance by engaging in academic overkill.

### 4. Synthesizing

The process of synthesizing is overlooked by a great number of students. Synthesis is an ongoing process, which, in the context of legal education, means pulling together disparate concepts into a comprehensible body of information. The process of synthesizing may be undertaken through a series of discrete steps. A few comments will help you to approach this process sensibly. The time to engage in synthesizing is at the end of each chapter in your book. This probably will be every one, two, or three weeks. Chapters in the casebook were created to place conceptually related topics together in the text. By taking one or two hours at these natural break points in the course, you can take advantage of logical divisions in the subject matter.

It is important to transform your study material from a case-oriented document to a concept-oriented one. The briefs and class notes as recorded in your notebooks reflect an artificial organization of the material, based on the chronology of the discussion and study. You need to create an outline that presents the ideas in a logical order that you can understand.

The first step in this process of synthesis is to reread your notes, particularly the highlighted portions of your briefs (as depicted in your postclass review). Then, extract from your earlier notes the rules, ideas, and principles you have identified. One convenient way to do this, which will support your subsequent outlining, is to place these statements on index cards. You do not need to write out case names or other citations, just the concepts. In the righthand corner of each card, jot down the day or days (because you may find that some ideas are discussed in more than one class) when the idea was discussed.

In the cases on intent in this chapter, you have already seen a number of concepts that you will need to understand:
- intent as a motive to cause harm
- intent to bring about consequences
- knowledge
- substantial certainty

- reasonable belief
- intent exercised by children
- intent exercised by insane persons

Reviewing your notes you may find other concepts. Whether you use note cards, make lists, or work from your notes, you should not overlook this step. Some students will utilize their computers during the synthesizing process, while others will do the job manually. In any event, the product should be a mass of information ready to be outlined.

Assuming your law school classes average about three cases per day, the discussion of *Garratt, McGuire,* and *Spivey* represents approximately one day's worth of law school work in one course. A typical class such as Torts will meet 28 to 30 times during the semester, and you will probably take five classes. This means that you now have covered about 1/150 of the information you will need to assimilate in the first semester alone.

### 5. Outlines

The bridge between classroom participation and studying for exams is outlining. Many students misunderstand the purpose of outlining, and therefore fail to benefit from the process. Others get too far behind in class preparation to properly utilize outlining techniques. Their last-ditch efforts before exams are too little, too late.

The course outline has two basic purposes: first, it is a continuation of the synthesis process. It represents a reduction of the vast amount of material into a manageable, organized format. Second, the outline allows you to transform the case-oriented classroom discussion into the topic-oriented summary of what you have learned.

You may outline material at the end of each chapter in the casebook after synthesis. Because the authors have grouped the material by chapters in a logical way, you will find it easier to grapple with ideas at these times. When you go back to study at the end of the course, you may find that some of your earlier impressions and statements were offbase. You may find it easier to revise your earlier synthesis and outline than to start from scratch.

Many students wait until later in the semester to do their outlines in order to give them the benefit of cumulative learning. Many find that their ideas early in the course have been modified by subsequent readings and discussions. The downside risk in waiting to do your outlines is that you may not have enough time at the end of the semester to do an adequate job. If you have been religious about reviewing and synthesizing the earlier material, however, preparing an outline should be a manageable process.

Different people use different outlining structures. Generally, a topic outline will be adequate, but you may need to use sentences as well to state rules of law with specificity. You probably will feel most comfortable with an approach to outlining that you already know. As long as you can organize major topics and subtopics in a systematic way, the particular format is not important. One of the most common outline formats is presented on page 69. This format provides eight levels of information, which should be sufficient for most law school outlines.

If you are using a personal computer, you probably already have access to an outline feature in your word processing program. The outline feature in WordPerfect, the most popular word processing program, can be turned on and off easily (the command is Shift + F4, 4 in WP5.1). If your word processor does not have an outline function, you can buy any of a number of outline programs (e.g., Think-tank). Such programs provide a greater degree of flexibility and efficiency than handwritten outlines. In addition, outliners can be revised easily, since they typically renumber automatically if you make changes.

It is critical to remember to create a topic-oriented substantive outline, rather than one based on the cases. You may place a case name at the end of a statement in your outline if it helps you to remember the context in which you studied the idea. Because professors are more interested in your knowledge of substantive legal principles than they are in hearing you recite case names, this approach makes more sense in exam preparation.

How do you put these general outlining principles to work? The form on page 70 presents a detailed organizational plan for a law school outline. As you can see, it focuses on concepts rather than cases, although cases are included along with class hypotheticals. The segment called "keys" is optional, but it may be useful to include in one place insights or hints to help you grasp the concept. Usually, the rule followed in the majority of jurisdictions is covered first, but frequently, one or more minority positions will need to be included as

## Model Outline Format

```
I.
    A.
        1.
        2.
        3.
            a.
            b.
            c.
                (1)
                (2)
                (3)
                    (a)
                    (b)
                    (c)
                        i)
                        ii)
                        iii)
                            a)
                            b)
                            c)
    B.
    C.
II.
III.
```

## Law School Outline Organization

```
                              OUTLINE

    I.   Topic #1

         A.   Principle #1

              1.   Rule--majority

                   a.   Elements, test, etc.

                        (1)  Examples

                        (2)  Cases

                        (3)  Hypotheticals

                   b.   Exceptions

                        (1)  Examples

                        (2)  Cases

                        (3)  Hypotheticals

                   c.   Keys

                        (1)  Terms defined

                        (2)  Comments

                             (a)  Professor

                             (b)  You

                             (c)  Others

                        (3)  Mnemonic devices, etc.

              2.   Rule--minority

              3.   Rule--others?

         B.   Principle #2

    II.  Topic #2
```

well. Minority rules may be discussed in the court's opinion, a dissenting opinion, note cases, or classroom discussion.

Using the information you have gathered on the three cases covered in this chapter, try your hand at producing an outline on intent. Since there is obviously more to the topic than you have had a chance to learn here (as the material in Appendix B suggests), proceed on the assumption that the universe of law on the subject of intent is contained in these three cases. After you have prepared your outline, look at page 72 to view a sample outline on the same subject. If your outline is substantially similar to the model, you are on the right track. If your outline is very different, you may want to reconsider your work product. In Chapter 5, on taking exams, you will have another opportunity to practice outlining, if you need it. Outlining is something most people have done since elementary school, so law students may overlook the fact that GOOD outlining is a skill essential to success in law school, because the outline is the vehicle through which you make all the information you have assimilated manageable.

The end product of your effort will be a document that reflects what you learned in the course you actually took. Even though you may need to do some research at the end of the semester to fill in gaps in your notes, if you have worked steadily throughout the semester you should have virtually everything you need to do your outline right in front of you when you need it. If you haven't prepared efficiently throughout the semester, the burden will be insurmountable. You will probably either cut corners on your outline, finish your outline with no time to study it, or resort to reading a commercial outline or one produced by a classmate.

Sometimes study groups prepare outlines by dividing subject matter among themselves. These individual efforts are collated, photocopied, and distributed to members of the group. If you accept the assumption that the importance of outlining is the process rather than the work product, you should agree that this approach is not sound. Group outlining will leave you highly informed about the areas you have outlined personally, and unclear about others you have not. It is a better practice for each person in the study group to prepare an outline individually, but work as a group to compare notes, discuss inconsistencies, pose hypotheticals, and look at thorny issues.

As you study, you may develop an outline of the outline, reducing the longer document into a shorter one as you master the material.

## Sample Outline

TORTS

I Intentional Torts
  a. Intent
     1. Substantial certainty that
        consequences will follow (scc)
        a. Reasonable knowledge
        b. D's state of mind
        c. Children (Garratt)
        d. Insane (McGuire)
     2. To cause harm (either/or)
        a. Motive
        b. May be more "wrong"
     3. Contrast
        a. v. knowledge of risk (neg.)
        b. Gun
           (1) Desire to kill v.
           (2) Pulling trigger in crowd (scc)
     4. Essential element in intentional torts
  B. Battery
     1. Elements
        a Harmful or offensive
        b. Intional
        c. Contact with another
        d. Unconsented

And that outline may be distilled further, until three or four major points trigger all of the knowledge derived from the original outline. Some students even tape their outlines and play them on the car radio while commuting.

Whereas outlining is an integral part of learning, it is possible to become so obsessed with the process of preparing the outiine that the objective of learning is overlooked. Never forget that the outline is a tool. Just as your briefs can be too long, your outline can say too much.

### 6. Checklists

Another useful device is the checklist. A checklist is a list of key words comprising a body of knowledge you need to know. This checklist may be broad, such as the main headings of your outline, or specific, such as in the elements of a tort. A checklist can help you avoid leaving out important points in your discussion. You can use mnemonic devices. Mnemonic devices use a series of letters representing concepts you want to remember in a word or phrase. If you ever took music, you learned that the lines on the treble clef were E, G, B, D, F because "Every good boy does fine," and that the spaces were F, A, C, E. In law you can use similar tools to help remember the large number of rules and principles you must know.

## C. Other Concerns

### 1. Memorization Versus the Big Picture

A common question posed by many first year law students is, "How much of my time should I devote to memorizing the law?" The simplistic answer is that you should focus more on the big picture than on memorization of case holdings. Getting the big picture means coming to grips with how the principles involved in the course fit together. It suggests an overall understanding of the material. And it is almost impossible to do well in law school without such an understanding. Thus, your professors all will admonish you not to simply memorize the black letter law.

On the other hand, it is difficult to get the big picture if you don't understand the underlying rules. And no matter how well you understand the rationale of proximate cause as discussed by the leading luminaries in the field of torts, if you can't remember the elements in a negligence suit, you might as well turn in your Gilbert's. In truth, there is a great deal of memorization in law school, but it is memorization within a larger context. It is different from cramming for a history exam in undergraduate school; in those days you could forget the facts you memorized as soon as you walked out of the exam. In law, you will be using many of these rules for the next 30 to 40 years. Your goal should be to internalize these concepts by learning how everything fits together.

### 2. Study Groups

Another question students ask is, "Should I study alone or with a group?" Part of the answer is that it depends on you. Some people study best alone, and find that the group merely slows them down. If the group's orientation is more social than study, the group will detract from the learning process. If one or more members of the group fail to do their share of the work, everyone is hurt. If the group serves simply to cut corners in studying, you might as well invest in a set of canned briefs and commercial outlines.

If the study group is properly utilized to supplement the individual efforts of its members, and if the group dynamics are good, study groups can have a positive effect on law school success. Learning the law frequently entails spirited discussion of the issues. You engage in such discussion in class, and informally when class is over. Study groups can provide another forum for dialogue on the issues.

There are two keys. All participants should be roughly equally prepared. Secondly, you must stick to the subject; if the discussion evolves into an anecdotal bull session, it ceases to be productive. A final note on study groups: your group doesn't have to be the same in each class nor does it have to be large. One or two good study partners will work better than a group of seven or eight duds.

### 3. Computers

The final question, which an increasing number of students ask, is, "Can I use my personal computer to help me study?" By all means, do it. In addition to the obvious application of typing memos and briefs, your computer can be used for outlining, taking notes (if you have a laptop model), organizing your schedule, managing your budget, and conducting your job search. Most schools will not let you type your exam on your computer because of the possibility that you could store notes in memory to call up during the exam. Personal computers have countless applications in law, and if you can begin to use them now, you should.

## D. Using the Library

Your school's law library is a vast resource, which is always available to you. During the next three to four years, you will spend countless hours doing legal research, studying, and reading. Determine at an early stage of your law school career how to exploit the library's collection.

Whether your library has as few as 100,000 volumes or over 500,000, there are a number of common parts. You will find reports containing published decisions of courts in different jurisdictions. You will also find law reviews and other scholarly journals, treatises (e.g., *Prosser and Keeton on Torts),* legal encyclopedias (e.g., CJS, ALR) and indexes (e.g., Shepard's). Not all the books are on the shelves either. The library will have many lesser used volumes on microfiche. It will also have access to electronic databases such as LEXIS and WESTLAW, as well as CD-ROM technology that permits the storage of vast amounts of information on compact disc. Finally, the library has special collections that relate to areas of emphasis in the law school curriculum, multimedia collections such as videotapes, and directories (e.g., *Martindale-Hubbell Legal Directory).* Furthermore, if your law library does not have a volume you need, it may be able to obtain the book through interlibrary loan from your university, public, or neighboring law library.

A library is more than books; it is people. The professional librarians are trained to help you with your scholarly endeavors; some of them may have a law degree in addition to a master's degree in library science. You should get to know the reference librarian and other members of the library staff, because they will be able to help you in ways you might not even anticipate as you begin your legal education.

If the library is books and people, it is also a place. It was designed to give you somewhere to study. A law library must, under the American Bar Association accreditation standards, be able to seat 60 percent of the student body at one time. Many law schools have gone beyond this requirement, providing ample study space, private carrels, and discussion rooms. Some libraries may be too noisy, too drafty, too dim, or too cramped. Such limitations may affect your use of the facilities. You should explore the physical layout of your law library in order to find a study area that works for you. If you can sign up for a study carrel, do so early before they are all taken. This may not be an option, however, if the school allocates a limited number of carrels to upper division students.

CHAPTER **5**
# Taking Exams

---

This chapter deals with law school exams. Probably no aspect of legal education produces as much stress as first year law school examinations. These tests are physically and intellectually draining. They can make you or break you academically. They are also the subject of considerable myth and misinformation. This chapter will explore four keys to successful exam taking: substantive legal knowledge, analysis, writing, and management of time and stress. Mastery of law school examinations requires the ability to do all these things well.

## A. The Role of Ongoing Study

The previous chapter suggests that an organized plan of ongoing study throughout the semester is the best way to prepare for law school exams. In undergraduate school and graduate school before, you may have succeeded in blowing off the semester until the night before the exam, and then cramming madly and somehow pulling out a decent grade. The chances of your repeating the feat in law school are highly unlikely. First, the learning process is very different here. You have to do more than just recite facts. During the second and third year, after you have learned to think like a lawyer, many of the steps that took forever during the first year will become second nature to you. For this reason, your study time will be reduced—although ongoing study still will work better than cramming. Second, there is just too much material to cover for short-term cramming to be a feasible approach to law school study. Not only is the volume of material vast, but the level of detail that you must comprehend is great. Third, the competition is too good. Because law schools accept only the best undergraduate students, the middle and bottom of the college curve is gone. And if you fall victim to lazy study habits, you will find yourself holding up the bottom of the class in law school. In fact, even if you study as hard as you can, you may still wind up in the middle of the class, although chances are you will not be at the bottom. The word is this: don't take chances. The stakes are too high. Your best shot at mastering law school exams is to prepare continuously throughout the semester.

## B. Review for Exams

### *1. By the Professor*

Many professors provide review sessions prior to exams. In these sessions, they give you some idea of what will be covered on the exam, how to study for their exam, and an overview of the substantive law. They may also discuss particularly difficult parts of the curriculum and answer questions. If your professor offers such a review session, take full advantage of the opportunity. Some professors will allow you to record these sessions. If they do, bring your tape recorder and leave your pencil at home. You can always transcribe the tape, so use the review session to actively listen to what the professor has to say.

Back in the old days, review sessions were unheard of. In fact, my Contracts class pleaded with Professor Loisieux to give us a review session because we were all so confused. After much gnashing of teeth, he relented. On the appointed day, we were all sitting expectantly in the classroom waiting for Professor Loisieux to arrive. When he did, a hush fell over the assembled throng. Now at last the truth. Instead of pulling stone tablets from his briefcase, Professor Loisieux looked around the room and smiled. Then he said, "Well, all year long you people have accused me of hiding the ball. There is no ball." And he walked out. The review didn't help much with the Contracts exam, but it has remained one of the most enduring and accurate lessons of law school. The lesson in its brevity teaches two things: First, there aren't any stone tablets. Second, to learn it, you have to do it yourself.

### *2. By Yourself*

Because the bulk of your study time will be spent working alone, it is important to find a study place that is comfortable, convenient, and free from distractions. Some law students move away from their families, take leaves from their jobs, and curtail regular activities during the exam period. This may not be an option for everyone, but it is important to create an environment where you can devote your full attention to study for substantial periods of time. The law library becomes packed during finals, and may prove to be a less hospitable study environment during exams than it was earlier in the semester. Plan out your study schedule from the last week of classes, through the reading period and exams. Try to block out periods of time to study, and designate what you plan to do at each stage. Allocate time according to the relative credits required in each course. Stick to your schedule.

Eat well and get plenty of sleep. Part of being mentally ready for exams is being physically prepared. If you are tired or weak, you will not perform as well. If you become sick during exams, do not try to take them. Call the dean in charge if you can't get out of bed, and supply medical documentation if necessary. Most deans do not look favorably upon butterflies in the stomach as sufficient grounds for postponing exams, but they will be understanding about legitimate illness. If you eat well and sleep well during this period, the chances of becoming ill are less.

After exams start, it is important to put the exams you have completed behind you, and move on to the ones ahead. There will be plenty of time for celebration after the last exam. Law school exams tend to be emotionally and physically draining, so a good meal and good sleep will help to put you back on track. If you had a particularly bad exam, do not worry about it now. You will be able to survive one bad grade, but if you let it affect your performance on other tests, you could be in trouble. Remember, too, that just because you thought you did poorly does not mean you did. Your reaction may arise from the fact that you saw clearly the complexity and difficulty of the issues addressed in the examination.

### 3. With Your Study Group

If you have a study group, schedule study group sessions as a balance to your individual work. As with your personal schedule, the study group schedule should be clearly spelled out, and adhered to. There may be a tendency to want to dissect completed exams rather than study for upcoming ones. Make every effort to avoid giving in to this temptation.

## C. Practice Exams

Most law school libraries keep on file past exams by your professors. At the very least, you should read through these exams in order to get a feel for what the professor is likely to ask this time around. You might spend some of your study group time discussing the old questions. The best use of old exams is to sit down and take them. Don't just answer the questions, but take the entire exam, adhering to the time limitations provided in the instructions. This will give you the opportunity not only to deal with the substantive questions, but also to get a feel for the professor's approach to the exam process itself. You will be able to ascertain, to a degree, whether you answer questions too quickly or too slowly. In some cases, the professor's exam will not be on file, or the professor will be new. If so, you may just have to look at exams prepared by other professors. However, you should be able to do practice exams for at least some of your classes.

## D. What Kind of Exam?

There are many different kinds of law school exams. Not surprisingly, you will approach different exam formats differently. Furthermore, generalizations about exam taking do not apply equally to all types of exams. Thus, before you begin to study for an exam, you should attempt to ascertain its organization and structure.

### 1. Essay Exams

The most common first year examination is the traditional essay exam. Tests are normally scheduled for two, three, or four hours, depending on the credit hours for the course. Essays may be 45 minutes, 1 hour, or more in length. The number of questions on a given test will depend on the length of the test and the individual questions. Longer questions, as you might expect, tend to cover more issues and utilize more complex fact patterns. The issues are also usually multilayered, so that most students will see the basic problem, and fewer students will catch more subtle questions. This may account for the phenomenon many law students experience: doing well on exams they are sure they flunked and performing poorly on exams they thought were easy. An exam may seem easy for someone who misses a number of significant issues and difficult for someone who recognized those issues.

Take a look at the sample essay question below, which was used in an actual first year Torts exam. You can see that the question involves a series of events, and you need not have gone to law school to recognize a number of injuries and potential lawsuits. The question asks, "Who is liable to whom?" (perhaps the broadest possible question "call"). It also calls for a discussion of theories, damages, and defenses, suggesting that specific points will be awarded for addressing these matters. Because of the complexity of long essays, your organizational skills are critical. It may help to label issues and subissues, as well as to underline key words and phrases.

Because you have not taken the entire Torts course, this question is probably beyond your ken at this point in time. Right now, you should read it to get a sense of the length and complexity of extended law school essay questions. You may want to return to it late in your first semester of law school as you begin to prepare for exams. Additional long essay questions may be found in Appendix E, pages 236–247.

## Sample Essay
## Exam Question

Construction was progressing on the new wing of the Camelot Law School. Although the project was far from complete, the faculty wing had been occupied prior to the beginning of the fall 1985 semester. A hallway connected the faculty offices with the rest of the law school; rooms along the hallway were still under construction.

The general contractor, Marvin Mercenary, had requested that his site supervisor, Joe D. Furious, protect the property by placing warnings in the hall to keep out everybody but faculty members, and to warn faculty using the hallway of potential dangers on the construction site. Furious put up two signs: one said "No students;" the other, "Be careful."

Furious also told his workers, Larry Comical, Klaus vonKurtson and Marjorie Schoolgirl, to keep the hallway clear and to avoid using sloppy methods in their work. Despite these admonitions, Comical left an open bucket of white paint in the hallway near the top of the stairs leading to the faculty offices. Schoolgirl and vonKurtson were carrying several sheets of plywood down the hall when vonKurtson stepped into the open paint bucket, causing him to lose his balance and drop his end of the load. Schoolgirl, being small of stature, could not hold on to her end of the plywood sheets, and she tumbled down the stairs.

At the very moment this happened, M. B. McManymen, Dave Fish, and Phyllis Bookends, faculty members at the law school, were returning to their offices from a faculty meeting in the law school. As they ascended the stairs, Schoolgirl and the plywood were descending at a great rate of speed due to the law of gravity. The faculty members did not notice the oncoming objects because they were involved in an intense discussion about the gravity of law.

At any rate, Schoolgirl's fall was broken when she fortunately landed on McManymen; McManymen's leg was broken when she unfortunately fell back down the stairwell. More unfortunately, the injury did not heal, and two years later cancer developed at the point of the break and her leg had to be amputated.

Meanwhile, the plywood struck Bookends, causing her to lose her balance. She instinctively reached out to grab something to maintain her footing. What she grabbed was an electrical cord hanging from the ceiling. Although there was no obvious exposed wire, Bookends was shocked as she held the cord. Fish, attempting to be civil, reached out to help her up, causing the current to proceed through his body as well. Bookends survived the incident, but she was in the second month of pregnancy and the child she was carrying did not. Nor did Fish, whose pre-existing heart condition was aggravated by the electric shock. The next day he collapsed and died of a heart attack.

The bucket of paint rolled down the stairs, coming to rest on the Torts notes of first year law student Gilbert Outline, who was studying at the foot of the stairs some 50 feet from the place Comical initially had left the bucket. Outline's notes were ruined; he failed the Torts exam and was dismissed from school for academic deficiency.

In addition, there was a statute in the state of Camelot, which provided that, "any building contractor who leaves an open container of paint in any enclosed area on a construction site shall be guilty of a misdemeanor." The legislative history indicated that fumes from open paint cans in enclosed areas had resulted in several explosions in recent years in the state of Camelot.

What tort liability issues are presented by this fact situation? Who is liable to whom? What damages are recoverable if the injured parties prevail? What theories of law are most likely

to be used by potential plaintiffs in subsequent lawsuits? What
defenses may be presented by potential defendants?

## 2. *Short Answer Exams*

A second type of exam is the short answer or short essay exam. In
this format, the questions are usually 10, 15, 20, or 30 minutes and
address a limited number of issues. A short answer test will have
many more questions and may limit the amount of space allocated for
writing your answer.

Short answer questions are problematic in that they are narrowly
drawn to cover a limited number of issues; if you miss the issue here,
you are out of luck. Sometimes short answer questions contain
enough issues that they could be long essays except for the fact that
you have only a limited amount of time to discuss them. The key to
answering short answers is to get right to the point, stating the
issue(s) immediately, and answering the question concisely and
clearly. There is less need to organize your answer than on a longer
essay, but logical thinking is still important.

The sample question below is an example of a fairly long short
answer question; we will return to it later in this chapter. Appendix
F, page 248, contains additional examples of short answer questions.
Some of them relate to topics addressed in this book; others deal with
problems you will not cover until later. Again, these sample questions
may prove valuable to you when you practice for exams later in the
first year in law school.

## Sample Short Answer Question

Sally Westchester decided to go shopping one day in
Manhattan. She took Metro North to Grand Central where she
disembarked, and started up Fifth Avenue, store by store.
Eventually, she turned down one of the cross streets as she
worked her way toward Madison Avenue and Bloomies. As she
was passing a construction site, she had to walk through a
temporary covered walkway separated from the street and the
construction by metal bars. The bars would permit a person
to pass through only with difficulty, especially a person
such as Sally laden with packages. On the construction side
of the passage was a chain link fence; in the street there
was a considerable amount of traffic.

About halfway through the passage, Sally looked up to see a scruffy looking man standing directly in her path. She clutched her purse tightly, but the man did not move. He stared at her for what seemed like an eternity, and then spoke, "Hey lady, you got a quarter for a cup of coffee?" Sally said nothing, but weighed the situation. Out of the corner of her eye she could see another man standing at the end of the passage from whence she had come, but she could not tell if he had any connection to the man who had spoken.

"Lady, you wouldn't want a poor homeless man to starve would you?" the man continued. Sally still said nothing, and the man, growing agitated, shouted, "You think you're too good to speak to me. You're lucky I don't break you like a stick, or smear that pretty makeup all over that pretty face." At this moment, Sally noticed that the second man had entered the walkway and was approaching her from behind. Summoning all her strength, Sally pushed the scruffy man in front of her as she ran to get out of the passage. He fell backwards between the metal bars and into the street, where he was struck and killed by a car carefully driven by Tom Tourist. Discuss the possible torts and defenses in this scenario.

### 3. Multiple-Choice Exams

A third exam format utilizes multiple-choice questions. Taking multiple-choice tests involves a specific skill that everyone has learned through standardized testing from grade school. Some students are clearly better multiple-choice test takers than others. Since the advent of the multistate bar examination in the mid-1970s, multiple-choice exams have proliferated at many schools.

On the next pages are three multiple-choice questions from a first year Torts exam. Although the fact patterns for many law school multiple-choice questions may be longer than these, they represent a standard format with four choices. Often you will be able to eliminate two of the options immediately, leaving two plausible answers. Multiple-choice questions tend to test your ability to make distinctions about fine points in the rules of law. Multiple-choice tests place much greater emphasis on the "black letter law" and less on the "big picture" than essay tests. Multiple-choice tests reward skill in taking standardized-type tests, while essay tests reward written communication skills.

Just as a poor writer will have difficulty on an essay exam, a person who struggled through the SAT, GRE, and LSAT will struggle through law school multiple-choice exams. If your skill in taking multiple-choice exams is weak and you know that you will be getting multiple-choice exams, try to get some practice, or assistance; otherwise multiple-choice tests will continue to be your Achilles heel. A guide that deals with multiple-choice test-taking skills generally, such as *Barron's Guide to the LSAT*, may prove helpful. Another possibility is to gain access to materials produced for bar review courses dealing with preparation for the Multistate Bar Exam, a multiple-choice test. Find out from your professors early in the semester if they plan to use multiple-choice questions (some may give a test that is part multiple-choice and part essay). You can expect between twelve and thirty multiple-choice questions per hour, depending on their length (the ones below are the two-minute variety).

## Sample Multiple-Choice Exam Questions

15. Smoke and soot from D's factory blew over P's property causing eye irritation and damage to his property. D showed that his factory could not be operated with a lower smoke and ash emission and that the neighborhood was mixed residential and industrial. P alleges that the factory is a nuisance and seeks an injunction and damages.

    a. P has shown that the interference with his property and health is substantial, and he is entitled to a directed verdict.

    b. It is for the jury to determine whether D's conduct is substantial under all the circumstances.

    c. The interference need not be substantial so long as it is unreasonable.

    d. The interference must be substantial and unreasonable. Both are questions of fact.

16. D built a high brick "spite fence" on his property line within six inches of P's building and thereby cut out light, air, and view of the residents. It was alleged that this was done maliciously and for the sole purpose of injuring P.

    a. There was no actionable wrong as P has no right to use D's property.

b.   D may not use his property to the injury of P when his only motive is spite and malice.

c.   The owner of land has a right to make any reasonable use of his property without liability.

d.   A lawful act is not actionable even though it proceeds from a malicious motive.

17.   P, a coal mine operator, built an earthen dam to hold waste water from its operation so that "tailings" could settle to the bottom before the water flowed into a stream. The dam was located above a narrow valley containing many small homes. P was aware that other such dams had broken in the past under pressure of flood water. Ds, residents of the valley, dynamited the dam in such a way as to permit the water to escape without flooding. P sues for trespass and resulting damages to the dam.

a.   Ds are not liable. Under the circumstances, they were entitled to use self-help to abate the nuisance.

b.   Ds are liable. They should have first notified the owner and demanded removal of the nuisance.

c.   Ds are liable. They used unnecessary force in abating the nuisance.

d.   P is entitled to no recovery as he is clearly the wrongdoer.

## E. The Examination

Whatever generalizations may be made about law school exams as a whole, every exam is an effort by an individual professor to test your knowledge of a legal subject. Professors vary in their approach to the law, testing methods, and grading criteria. Long before you sit down to take an exam, you should attempt to get some feel for the professor's mind-set. What has the professor said about this exam? What points has the professor emphasized and de-emphasized in class? What concepts recur periodically throughout the course? What are the professor's old examinations like (because many law schools keep old exams on file in the library, you can frequently obtain these documents)? What do former students of the professor say about their experiences in his or her examination? If you look at these questions, you may be able to anticipate the exam. Certainly, the professor may fool you, but generally professors are somewhat predictable.

### *1. Beforehand*

Find out in advance what materials you can have with you in the exam room. Although most first year exams are not open book, some courses that rely heavily on statutory material (e.g., Civil Procedure) may permit those materials to be used in the exam. Make sure you know whether you will need pencils, pen, paper, or other supplies. Law schools usually provide blue books and answer sheets, but may or may not supply you with scratch paper on which to take notes. Having a watch or clock with you is an absolute necessity. And, of course, because law school exams are graded anonymously, don't forget your anonymous number.

Get plenty of sleep the night before the exam. Eat a good meal before you take the exam. Make sure to arrive in plenty of time. Go to the bathroom before the exam begins. Despite the fact that you can leave during the exam if nature calls, you can ill afford the time during the test. These logistical suggestions are as important to effective test taking as drafting a good answer. When you sit down in the exam room, get comfortable and relax.

### *2. Instructions*

When you get the exam, read the instructions and allocate your time among the questions. Remember to stay on schedule. If you get behind, you are dead. It is probably best to answer the questions seriatim rather than to spend time trying to decide which question to answer first.

### *3. Read the Question*

When you start on the first question, read it once through, underlining key words and making notes. Try to get a picture of the problem. Who are the parties? What is the history of the case? What are the basic facts? And, most importantly, what question or questions does the professor ask at the end? Your mission is to answer the question the professor asked rather than the question you would have preferred. The question itself gives you information about how to write the answer. For instance, the question may say, "You represent the plaintiff in this case. Against whom would you proceed? What actions would you bring? What arguments would you make? What arguments and defenses do you anticipate from the other side?" Or, "As law clerk for the judge in this case, draft an opinion based upon the issues presented in these facts, explaining how the court should decide and why." Or my favorite, "Discuss." If only law students would read the question carefully, they would obtain insights into their answer.

### 4. Organize

Read the exam question again, outlining your answer as you go. Note unusual or salient facts, problems, or issues. Unlike on those Poli Sci exams in college, you can't just start writing and hope to say something memorable. On the other hand, you can't spend so much time organizing that you don't have time to write your answer. A well-organized essay will inevitably account for several points on your final grade. What do you want to say? How do you want to say it? What logical arguments can you make? What counterarguments can you make?

Don't spend so much time on the outline that you don't have time for your real answer, leaving all your good points on the scratch pad. Some students devote as much as one third to one half of the allocated time to reading and organizing their thoughts. Some people write faster than others; if your handwriting is more deliberate, you may not have the luxury of spending much time organizing your answer. If nature has afflicted you with a slow hand, you have to compensate by reading faster and organizing mentally in order to stay even.

One way to think of this organization step is to picture your professor as someone who is intelligent but ignorant of the law. Your job is to take him or her by the hand and walk through the problem, explaining as you proceed. It is wise to discuss the most important issues first, followed by subissues and secondary issues. If you run short on time, you can give a quick sketch to minor issues having already addressed the major ones fully.

Before proceeding to discuss the specifics of exam taking, it is necessary to read one more case, *Katko v. Briney*. *Katko* involves the privilege of defense of property, a variation of self-defense. A valid privilege will excuse an otherwise actionable tort. A person is privileged to exercise force to defend himself or others, even deadly force in response to deadly force. Other nuances of self-defense can wait for Torts class. The question raised by *Katko* is whether one may use deadly force to protect property. Before proceeding, you should read and brief this case.

*Katko v. Briney*

## 4. DEFENSE OF PROPERTY
### KATKO v. BRINEY

Supreme Court of Iowa, 1971.
183 N.W.2d 657.

MOORE, C. J. The primary issue presented here is whether an owner may protect personal property in an unoccupied boarded-up farm house against trespassers and thieves by a spring gun capable of inflicting death or serious injury.

We are not here concerned with a man's right to protect his home and members of his family. Defendants' home was several miles from the scene of the incident to which we refer infra.

Plaintiff's action is for damages resulting from serious injury caused by a shot from a 20-gauge spring shotgun set by defendants in a bedroom of an old farm house which has been uninhabited for several years. Plaintiff and his companion  *  *  * had broken and entered the house to find and steal old bottles and dated fruit jars which they considered antiques.  *  *  *

The jury returned a verdict for plaintiff and against defendants for $20,000 actual and $10,000 punitive damages.

After careful consideration of defendants' motions for judgment notwithstanding the verdict and for new trial, the experienced and capable trial judge overruled them and entered judgment on the verdict. Thus we have this appeal by defendants.  *  *  *

[The house was inherited from Mrs. Briney's grandparents and had been unoccupied for some time. There had been a series of intrusions.] Defendants through the years boarded up the windows and doors in an attempt to stop the intrusions. They had posted "no trespass" signs on the land several years before 1967. The nearest one was 35 feet from the house.  On June 11, 1967 defendants set "a shotgun trap" in the north bedroom.  After Mr. Briney cleaned and oiled his 20-gauge shotgun, the power of which he was well aware, defendants took it to the old house where they secured it to an iron bed with the barrel pointed at the bedroom door.  It was rigged with wire from the doorknob to the gun's trigger so it would fire when the door was opened.  Briney first pointed the gun so an intruder would be hit in the stomach but at Mrs. Briney's suggestion it was lowered to hit the legs.  He admitted he did so "because I was mad and tired of being tormented" but "he did not intend to injure anyone."  He gave no explanation of why he used a loaded shell and set it to hit a person already in the house.  Tin was nailed over the bedroom window.  The spring gun could not be seen from the outside.  No warning of its presence was posted.  *  *  *

[Plaintiff] entered the old house by removing a board from a porch window which was without glass.  *  *  *  As he started to open the north bedroom door the shotgun went off striking him in the right leg above the ankle bone.  Much of his leg, including part of the tibia, was blown away.  Only by  *  *  *  assistance was plaintiff able to get out of the house and after crawling some distance was put in his vehicle and rushed to a doctor and then to a hospital.  He remained in the hospital 40 days.  *  *  *

There was undenied medical testimony plaintiff had a permanent deformity, a loss of tissue, and a shortening of the leg.  *  *  *

The main thrust of defendants' defense in the trial court and on this appeal is that "the law permits use of a spring gun in a dwelling or warehouse for the purpose of preventing the unlawful entry of a burglar or thief."  *  *  *

Instruction 6 stated:  "An owner of premises is prohibited from willfully or intentionally injuring a trespasser by means of force that either takes life or inflicts great bodily injury;  and therefore a person owning a premise is prohibited from setting out 'spring guns' and like dangerous devices which will likely take life or inflict great bodily injury, for the purpose of harming trespassers.  The fact that the trespasser may be acting in violation of the law does not change the rule.  The only time when such conduct of setting a 'spring gun' or a like dangerous device is justified would be when the trespasser was

committing a felony of violence or a felony punishable by death, or where the trespasser was endangering human life by his act."
* * *

The overwhelming weight of authority, both textbook and case law, supports the trial court's statement of the applicable principles of law. * * *

Restatement of Torts, section 85, page 180, states: "The value of human life and limb, not only to the individual concerned but also to society, so outweighs the interest of a possessor of land in excluding from it those whom he is not willing to admit thereto that a possessor of land has, as is stated in § 79, no privilege to use force intended or likely to cause death or serious harm against another whom the possessor sees about to enter his premises or meddle with his chattel, unless the intrusion threatens death or serious bodily harm to the occupiers or users of the premises. * * * A possessor of land cannot do indirectly and by a mechanical device that which, were he present, he could not do immediately and in person. Therefore, he cannot gain a privilege to install, for the purpose of protecting his land from intrusions harmless to the lives and limbs of the occupiers or users of it, a mechanical device whose only purpose is to inflict death or serious harm upon such as may intrude, by giving notice of his intention to inflict, by mechanical means and indirectly, harm which he could not, even after request, inflict directly were he present." * * *

The facts in Allison v. Fiscus, 156 Ohio St. 120, 100 N.E.2d 237, decided in 1951, are very similar to the case at bar. There plaintiff's right to damages was recognized for injuries received when he feloniously broke a door latch and started to enter defendant's warehouse with intent to steal. As he entered a trap of two sticks of dynamite buried under the doorway by defendant owner was set off and plaintiff seriously injured. The court held the question whether a particular trap was justified as a use of reasonable and necessary force against a trespasser engaged in the commission of a felony should have been submitted to the jury. The Ohio Supreme Court recognized plaintiff's right to recover punitive or exemplary damages in addition to compensatory damages. * * *

In addition to civil liability many jurisdictions hold a landowner criminally liable for serious injuries or homicide caused by spring guns or other set devices. [Citations] * * *

[The court declined to rule on whether punitive damages were allowable in this type of case because defendant's attorney had not raised that issue in the trial court.]

Study and careful consideration of defendant's contentions on appeal reveal no reversible error.

Affirmed.

LARSON, J., dissented, noting that the trial judge's instructions "failed to tell the jury it could find the installation was not made with the intent or purpose of striking or injuring the plaintiff," and that the principle espoused by the court had never been applied to a burglar, but only "in the case of a mere trespasser in a vineyard."

---

1.  The Brineys had to sell 80 acres of their 120-acre farm in order to pay the judgment in this case. Their appeal to equity to block enforcement of the judgment failed. See Briney v. Katko (1971) 197 N.W.2d 351. Further background about the case can be found in Palmer, Katko v. Briney: A Study in American Gothic (1971) 56 Iowa L.Rev. 1219.

2.  A strange development later arose between the parties. When the 80 acres were put up for judgment sale and there were no bids above the minimum price of $10,000, three neighbors purchased the land for a dollar more, expecting to hold it for Briney until he won his appeal. When he did not win, they leased the land back to him for enough to pay taxes and their interest costs on the money they had borrowed. Some years later the neighbors decided to sell. One of them bought the property for $16,000 and sold it to his son for $16,500. Briney and Katko then got together and jointly sued the neighbors to establish a constructive trust on their profit. Just before the case came to trial, it was settled for a sum large enough to pay the remainder of Briney's judgment to Katko.

3.  The United Press International reported the results of the trial court decision in this case stating in part that Katko was "shot and seriously injured in the *home* of Mr. and Mrs. Edward Briney." (Emphasis added.) A public outcry about the decision resulted in the introduction of "Briney Bills" in several state legislatures. The Nebraska Legislature enacted a self-defense act that provided in part that "no person * * * shall be placed in * * * jeopardy * * * for protecting, by any means necessary, himself, his family, or his real or personal property * * *." The statute was held to be unconstitutional by the Supreme Court of Nebraska on the unusual ground of improper delegation of sentencing authority. See State v. Goodseal (1971) 186 Neb. 359, 183 N.W.2d 258, certiorari denied 404 U.S. 845.

4.  As in the case of self-defense, the privilege to defend property is limited to the use of force reasonably necessary to the situation as it appears to the defendant. Here again a reasonable mistake as to the necessity will protect him. Smith v. Delery (1959) 238 La. 180, 114 So.2d 857; Bunten v. Davis (1926) 82 N.H. 304, 133 A. 16. But a reasonable mistake as to the existence of the privilege will not, as when the invader is on the land as a matter of right.

5.   What constitutes reasonable force is normally a question for the jury, but there are several recognized limitations.   When the invasion is peaceful and occurs in the presence of the possessor, the use of any force at all will be unreasonable unless a request has been made to depart.   Chapell v. Schmidt (1894) 104 Cal. 511, 38 P. 892 (defendant caned elderly person who was picking flowers) ; Emmons v. Quade (1903) 176 Mo. 22, 75 S.W. 103. A request does not have to be made, however, when the conduct of the intruder would indicate to a reasonable person that it would be useless or that it could not safely be made in time.   See Higgins v. Minaghan (1891) 78 Wis. 602, 47 N.W. 941; State v. Cessna (1915) 170 Iowa 726, 153 N.W. 194.

6.   When the invasion occurs in the presence of the possessor he may repel him by use of physical force short of infliction of serious bodily injury.   See Palmer v. Smith (1911) 147 Wis. 70, 132 N.W. 614; Ulmer v. Seelman (1909) 159 Mich. 253, 123 N.W. 1124; McIlvoy v. Cockran (1820) 9 Ky. (2 A. K. Marsh.) 271.

7.   *Use of Force Calculated to Cause Death or Serious Injury.*   The principal case caused a good deal of re-thinking about when, if ever, force calculated to cause death or serious injury may be utilized to defend possession.   It is one of the few cases in which a burglar or a thief was able to recover civil damages from his intended victim.

A.   When the privilege of self-defense enters the picture in that the invader threatens the personal safety of the defendant or his family, the defendant may use deadly force if it is necessary in the circumstances.   This is likely to occur when the invader attempts to enter the homestead at night.   See Tipsword v. Potter (1918) 31 Idaho 509, 174 P. 133; Coleman v. New York & N. H. R. Co. (1870) 106 Mass. 160.

B.   Still another privilege may also apply.   There is a privilege to use reasonable force to prevent the commission of a crime.   With a serious felony like burglary the amount of permissible force is greater, and some courts permit a deadly force.   See Scheuerman v. Scharfenberg (1909) 163 Ala. 337, 50 So. 335; Gray v. Combs (1832) 30 Ky. 478.

C.   In Ilott v. Wilkes [1820] 3 B. & Ald. 304, 106 Eng.Rep. 674, it was held that a landowner who placed spring guns on his land to keep off poachers was not liable to a trespasser who was shot.   The result of this decision was a storm of public disapproval, which led to an act of Parliament making the setting of such devices a crime.   In Bird v. Holbrook [1824] 4 Bing. 628, 130 Eng.Rep. 911, a case which arose before the statute was passed, but was decided afterward, the court overruled the Ilott case and a defendant who set a spring gun was held liable to a trespasser.

D.   Most American courts such as the main case and the Restatement (Second) of Torts § 85, have followed Bird v. Holbrook.   Many jurisdictions have placed the restrictions on the use of deadly force in their state statutory codes.   See statutes collected in Posner, Killing or Wounding to Protect a Property Interest (1971) 14 J. L. & Econ. 201, 228–232.   Some statutes and some cases appear to allow the use of deadly force against serious invasions of property, such as burglary, that may be costly to the possessor. There is also some authority that the right of peaceful habitation may be protected by the use of deadly force. See Model Penal Code § 3.-06(d)(i) (1962). Compare Bramble v. Thompson (1972) 264 Md. 518, 287 A.2d 265 (german shepherd).

E. The general rule prohibiting deadly force is modified in some states by permitting it if defendant gives the plaintiff clear notice of the danger. See Starkey v. Dameron (1933) 92 Colo. 420, 21 P.2d 1112 (dictum); State v. Marfaudille (1907) 48 Wash. 117, 92 P. 939. This is especially likely to occur when defendant's use of force involved a vicious dog. See Hood v. Waldrum (1968) 58 Tenn.App. 512, 434 S.W.2d 94; Sappington v. Sutton (Okl.1972) 501 P.2d 814. Compare Loomis v. Terry (1837) 17 Wend. (N.Y.) 496, 31 Am.Dec. 306 (no warning, defendant liable). Barbed wire may give notice in and of itself. See Quigley v. Clough (1899) 173 Mass. 429, 53 N.E. 884. What privilege is operating in these cases? See also Hart v. Geysel and notes.

In some jurisdictions even posted warnings will not protect the landholder if he would not be privileged to use this amount of force were he there in person. See State v. Plumlee (1933) 177 La. 687, 149 So. 425; State v. Childers (1938) 133 Ohio St. 508, 14 N.E.2d 767.

F. Another line of defense that may work for the landholder is the argument that he intended only to frighten and not to injure the intruder. See Allison v. Fiscus (1951) 156 Ohio St. 120, 100 N.E.2d 237, discussed in the principal case.

8. The limitations on the possessor's privilege may also restrict his power to eject the plaintiff from his property into a position of unreasonable physical danger. Thus a tramp stealing a ride on a railroad train cannot be thrown off at forty miles an hour. Chesapeake & Ohio R. Co. v. Ryan (1919) 183 Ky. 428, 209 S.W. 538; Kobbe v. Chicago & N. W. R. Co. (1928) 173 Minn. 79, 216 N.W. 543.

In Depue v. Flatau (1907) 100 Minn. 299, 111 N.W. 1 this was extended even further. Plaintiff, a travelling cattle buyer, called at defendant's farmhouse on a cold winter evening, and was asked to stay for dinner. During dinner plaintiff was overcome by a "fainting spell," and became very weak and seriously ill. He asked permission to stay over night, which was refused. Defendant led him out to his sleigh, put him into it, adjusted the robes around him, and threw the reins, which he was too weak to hold, over his shoulders. Defendant then started the horses on the road to town. Plaintiff was found the following morning by the side of the road about three-quarters of a mile away, badly frost-bitten, and nearly frozen to death. Defendant was held liable. Suppose the landowner places a drunken guest in his car to go home?

9. On the other hand, if the plaintiff's presence endangers the personal safety of those on the premises, the privilege of self-defense, or that of defense of third persons, may justify the ejection. In Tucker v. Burt (1908) 152 Mich. 68, 115 N.W. 722, plaintiff, a member of the family of the janitor of an apartment house, fell ill with a highly contagious and infec-

tious disease. Defendant, the owner of the building, ejected her. She was able to get to a hospital in a taxi. It was held that defendant was not liable.

10. See Bohlen and Burns, The Privilege to Protect Property by Dangerous Barriers and Mechanical Devices (1926) 35 Yale L.J. 535; Hart, Injuries to Trespassers (1931) 47 Law Q.Rev. 92, 101–105; Note, (1972) 24 S.C.L.Rev. 133; Annot. (1973) 47 A.L.R.3d 646.

Don't open your answer with a rambling preamble or restatement of the facts. Don't use any unnecessary introductory or transition language. You don't have to say, "There are three issues in this problem. I will now discuss these issues in order." Nor do you have to say, "The first issue is whether...." It is enough to say, "Was Farmer Jones justified in setting a spring gun in his home to protect it against burglars while he and his family were on vacation?" There is no magic in the order of presentation of issues in a multi-issue exam question. You may discuss the issues chronologically, by type of action, by plaintiff, by defendant, or in the relative order of importance as you see it. Sometimes you have to discuss a preliminary issue before addressing a major issue, or you have to talk about a major issue before tackling one or more subissues. However, there should be some structure to your approach. A random approach generally will not work because the professor reading the question will not have any idea where your answer is going and may conclude that you do not understand the problem. A stream of consciousness style like that of James Joyce is unlikely to produce satisfactory results in law school.

### 5. IRAC

Some commentators have suggested a system called IRAC for answering law school essay exam questions (I = issue, R = rule, A = analysis, C = conclusion). This approach bears a startling resemblance to the case brief discussed previously. As an approach to questions generally, IRAC can be quite useful. However, students can become bogged down in the methodology of IRAC, particularly on complex, multi-issue questions. They sometimes forget what questions the professor has asked, and their analysis may deal with discrete subissues while neglecting to analyze the relationship among the various issues, or it may fail to perceive, for instance, that the issue in the question is how to characterize the issue itself. It is sufficient to say that all essay exams present legal issues, that they require explication of the law, that they anticipate some rational analysis, and that the conclusions you reach should be supported by your reasoning.

As for spotting issues, your facility will depend upon how well you know the material generally, and how adept you have become at spotting issues. Much of the classroom experience during the first year reinforces the learning of issue spotting. Professors frame the issues through hypotheticals, through the Socratic questioning of students, and through comments. You can practice spotting issues with classmates, or try to predict the salient issues as you study. When you sit down with the exam, you either see the issue or you don't. If you don't, there is absolutely nothing you can do about it, because your discussion is neither right nor wrong, only missing. When in doubt, err on the side of inclusion. Remember, however, that to call something an issue that is not can be damaging too. Some professors include "red herrings" in exam questions; these are facts that lead you to think that a particular problem exists, which on closer analysis proves not to be a problem at all.

I offered this "red herring" on the short answer question involving Sally Westchester and Scruffy Man, included earlier in the chapter on page 83. The question says specifically that Tom Tourist was NOT negligent, but the facts also indicate that Tom's car struck Scruffy Man when Scruffy fell into the street. A number of students could not resist the opportunity to analyze Tom's negligence. On another question from the same test Bob and Otto Palindrome were harmed in various ways by Bob's ex-girlfriend, Allie Stalker. (In case you were wondering, professors do sit up nights thinking of these names.) The question asked what lawsuits Bob could bring against Allie. Again, a number of people got sucked in to a discussion of Allie's liability to Otto. Sometimes the facts will use a buzzword that conjures up memories of a particular case or rule that does not apply to the question at hand at all.

Assuming that you have seen the issue, the next step, as it was in class, is to state the issue succinctly and clearly. The statement should cut to the heart of the problem, and be expressed as narrowly as possible to cover the facts in the case. The wording of the question itself may give you guidance as to how to frame issues on an exam.

After articulating the issue, you should state the applicable law: "In a majority of jurisdictions, a landowner may not use deadly force to protect the property against damage from intruders. A small minority of states would allow such force to be used." State only the law that is applicable to the issue. For instance, you don't need to add, "The homeowner may use deadly force in his home in defense of himself or his family, although a majority of states require the owner to retreat prior to exercising such deadly force." The facts establish that Jones's family isn't in the building where the intrusion took place, so the issue of self-defense doesn't arise.

Next, apply the specific facts to the law you have stated: "Here, no one was in the house when the burglar was injured by the spring gun. A spring gun may be considered a deadly force. In fact, it killed the burglar. A number of cases, such as *Katko v. Briney,* have established that the use of a spring gun, even if it does not actually kill an intruder, can be considered a deadly force because it had the potential to kill."

A good answer always anticipates the counterargument. "It may be argued that since Farmer Jones placed the gun so that it was pointed at the door two feet above the ground, he intended to use only nondeadly force. However, this argument is unpersuasive because a gun is highly likely to kill at any height. Jones's weapon would have been pointed chest high at a four-year-old."

Finally, your answer should state a conclusion: "Therefore, Farmer Jones was not justified in using a spring gun to protect his house while he and the family were on vacation." The conclusion itself is less important than the rest of the answer. It is important that the conclusion be supported by your analysis, but the "right" answer will mean little if your statement of the law is inaccurate or your logic flawed. It is possible for different students to reach different conclusions based upon the same set of facts. In fact, exam questions are seldom clear-cut. The answers could go either way.

### 6. Logic

It is important for you to construct a logical answer. The basic analytical tool used on law school exams is the syllogism. Your statement of the law is the major premise: "People who use spring guns to defend their property and cause injury to another may be held liable." The minor premise refers to the facts in the question: "Farmer Jones used the spring gun to defend his property and killed the burglar." The conclusion follows logically from the two premises: "Therefore, Farmer Jones may be held liable."

You do not have to have studied logic in college to handle this kind of analysis successfully. A few helpful hints may make it easier for you to master the process.

First, remember to use deductive logic. The conclusion must be deduced from the law as applied to the facts. Inductive or inferential logic can get you into trouble on law school exams. For instance, if the burglar was injured by Farmer Jones's spring gun while Farmer Jones was on vacation, it might be inferred that Farmer Jones set up the device. Maybe he did and maybe he didn't. The facts suggest that he did, and if there are enough facts, the inference may be a strong one. But a strong inference will never replace a sound deductive conclusion.

Second, avoid making unwarranted assumptions. Assumptions in the context of the law school exam question are facts not stated in the question that are taken by the reader to be true. We all make certain basic assumptions about the facts: "The case took place in an American jurisdiction." "The burglar was there for unlawful purposes." The problem arises when we assume too much: "Farmer Jones feared for the safety of his property and family because of rampant crime." Some students rewrite exam questions assuming away problems they do not wish to address: "Assuming that Farmer Jones set the spring gun for the purpose of protecting his family and forgot to turn it off when they went on vacation, his defense of them may have been justifiable." On the other hand, if the facts are ambiguous, it may be necessary to analyze the situation using different assumptions: "Assuming Farmer Jones was attempting to protect his family, his conduct may have been justified. However, if he was protecting the property alone, his conduct was probably improper."

Third, be prepared to argue in the alternative. On many law school exams, either the facts will lie somewhere between two rules that produce contrasting results, or the facts will fall between two fact patterns that produce different results under the same rule. This "on the one hand, on the other hand" approach is reminiscent of the character Tevye in *Fiddler on the Roof* trying to grapple with his daughter's impending marriage: "On the one hand...On the other hand..." Or *Hamlet*, who saw both sides of every question: "Whether 'tis nobler in the mind to suffer/The slings and arrows of outrageous fortune/Or take up arms against [them]."

Don't get sucked into a conclusion not supported by the facts: "Birds are animals. The burglar is an animal. Therefore, the burglar is a bird." Beyond your analysis itself, the effectiveness of your answer may depend on a number of other factors. Some of these factors should be apparent; others are more subtle.

## F. Writing

### *1. Grammar and Style*

Although the heart of your exam is undoubtedly the quality of your analysis, other factors may contribute enough points to make the difference between a good or mediocre paper. Probably the most important of these factors is writing style. If you can't write clearly, your grades will always fall behind your knowledge. To those who argue that this is law school, not freshman English, the best answer is probably that the fundamental skill of lawyering is communication, which involves both written and oral persuasion. More to the point, if the professor can't understand what you are talking about, you won't get a good grade. Every semester I have students who come in to review their exams, and attempt to point out that they knew what they were talking about. I respond that the very fact that they have to explain what they have written in order to make it comprehensible to me demonstrates the inadequacy of their answer. Since the professor may be reading one hundred or more papers, vague, poorly expressed ideas and convoluted prose can be painfully difficult to follow. If the professor cannot follow your train of thought, your exam grade will be derailed quickly.

The basic principles of effective writing should not be new. Use clear, concise prose. Avoid complex sentences. Place the central thought in each sentence at the beginning of the sentence and the most important sentence in each paragraph at the beginning of the paragraph. Avoid long, flowery transitions and lead-ins. Use the active rather than passive voice. Stay away from legalese. If you aren't sure what a word means, don't use it. Say it one time. In short, be brief.

Another common problem on exams is grammar and spelling. It is likely that your sentence construction will not be as clean under the time constraints of the law school examination process as it would have been in less stressful situations. Your writing may, at times, be awkward. Such lapses are unavoidable under the circumstances, and you should not spend valuable time trying to make a problematic sentence sound like it came from a Pulitzer-prize-winning novel. On the other hand, there is no excuse for abandoning fundamental rules of grammar and construction. The same thing may be said of spelling errors. Although many professors claim that they do not grade grammar and spelling, they may make unconscious assumptions about your ability that may influence their willingness to give you the benefit of the doubt on a questionable response.

One difficulty with these suggestions is that if you don't know good grammar or how to spell, you may not be able to identify your own problem. And if you haven't learned these matters in 16 or more years of school, nothing you can do the night before exams or during exams can help you. If you have writing problems, you should seek remedial help before the time of exams. This may be a concern of yours if you did not do much writing in undergraduate courses, or if you have always had difficulty writing.

## 2. Legibility

Another aspect of writing is legibility. Although law school professors do not give awards for penmanship, it is important to produce a blue book that the professor can read. Because law school essay exams are long, they strain the hand, and because time is limited, students often rush to finish. Both of these phenomena can have an adverse effect on handwriting. Of course, some people just write almost illegibly regardless of the pressure.

The profs may tell you that they do not penalize bad handwriting, but the truth is that if they are reading 80 or more essay exams, and they can't read what appears on the page, the writer inevitably loses points. If the page looks like Arabic, Russian, or Sanskrit to the eye, the professor may overlook the brilliance of the answer. Take a look on page 101 at two handwriting samples from a recent law school test, and imagine yourself reading 20 or more pages of each.

## Which Exam Would the Professor Want to Read?

DID THE SCRUFFY MAN AND HIS
POSSIBLE ACCOMPLICE JOIN TO FALSELY
IMPRISON SALLY? FALSE IMPRISONMENT
OCCURS WHEN A DEFENDANT CREATES
BOUNDARIES THAT RESTRICT A PLAINTIFF
FROM LEAVING OF HER OWN FREE WILL.
THE PLAINTIFF IS NOT AWARE OF ANY
REASONABLE MEANS OF ESCAPE. THE
PLAINTIFF MUST BE AWARE OF THE
CONFINEMENT OR SUFFER DAMAGES.
FORCE IS NOT NECESSARY TO CONTAIN
THE PLAINTIFF. HERE, THE SCRUFFY

False Imprisonment could be charged against
the two men for their action restricting her
in a confined space – taking no action to
let her go + doing all against her will. Sally
found no reasonable, safe way to exit –
(the bars, the traffic, etc.)
But we'd have to prove the 2 men had the
necessary intent: knew that they were causing

As an exam taker, try to write legibly. Don't crowd your answer; the law school will give you as many blue books as you need. Label different parts of your answer, and highlight important words. Write on one side of the page in case you need to come back later and add to or change your answer. Write on every other line. In other words, unless you are given a limited amount of space, spread out your answer on the page.

## G. Time

Perhaps the greatest failing of many law students is an inability to manage time during the exam. You may assume that on law school exams you will run out of time more than you will walk out early. If you were the last one to leave the examination room in previous educational incarnations, prepare yourself now for a formidable struggle against time limits in law school. If this is a problem for you, practice answering law school exam questions, particularly those of your professors that may be on file, prior to the exam. Students who have previously taken the same professor can tell you whether the professor's exams are normally difficult to complete in the time allotted. By doing a little preliminary investigation, you can identify potential problem exams in advance. Forewarned is forearmed!

In the exam itself, you have to get a grip on the time. Never just start answering the first question on the test. Carefully read the instruction sheet, because it usually describes the number and type of questions, as well as the time allocations or point values for each. In some cases the professor may have provided this information in advance; regardless of such information, rely only on the actual instructions in the test book. Look through the test book to see how many pages are included, and how much reading you will have to do. Many law school exam questions are long and convoluted, with complex facts and many issues. As you might expect, it is usually the case that the more time you are given to answer the question, the more complicated the question will be.

Don't panic! Remember that somebody (your diabolical professor) thought this exam could be answered in the time allotted. Even if the professor misjudged the time needed, everybody in the exam room has exactly the same amount. Your grade will not be based on some absolute value.

On your college history exam, there may have been 100 multiple-choice questions that look something like this: "In what year was the Declaration of Independence signed? (A) 1776 (B) 1876 (C) 1678 (D) 1767" The answer, of course, is (A). If you got the other 99 questions right, your score was 100 and you got an A on the test. If you missed 11, you got a B. On a law school exam, the professor might have 200 possible points, with the best paper in the class scoring 125. Even on multiple-choice exams, which are frequently modeled after multistate bar exam questions, it is possible to miss a number of answers and still do well on the test. Thus, the question is not what you could say if you had an unlimited amount of time and resources to produce an answer. The question is what you do say in three hours, or whatever time is provided, compared to what other examinees say in the same amount of time.

Think of yourself as a practicing lawyer, sitting in your office. A client comes in and tells you his problem. He was driving down the street in his brother's car when the brakes gave out and he ran into another car that had just run a red light. The doctor had improperly set his broken wrist and he has had to give up his career as a concert pianist. His brother also refuses to speak to him anymore. You explain to the client that he may be able to sue the driver of the other car on a negligence theory, but that under the state's comparative negligence statute, the brother, the brother's mechanic, or the manufacturer of the car might be partially responsible. You tell him that these potential defendants can be expected to compensate him only for the injuries that flow directly from their conduct. You may or may not be able to convince a jury that the subsequent negligent act of the doctor was foreseeable. The doctor can in no way be held responsible for the damage to your client's brother's car, but he may be sued for the damages caused by his subsequent negligent conduct. You tell your client that the fact that the doctor did not know he was a concert pianist, whose career was ruined by the accident, will not preclude recovery, citing the famous "egg-shell skull" case. The client agrees to have you represent him and leaves the office.

You then go into your law library to begin conducting research to develop your case. The spontaneous legal advice you gave your client was based upon the facts presented to you in the client interview. Your answer does not represent a final statement on the problem, and certainly not the level of knowledge you will have attained by the time the case goes to trial. But you had better at least be in the ballpark recognizing the client's problem and offering him legal advice. The law school exam question is like the client interview in that you are presented a problem you have not seen before, and you must identify the issues, articulate the applicable law, and make the basic arguments.

The point is this: you are not expected to write a brief that would be filed with the United States Supreme Court. You only have to answer the question within the framework of the time provided. You do well on the question if you give a better answer than the average law student within that time period; you will do poorly if your answer is worse.

### H. Test Anxiety

Everyone feels nervous before examinations. The physical symptoms may vary from a knot in the stomach, to loss of appetite, to irritability, to loss of sleep, to a host of other reactions. More than a few of us have felt the primal fight-or-flight response when we go into the examination room. And rare is the law student who does not recall reading a question and drawing a complete blank.

These are all ways our body deals with stress, and exams are stressful. But if we did not respond to stress as we do, we would not get that jolt of adrenalin that helps us perform at our most efficient level at such times. As disturbing as it is, we need stress; we use stress; we overcome stress. Stress is normal. See pages 129–135, for a more general discussion of stress in law school.

For a small number of law students, stress levels prior to or during exams can become so heightened that they simply cannot perform. For them, stress is an enemy and not an ally. They may become so sick that they are incapacitated. They may become so agitated that they cannot sleep or study. They may feel so overwhelmed in an exam that they stare at a wall for three hours or run out of the room although the exam is only half over. Take heart: this will probably not be you. You will take a few deep breaths and make the best of things. You will do what you have to do. You will survive, even succeed.

Those students whose test anxiety is so severe that they are incapacitated must do something about the problem or they will not stay in law school for long. If you have a history of test anxiety, experience the severe reactions described above before exams begin, or have recently suffered through other highly stressful events, such as a divorce or job layoff, try to stay tuned in to your own feelings. Talk to someone before an exam crisis occurs. Take measures to reduce stress in your life. One of the best things you can do is be prepared. If you get to the exam and suffer from an anxiety attack, contact the dean or administrator on duty (not the professor because the exams are anonymous). If you wait until later, the response will probably be, "Too bad; that's life." Avoid disaster while you can.

## I. Practice Questions

Enough talk. It's time to practice your exam-taking skills. If you prefer, you can continue to Chapter 6, and return to this material later. To do justice to these practice exercises, you should give yourself several hours of uninterrupted time. You may be able to divide the material into as many as three separate sessions if your schedule is tight. Either way, the practice will help you to be a better test taker.

### 1. Problem 1—Sally Westchester

Recall the question about Sally Westchester and Scruffy Man on page 83. Recall also the four cases you have read in this chapter. Review also the materials on intent and battery that appear in Appendix B, page 158. The only other information you need to know is that there is an issue of false imprisonment in this fact pattern. False imprisonment is the intentional, unconsented confinement of an individual within boundaries set by the defendant without reasonable means for the plaintiff to escape. There's a little more to it than that, but for now, this definition should suffice. After you have reviewed the material, sit down and answer the question in the 30 minutes designated.

* * * * * * * * * * * * *

If you have finished, let's look at your answer.

This problem implicates several intentional torts, including assault and battery, which have been mentioned in the cases, and false imprisonment which is defined in the text above. A good answer would have talked about each of these issues. There are peripheral negligence issues as well, negated as to Tom and lacking facts as to the construction company. A reading of the entire question should alert the examinee that the main thrust of the professor is to test intentional torts. Looking at the specific issues (and understanding that you have not studied these various torts in detail), the professor would look at the following:

*Assault*—Were Scruffy's words alone enough to bring about apprehension of imminent battery? Probably not. In fact, they may have negated intent. But if they didn't, circumstances (the passageway, the other guy, Scruffy's hostile conduct) may be enough to cause Sally to reasonably anticipate harmful or offensive contact. Scruffy's ability to carry out the battery is not a problem.

*False imprisonment*—Scruffy cuts Sally off on three sides. The other guy is coming up from the rear. We know she can get through the bars sans packages, but the law doesn't require her to imperil herself or abandon her property. We don't know if the two men are acting in concert, but if they are, this may be a confinement. If not, the danger posed by the second man (as seen through Sally's eyes) may effectively negate that exit as a means of escape (the means of escape must be reasonable). But really, Sally doesn't even ask if she can get by; she just pushes Scruffy aside. It's hard to imagine false imprisonment without more facts. If there is a restraint, however, it doesn't matter how long.

*Battery*—As to Sally pushing Scruffy, clearly the elements of the tort are met. She intentionally caused harmful touching of Scruffy's person without his consent. Her motive does not have to be to cause harm; she only needs to know with substantial certainty that her act will bring about contact with Scruffy's body (as in *Garratt*) If these elements are present, Sally is liable for the harm to Scruffy, and in intentional torts, if she is liable, she is liable for all physical consequences flowing from her battery (here the death of Scruffy). You might argue that, as in *Spivey*, the result was unforeseeable, and that such consequence could not have been known with substantial certainty. In all likelihood, unless Sally's conduct was privileged, she will be held liable.

*Self-defense*—If Sally is privileged, the battery is excused. The question turns on whether her belief was reasonable as to the danger and whether the force she used was excessive. Her possible mistake as to the threat posed by the second man is allowed (i.e., she perceived him as a threat even if it turns out he wasn't one). Arguments can be made either way as to the reasonableness of her fear. As to force, she is allowed to use force equal to that threatened. Here, she used nondeadly force against nondeadly force. The fact that Scruffy fell into traffic does not make Sally's force deadly. The requirement to retreat prior to exercising the privilege of self-defense may mean that Sally should have taken steps to avoid confrontation before exercising her privilege, if she could do so without increasing her danger. But could she?

*Defense of property*—As in *Katko* she has a privilege to protect her property, but unlike *Katko* she is personally in danger along with her property (as when a burglar breaks into your house as opposed to an unoccupied building). But her privilege is no greater as to her property than as to her person.

*Negligence of the contractor*—Although there are no facts in the problem to suggest possible liability, the property owner is certainly a possible target of an injured person.

*Negligence of Tom*—The facts said he was driving carefully, so a discussion of this possible action is off base.

In light of these comments let's look at two actual student answers, reproduced below. The first answer was one of the best in a class of eighty. It is clear, direct and easy to understand. The issues and the relevant law are articulated accurately. The analysis is sound. The second answer was one of the poorer papers in the class on this question. The writer just never seems to get going. You will note that even the "good" answer does not hit all the issues addressed in the comments. It just covers more of them, and better. Following the two sample answers is an evaluation checklist. Use it to rate the two answers and then your own answers. If you can be brutally honest with yourself, such self-evaluation can be an effective tool for improving your test-taking skills.

QUESTION 2

WE HAVE 2 ISSUES OF INTENTIONAL TORTS, AND 1 ISSUE OF NEGLIGENCE. THE POSSIBLE INTENTIONAL TORTS THAT MR. SCRUFFY COMMITTED AGAINST SALLY ARE THOSE OF ASSAULT, AND FALSE IMPRISONMENT.

THE FACT PATTERN FAILS TO ESTABLISH A PRIMA FACIE CASE OF <u>FALSE IMPRISONMENT</u> BECAUSE IT IS UNCLEAR WHETHER MR. SCRUFFY WAS IN FACT RESTRICTING SALLY'S MOVEMENT. WE DO NOT KNOW WHETHER THE SECOND MAN WAS INVOLVED OR NOT. IT CAN BE ARGUED THAT SCRUFFY INTENDED TO RESTRICT SALLY'S MOVEMENTS, BUT SINCE NO SPECIFIC REQUESTS WERE MADE BY SALLY TO PASS ALONG HER WAY. WE CANNOT BE CERTAIN. IT IS CERTAIN THAT SALLY FELT RESTRICTED, BUT THIS IS NOT SUFFICIENT TO ESTABLISH A PRIMA FACIE CASE.

THERE IS, HOWEVER, SUFFICIENT EVIDENCE OF ASSAULT. SCRUFFY'S COMMENTS WERE DESIGNED TO PUT SALLY IN FEAR AND APPREHENSION OF A BATTERY, THEREFORE HE HAD INTENT. SALLY CLEARLY FELT THREATENED BY A LIKELIHOOD OF IMMINENT OFFENSIVE CONTACT TO HER. THERE IS A CAUSAL LINK BETWEEN SCRUFFY'S WORDS AND SALLY'S FEAR AND APPREHENSION. IT IS OFTEN HELD, HOWEVER, THAT WORDS ARE NOT SUFFICIENT TO ESTABLISH ASSAULT. IN THIS CASE, HOWEVER, SCRUFFY IS STANDING IN SALLY'S WAY AND SHOUTING AT HER MENACINGLY. HE ALSO SPECIFICALLY MENTIONS PHYSICAL HARM TO HER.

IN ADDITION TO SCRUFFY'S INTENTIONAL TORTS, SALLY COMMITS AN ACT OF <u>BATTERY</u> AGAINST SCRUFFY. ALTHOUGH SHE HAS INFACT COMMITTED A BATTERY (INTENDING TO TOUCH SCRUFFY, OFFENSIVELY TOUCHING SCRUFFY, CAUSING HARM AS A RESULT OF HER ACTIONS), SHE IS ABLE TO CLAIM AN AFFIRMATIVE

DEFENSE OF <u>SELF DEFENSE</u>. ALTHOUGH SCRUFFY DIED AS A RESULT OF SALLY'S BATTERY, THIS WAS CLEARLY AN ᴀ ACCIDENTAL RESULT. THERE IS NOTHING TO INDICATE THAT SALLY USED DEADLY FORCE. IT MAY BE ARGUED, HOWEVER, THAT SHE USED UNREASONABLE FORCE, OR PERHAPS SHOULD NOT HAVE USED ANY FORCE. THE ORDINARY PERSON IS SALLY'S SHOES WOULD PROBABLY HAVE ACTED SIMILARLY.

SCRUFFY'S DEATH IS ACCIDENTAL AND TOM TOURIST IS PROBABLY NOT LIABLE FOR THIS TRAGEDY.

SALLY MAY ALSO FIND NEGLIGENCE IN THAT THE CONSTRUCTION CONTRACTOR HAD A DUTY TO PROVIDE AN ADEQUATE WALKWAY ALLOWING PROPER SPACE AND THAT A BREACH OF THIS DUTY RESULTED IN SOME DAMAGE (LOST PACKAGES, MENTAL DISTRESS (VOMITING) FOR WHICH SHE MAY BE LIABLE

## Question 2.

Sally W. was assaulted by scruffy because he placed her in fear of imminent battery, sally Then used an amount of force that may have been excessive but because she was put into fear by scruffy's threats and his relevant size and probable ability to harm her she was justified under the doctrine of self defence. Scruffy's death while arguably tragic was not ~~s~~ caused by a tort on Sallys part (She was acting as one reasonably so situated would under the circumstances) but may have been caused by the negligence of the construction company for not making the (cite) safe enough by limiting the width of the side walk area, but not fencing the side facing traffic. This may be because they undertook to control the flow of pedestrian traffic and didnt follow through or because they had a duty to the

pedestrians because they were negligent
in leaving the site only partially
protected but obstructed and unsafe.
(Also could be negligence per se if in violation of OSHA
    Tom Tourist is not liabel. Statute)

So long as he didn't have a (last) clear
chance to stop. Which if Leo were
driving carefully would have.

    The man following had no duty to
any-one unless he were in on a
         joint venture with scruffy to rob
                    Concert
other pedestrians or whatever
although this is a stretch.

# Critique Form

### Evaluation

Points

      (1)   Issues

_____(10)   Did the person state the basic issues?

      (2)   The law

_____(20)   Did the person correctly state the law?

      (3)   Analysis

           How did the person apply the law to the facts in the

_____(40)   case?

      (4)   Conclusion

           Did the person reach a conclusion on each issue?

_____(5)   What was it?

_____

_____

      (5)   Other factors

_____(5)   a.   Was the answer well organized?

                Did it make sense?

_____(5)   b.   Was the answer logical?

                Did it apply a rational, deductive analysis?

_____(5)   c.   Was the answer well written?

                Were there grammatical, spelling, or

                structural errors?

_____(5)   d.   Did the answer deal with the problem on a

                superficial issue or address the complexities?

_____(5)   e.   Was the answer persuasive?

_____

Total 100

## 2. Problem 2—Ronnie and Nancy

In this problem (which, in the 90s, might be dubbed Bill and Hillary), you get to look at another body of law. This problem involves the issue of strict liability for abnormally dangerous activities. Appendix C, page 177, contains cases and material taken from the same Torts casebook as the previous cases in this chapter. You should read and brief the cases, and then prepare and study an outline on the subject. When you think you are ready, take twenty minutes to answer the question below (no notes please, and don't turn the page to look at the model answer).

*********** 

After you are finished writing, read the answer, comparing it to your own. Then critique yourself using the evaluation form tailored to this question. For the next problem, you will use the generic evaluation form, but this one gives you an idea how to flesh it out.

## Practice Question and Answer

Ronnie and Nancy maintained a pond on the ranch that was used to water cattle. The pond was on the land when Ronnie and Nancy bought the land several years earlier. The pond was man-made, having been created by an earthen dam on a small creek. Through no negligence on the part of Ronnie and Nancy, the earthen dam broke after several weeks of unseasonable rain.

Water from the pond produced a flash flood damaging property for several miles downstream before the creek bed emptied into a larger stream. The damage included the Ferraro Bait Shop minnow tanks and worm troughs, three autos at Hart's Used Cars, and some vestments belonging to a Rev. Jacks at the Church of Freedom, PAC. Wally Mondell, who was camping in the dry creekbed, was swept away by the flood while he slept.

The cattle on Ronnie and Nancy's ranch stampeded when the dam broke. They broke through the fence on the ranch and ran onto Jeannie K's truck farm where they trampled several thousand head of cabbage.

Consider the issues raised in this fact pattern and discuss them in terms of strict liability theories of recovery.

# Answer

This question deals with two primary issues involving strict liability for damages caused by 1) the breaking of the dam and 2) the stampeding cattle. In each situation the issue is whether liability should attach for certain conduct absent a showing of negligence because of the nature of the instrumentality causing the injury. The concept of strict liability holds liable owners of animals trespassing and persons who engage in abnormally dangerous activities if their animals or activities cause harm, regardless of fault. The rationale behind the strict liability theory is that the defendant is in a better position to bear or insure against the loss than the innocent plaintiff in part because the defendant controls the instrumentality, in part because he benefits from its use. In this question, the application of the general rule is slightly different in each situation.

1) The breaking dam--the traditional rule articulated in _Rylands v. Fletcher_ imposes strict liability on the owners of land for the nonnatural use of the land causing damage to the property of another. Lord Cairns modified Judge Blackburn's rule in the lower court that one is strictly liable whenever he brings something dangerous on his land, it escapes and causes damage. The Cairns view limited liability to things or activities unduly dangerous and inappropriate to the place maintained in light of the character of that place and its surroundings. Many American Courts rejected _Rylands_ by mistakenly using the Blackburn view, although many of those courts later accepted the doctrine under the rubric of "absolute nuisance." An additional issue is whether the unseasonable rain was "an act of God" cutting off liability. If unforeseeable, sudden or destructive, the outside force may act as a superceding, intervening cause; here, it probably does not.

In this fact pattern, Blackburn's view would probably hold Ronnie and Nancy liable to Ferraro's Bait Shop, Hart's Used Cars, and Rev. Jacks because the water was a dangerous thing brought on the land; it escaped and caused damage. However, under the Cairns view, it is unlikely that a jury would find a cattle pond inappropriate to the place in light of the surroundings, if the ranch is in a rural area where cattle ponds are common. The heirs of Wally Mondell will have greater difficulty because Wally's conduct placed him in the path of the water. Did Wally have full knowledge of the danger? Probably not. Although contributory negligence is not a factor in strict liability, plaintiff's conduct may bar recovery if it is sufficiently reckless. If Ronnie and Nancy are negligent, that is another matter, but absent a showing of inappropriate use strict liability is unlikely to be applied.

2) The stampeding cattle--at common law, owners of livestock have been held strictly liable for damages caused by the livestock trespassing on the land of another. This issue was complicated by the passage of "fencing in," "fencing out," and "free choice" statutes. Under "fencing in" statutes the defendant has the burden of fencing his cattle in; under a "fencing out" statute, the plaintiff has the burden of fencing out the cattle of defendant. A "choice" statute would allow the community to choose either option.

The answer to this question depends upon the statute involved. If there is no statute, Ronnie and Nancy are probably liable to Jeannie K., because under the general rule their cattle escaped and caused the damage. If there is a "fencing in" statute, they are probably liable also because the defendant's duty is to keep the cattle fenced in and he did not, while the plaintiff has no duty to keep the cattle out. If the cattle escape and do damage, the defendant should be liable. If there is a "fencing out" statute, Ronnie and Nancy may be relieved of liability if Jeannie K. has not fenced her property in order to keep the cattle out. If she has met this burden, however, she may recover for damages caused by the cattle, although the facts here do not indicate which is the case.

# Evaluation

Points

(1)  Issues

Did the person state the basic issues?

_____(5)      a.   Flood

_____(5)      b.   Stampeding cattle

(2)  The law

Did the person correctly state the law?

_____(10)     a.   Rule in <u>Rylands</u>

i. Blackburn view

ii. Cairns view

iii. American "misinterpretation"

iv. English view

_____(10)     b.   Rule on trespassing cattle

i. General rule

ii. Fencing statutes

(3)  Analysis

How did the person apply the law to the facts in the case?

_____(20)     a.   The flood

_____(20)     b.   Stampeding cattle

(4)  Conclusion

_____(5)      Did the person reach a conclusion on each issue? What was it?

a.   The flood_____

b.   Stampeding cattle_____

(5)  Other factors

_____(5)      a.   Was the answer well organized? Did it make sense?

_____(5)          b.    Was the answer logical?

Did it apply a rational, deductive analysis?

_____(5)          c.    Was the answer well written?

Were there grammatical, spelling, or structural errors?

_____(5)          d.    Did the answer deal with the problem on a superficial level or address the complexities?

_____(5)          e.    Was the answer persuasive?

_____
Total (100)

### 3. Problem 3—Sam Student

Our final practice question involves another legal question, whether the violation of a statute can be used to establish a breach of the standard of care for a defendant whose conduct unintentionally causes harm to another. Individuals are normally supposed to take reasonable precautions to avoid injuring others, and if they fail to do so, they can be held liable for the harm they cause. In these questions, the defendant has not only caused the plaintiff's injuries; she has also violated a statute that arguably establishes a standard of conduct. The cases and materials appear in Appendix D, page 208. As with Problem 2, read, brief, outline, and review the material. When you have finished, take twenty minutes to answer the question (again, no peeking).

\* \* \* \* \* \* \* \* \* \* \* \*

After you have answered the question, look at the model answer, and then critique your answer using the evaluation form that appears on page 112. By now, you should be able to evaluate your progress. If your test-taking skills are wanting, make sure you get more practice before you undertake the real thing. Many universities have test-taking labs. Professors and student mentors are frequently willing to offer advice. Just don't ignore the symptoms. Since most readers of this book either have not yet or just recently begun law school, these exercises are less a measure of your knowledge than your ability to communicate your thoughts on paper. For now, that should be enough of a head start to permit you to begin your legal education with confidence.

## Practice Question and Answer

```
     Sam Student decided to fly his kite while at the beach one
day. He did this despite knowledge of a local ordinance that
prohibited kite flying on the beach and punished offenders with a
$25.00 fine. Sam was not holding onto the kite string very
tightly and when an unexpected strong gust of wind materialized,
it blew the kite out of Sam's hands. The wind carried the kite
about 5 miles until it crashed into the windshield of Pete
Plumber's truck, which Pete was driving at a speed 10 miles above
the legal limit. The kite shattered the glass and forced Pete to
cancel all of his afternoon appointments. Discuss Student's
liabilty to Pete.
```

# Model Answer

The first issue is whether Sam may be liable to Pete for damages in tort due to his violation of a statute prohibiting kite flying on the beach. Generally, one may be held civilly liable for statutory violations if the statute provides a standard of conduct. The test is whether the plaintiff was in the class of persons the legislature intended to protect by passing the statute, and whether the harm that resulted was the type the legislature intended to protect against.

Here, there is no information about the legislative intent. However, if the purpose of the legislature had been to provide for the safety of people on the beach (e.g., being run over by people trying to get or keep their kites up), the harm to Pete would probably not be within the scope of the legislative intent; nor would Pete be within the protected class. If the legislature meant to provide some broader protection against errant kites, then Pete may be within the class and the harm exactly what the legislature contemplated. However, the statutory language limiting the prohibition to "on the beach" suggests that such a broad interpretation is not warranted. Even if the legislature, in response to injuries caused by loosed kites on the beach drafted narrow language limited to kite flying on the beach, it is unclear whether an injury occurring 5 miles away caused by an unexpected gust of wind was contemplated. The answer may turn upon how common such strong gusts of wind were on this beach; in other words, was the propulsion of Sam's kite this distance a foreseeable event, which the legislature contemplated in drafting the statute.

It is likely that Sam will not be held liable in this case because the statute was not intended to protect the class of persons of which Pete is a member or against the harm that occurred.

If the statute applies, however, an additional question arises, whether Pete is contributorily negligent for exceeding the speed limit. Using the same test for civil liability in case of statutory violation, exceeding the speed limit is not likely to provide a basis for contributory negligence. Pete could have hit the kite at any speed, so violation of the statute was not a cause of the injury. Thus Pete cannot be found contributorily negligent in this case.

## J. Conclusion

In the end, it's just you and the exam book. For the most part, in law school there are no homework assignments, no pop quizzes, no bonus projects to factor in with the final exam, to produce your final grade. Everything comes down to this three-hour intellectual duel. Assuming that you have prepared throughout the semester and studied effectively in the days preceding the exam, you now have an opportunity to demonstrate how much you know. Taking law school exams requires a special set of skills. Some students who are very good in classroom discussions perform poorly on tests. Every year, many students fail to establish on paper what they know in their heads. On the other hand, there are some students who get better grades, not because they know more but because they know more about taking tests.

CHAPTER **6**
# Avoiding the Pitfalls of Law School

The road through law school, like the road to hell, is paved with good intentions. Victory here is never absolute. There always is one more case you could have read. Another source you could have checked. An additional hour you could have studied. There probably is not a lawyer alive who would not have done something or other differently in law school to improve his or her performance.

In law practice, you develop your skills as a lawyer through experience. If you are a trial lawyer, you argue cases in court. If you are an estate planning lawyer, you draft increasingly complex instruments. As a new lawyer, your mistakes will be corrected by senior lawyers, judges, and your own desire to improve. Competence is a constantly receding goal.

In law school you only get one chance. Whereas you certainly can improve your performance after a disastrous first year, you do not have the luxury of years to hone the skills needed for success. This chapter addresses some common pitfalls for the unwary law student, and offers suggestions on how to avoid them. It deals with time management, money management, stress management, alcohol and substance abuse, and other problems.

## A. Time Management

Time management is the most pervasive problem you will encounter in law school. Not only is the work voluminous, but also the need to make choices is inevitable. Your ability to get a grip on your schedule and discipline yourself to establish a flexible but workable routine will have a major impact on your success in law school.

**121**

## *1. Common Difficulties*

Law students procrastinate. They are overwhelmed by choices they have to make. They are overcommitted. All these difficulties are related. We often procrastinate when we have many things to do; we simply don't do the most onerous tasks. We make too many commitments because we can't make decisions, and so just say yes to everyone. In the most basic sense, time management is learning to make decisions in a timely way about matters important to us, and acting upon those matters when it is most advantageous to do so. Law school imposes an entire set of inevitable demands that can only be controlled, not eliminated. Although it may be easy to recognize the objectives of time management, it may be more difficult to become an effective manager of time.

## *2. A Time Management Model*

If you are a full-time law student, you will have approximately 33 months separating first year orientation and graduation. If you had a full-time, 40-hour-per-week job, you could expect to spend 5,500 hours on the job during this 33-month period. Many lawyers work considerably more hours than this. On the other hand, a law school will prescribe roughly 1,300 hours of classroom work. If you spend 3 hours outside class for each hour in the classroom (a suggestion that many professors offer but few students accept), you would still spend less than the time demanded by your full-time job on legal studies. To be sure, because of semester breaks, summer jobs, and vacations, the actual work load during school is greater. (If you are carrying 15 classroom hours per week, and spending 3 hours outside class, your work load is actually about 60 hours per week.) The point, however, is that there are plenty of hours to go to law school and lead some semblance of a normal life. If there are 24,000 hours during the 33 months of your legal education, and you spend 12,000 of them eating, sleeping, and grooming, you still have 12,000 hours left for school, work, play, and commuting.

The evening law student may not have such a good situation. Even carrying a reduced load of 10 or 11 classroom hours, applying the 3:1 study to classroom ratio, the evening student is frequently carrying two full-time jobs during periods when school is in session and only one during breaks. Such a schedule requires significant sacrifices, careful planning, and dogged perseverance. Pursuit of a part-time legal education is not for those who are marginally committed or perennially disorganized.

What you must do is *hire yourself* as a law student. Get out of the student mentality and think of your job as attaining a legal education. Make the commitment to yourself that you will spend a minimum of some specified number of hours per week over the next 33 months (45 months if you are an evening student). Give yourself two weeks vacation per year and appropriate holidays, but otherwise go to work every day as a law student. And pay yourself. Once a month, reward yourself with some treat as compensation for doing your job. Your pay might be something esoteric, like dinner and a movie; physical, like a new article of clothing; edifying, such as a (nonlegal) book to read; or psychological, like vegging out in front of the TV. This is not the only relaxation you can have during law school; it is one form of R&R that acknowledges your ongoing work.

Your friends, family, and loved ones must understand your commitment to law school. Just as they should know the demands of any job you take, they need to know the demands of this job, so they will not make competing demands (too often). If you use your time well, there will be time for relationships. Whether you "work overtime" or bring your work home with you is a separate question.

Some readers may question the need for a device such as the one just described. Some readers may possess the discipline to do their work without creating the fiction to assist them. Unfortunately, many do not. This exercise forces those students to make commitments to set aside the large blocks of time required for law school, while maintaining a big picture of how law school fits into their broader existence.

### 3. Establish a Schedule

A second technique for managing your time is to establish a weekly schedule. There are many commercial products, such as the "Weekly Planner" that you can buy. If you have a personal computer, a number of programs, such as "Lotus Organizer," have scheduling features. You may have developed your own system over the years in school or business. Whatever system you use, set up and follow a weekly schedule. Make sure the schedule is workable. If you don't allow yourself enough time to get from home to school each day, you will always be late. If you stop to get coffee each morning in the student lounge, put it in the schedule. Set aside blocks of time to study.

You walk a fine line, when you schedule your time, between inflexibility and anarchy. No schedule can be inelastic; things come up that you can't anticipate. On the other hand, if the schedule is honored more in its breaking than in its observance, it is useless. As a rule of thumb, the schedule should represent accurately your actual utilization of time. If more than 10 percent of your time is spent on unplanned activities, you need to get better control of your schedule.

### 4. The Daily List

A third simple device for time management is the daily list. While your schedule may govern the allocation of major blocks of time during the day, you still must find a way to deal with the urgencies of the day. Every morning, when you get up, make a list of the nonroutine things you have to do that day. Routine things (e.g., reading the paper, getting the mail) should already have a place in the schedule. Nonroutine matters, such as class assignments and personal obligations, should be included on your list. Then, rank the items in their order of importance, with the things that absolutely must be done today at the top and matters that you hope to finish today at the bottom. Within the times allocated for the appropriate activities, take care of the things at the top of the list first and handle the less important matters if you can. If some item stays at the bottom of your list for a period of weeks, drop it from the list, because you will never do it.

### 5. A Tickler System

In law practice, you may utilize a device called a tickler system. A tickler is a perpetual calendar that reminds you of critical dates. You can set up a tickler file now with a 3 × 5 card box, index cards, and tabs. Whenever you need to remind yourself of something, put a card in the box. The tabs include 31 days (for the current month), 12 months, and 5 years (see a sample tickler system, page 125). At the end of each month, divide the cards under the *next* month by day. At the end of each year, divide the cards under *next* year by month, and add a new tab at the end. A tickler can help you make appointments, remember birthdays, organize a study schedule, and meet deadlines

## Tickler System

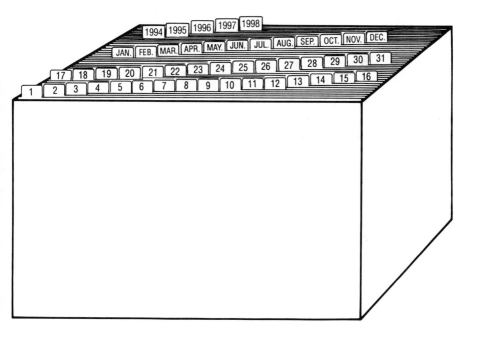

for papers, registration, and so on. You can also use a commercial software program; you do not have to be a computer whiz to apply this easy study aide.

## B. Money Management

Several years of service on a law school academic standards committee have produced these observations. Next to personal and family problems, money problems are most commonly cited by students in academic difficulty as a cause of their plights. Financial worries overwhelmed their consciousness and eliminated any possibility for effective study. These comments are intended for every law student who cannot sit down and write a check for $60,000 without grimacing.

In 1994, law school tuition ranged from just over $1,000 to more than $12,000 per semester. In addition, the cost of living for housing, food, transportation, entertainment, and other expenses will run $7,000–$12,000, or more, depending upon your location, lifestyle, marital status, and pre-existing obligations. Before you begin law school, you should budget carefully, considering your needs, law school expenses, and sources of income.

### 1. Financial Planning

Many students enter law school without a clear financial plan. They literally live from hand to mouth day by day. They are forced to take jobs in restaurants to pay expenses, constantly fight with family to obtain financial help, and frequently ignore school work because they are struggling with financial matters. If you prepare a realistic budget and the numbers just don't add up, it is probably better to postpone law school for a year or two or, after having started, take a leave of absence than to continue your legal education with inadequate resources. If you are committed to the idea of attending law school, make arrangements to set aside a portion of your earnings in a money market or other savings plan until you have saved enough to enter law school with some degree of financial security.

### 2. Financial Aid

There are alternatives to deferring law school enrollment that you should consider also. First, talk to the financial aid officer at the law school(s) where you are admitted to determine whether the school can put together a package with which you can live. The Financial Aid Office may be able to combine scholarships, work-study, and student loans in such a way that you will be able to survive. Most law students are not supported by their parents and therefore qualify for higher loan limits than younger students living at home. Convincing the Financial Aid Office that you are not in the same boat as an undergraduate student may prove problematic at some schools. One caveat concerning student loans deserves mention: the more you borrow, the more you have to pay back. A heavy debt load at graduation may force you into career choices you would not otherwise make. Because loan repayment commences with graduation from law school, there is great pressure to obtain the highest paying job possible immediately after graduation in order to pay the bills. For instance, many students do not pursue prestigious federal/judicial clerkships because the pay may be less than half what they could make in large law firms.

### *3. State Versus Private Schools*

If you wish to avoid going into hock up to your eyeballs, you may consider attending your state law school instead of the expensive private school you always dreamed about. Most state law schools have sound programs and excellent resources. The best state law schools compare favorably with the leading private institutions. At many state schools, tuition pays for only a portion of the cost of running the law school, so tuition is only a fraction of that of a private school, which must cover its operating expenses with tuition revenue.

### *4. Working*

Consider working full-time and going to school at night. Many law schools have evening division programs for students who choose not to go to school full-time. Whereas a part-time education takes four years and terrific discipline, the educational experience is substantially the same as that of a full-time program. Some schools permit you to change from one division to the other depending on your needs. Remember, however, that full-time students take 14–16 semester hours, while part-time students take 10–11. Thus, as a part-time student, you take only 1–2 fewer courses per semester than your full-time counterparts. The main advantages of enrolling in a part-time program are that you can carry a full-time job, and that the tuition is only about three-fourths of that for a full-time student.

American Bar Association standards limit full-time law students to 20 hours of outside employment per week. Many law students clerk in law firms during their second or third year of law school (see Chapter 8). The same ABA standards discourage first year students from working at all. By the second year, you should know whether you will be able to handle outside employment and still keep up with your law school work. Furthermore, after the first year you can adjust your course load to accommodate your work schedule by bunching your classes on certain days, taking a lighter load in some semesters, or attending summer school.

During the first year, your schedule is inflexible, and you really don't know how much time it will take you personally to do the work necessary to succeed at this enterprise. It makes more sense to hold off working until after the first year is over if at all possible. If you must work, try to find a job with flexible hours so that you can take time off to study for exams, prepare for moot court, and meet other law school obligations. Some students have successfully located positions that allow them to study while they work (e.g., night security guard, police dispatcher in a rural police department). Try to find a job that is close enough to the law school that transportation is not a problem. Avoid work that is physically or emotionally taxing. Some students engage in entrepreneurial activity, running their own businesses (e.g., computer consultant, writer, private investigator), so that they can control their schedules better. In short, don't work unless you have to, but if you do, try to pick something that you control or that doesn't impinge on your law school work.

### 5. Scholarships

A final comment on financing your legal education involves scholarships. If you are resourceful, you may be able to identify scholarship money that is not available through the university, law school, or Financial Aid Office. Many private organizations offer scholarships to individuals who meet special criteria. These include private foundations, religious organizations, ethnic and cultural support groups, states and municipalities, the military, and other institutions. If you can identify such independent funding for your legal education, you may be able to avoid many of the pitfalls described above. Every year in the United States, countless scholarships go unclaimed because no one applied for them. For more information on student financial aid, see *Barron's Guide to Law Schools.*

### *6. Budgeting*

Once you are in school, money management involves keeping track of your finances. The time management section of this chapter suggests hiring yourself as a law student. To carry this analogy further, the business entity hiring you as a law student is "your future." As in any business, this one must be properly capitalized, as the preceding section indicates. The enterprise also needs to be run in a businesslike fashion. This means that you operate as efficiently as possible within a budget and keep accurate financial records.

If you have a personal computer, there are a number of excellent and inexpensive personal financial management software packages (e.g., "Quicken") on the market that allow you to keep track of your finances. These systems are usually easy to use and require no formal accounting training to operate. Manual systems depend largely on your business/financial/accounting acumen. As with any business, "your future" depends on adequate cash flow. You have to have enough money in the bank at times when bills are due in order to pay them. Even students who have addressed the problem of financing their legal education may face short-term difficulties if they cannot get to their resources when the rent is due, the tuition bill arrives, and other expenses arise.

On the whole, you will find the law school experience much less painful and probably more meaningful if you get a grip on your finances from the start. If you have financial problems, don't wait until disaster is impending to seek help. After all, law school gives you enough to worry about without having to struggle with money matters on an ongoing basis.

### C. Stress Management

The point has already been made that law school is a high stress environment. Everything seems designed to produce anxiety, particularly during the first year. You will often hear the argument that learning to survive the pressures of law school will prepare you to cope with the pressures of practice.

Understanding that law school is stressful is one thing; doing something about it is quite another. Different people cope with this stress with varying degrees of success. Because stress can effect your performance, it is important to develop effective stress management skills.

One misconception is that all stress is bad. On the contrary, stress is a motivator. It helps us to deal with the problems and conflicts that life throws at us. The only truly stress-free state is death.

You need to make stress work for you. If the pressure isn't great enough, you have no motivation to act. If it is too great, you may be immobilized and unable to act. The following suggestions are designed to help you manage stress. Some of the ideas presented have been discussed already in this book in conjunction with other issues; others are introduced for the first time as techniques to deal with stress generally.

### 1. Responsibility

*Take responsibility for what happens to you.* Victims are almost always more stressed out than those who accept responsibility for their own decisions, because victims don't have any control over what happens to them. For instance, the victim would say, "That #!)/[* > Munneke gave us too much to read in Torts again," instead of "I didn't read my Torts last night." When you decide that you are in control of your own destiny, you will feel better equipped to deal with whatever obstacles law school throws at you.

### 2. Commitment

*Believe in something.* Dr. Ted Edwards, who runs The Hills Medical Sports Complex in Austin, Texas, and who has spoken to lawyers all over the United States on stress management, has stated repeatedly that individuals who are committed to something are less likely to have strokes, heart attacks, and other stress-related illnesses than those who are not. For some people, this may be a belief in God or some secular value system. For others it may be commitment to a cause or to family or loved ones. As much as drifters make popular movie heros, they may not fare as well on the streets of life as they do on the silver screen. In law school, the translation of this principle is fairly simple. Those who have a strong sense of purpose find it easier to endure the pressure than those who don't.

### 3. Little Aggravations

*Don't sweat the small stuff.* One of the difficulties with stress is that it doesn't always come out in response to what is really bothering you. The week before your brief is due, you yell at your spouse for being 15 minutes late getting home from work. You threaten to sue the grocery checker for neglecting to give you credit on your Peter Pan peanut butter coupon. You make obscene gestures at drivers who impede your progress in traffic with seeming maleficent purpose. You may do all sorts of uncharacteristic things in response to what is going on at school.

It is important to remember that stress is cumulative. All the pressures add up. Studies have shown that individuals who experience a large number of stressful events in their lives within a year often fall victim to physical illness shortly thereafter. If you let the little things get you down, it will be harder to deal with the one big stress you can't escape: law school.

When you feel like blowing up at someone or something, count to ten. Yes, just like your mother told you when you were a little kid. Wait a few seconds, take a deep breath, and think about whether it's worth it to waste your valuable anger on something like this. If it is, by all means, give them hell. Sometimes you just need to get a load off your mind. Sometimes those who do not know how to express their anger, frustration, or unhappiness, or who refuse to recognize their stress, have as much of a problem as those who express their anger too easily.

### 4. Signs of Stress

*Learn to recognize the signs of stress.* Although we all react to stress somewhat differently, there are a number of common symptoms that can signal us that the stress level is high: tightness or tension across the shoulders and the neck region, bulging blood vessels in our temples and neck, clenched teeth, clenched fists, sweaty palms, a knot in the stomach, heart palpitations, feelings of rage or panic, or compulsive behavior such as craving for cigarettes, food, drugs, or alcohol. If you know how to recognize these stress reactions in your own body, you can frequently cope with the anxiety even if you are not aware of the stress cognitively. A lawyer I know found that she was digging her fingernails into her palms at times she didn't even know she was under stress. However, she learned that when she did this, there usually was something bothering her.

### 5. Stoicism

*A little stoicism goes a long way.* Learn to accept the things you cannot change. Every indignity is not your personal war. Pick your battles and save your anger. We all feel a little like David Banner (a.k.a. "The Incredible Hulk") who responds to the bad guy twisting his arm, "Please don't do that. You really wouldn't want to see me when I'm angry."

### 6. Causes

*Recognize what causes your stress.* In law school, this means recognizing the times when you face the most stress: when you get behind, when you take exams, when major assignments like briefs are due, when you have to speak in class or do an oral argument, and when you have trouble understanding something. Although you can do something about some of these stressors (like getting too far behind), many of them are just part of law school. To the extent that you know what they are and when to expect them, you will find it easier to cope.

### 7. Coping

*Learn some simple coping mechanisms.* Deep breathing can lower your heart rate and blood pressure and actually reduce stress. When you recognize signs of stress, take several deep cleansing breaths, breathing in slowly through the mouth with the diaphragm and breathing out through the nose. If you can, sit down. If you can't, drop your shoulders and open your palms. Close your eyes and fantasize about something wonderful. Massage the spots where you feel the stress (e.g., temple, jaws, shoulders).

### 8. Exercise

*Get some exercise.* One of the best ways to get rid of stress is to work it out through exercise. The opportunities for physical exercise are virtually unlimited: tennis, basketball, running, jogging, walking, aerobic dancing, sex. Many law schools have intramural programs, tennis and golf matches, and exercise classes. There always are health clubs, exercise centers, weight rooms, and leagues sponsored by your local parks, Y.M.C.A., or other organizations. Whatever you decide to do, whether it is an individual or group activity, just try to get out regularly during law school. You will find it much easier to survive.

### 9. Diet

*Eat well.* There is a difference between eating much and eating well. Many law students experience eating disorders; some of them balloon whereas others waste away. Many students subsist on junk food, particularly those who work all day, go to school at night, and grab a "Big Mac" in between. A well-balanced, high protein, low fat, low cholesterol diet can actually contribute to stress reduction. Switch to decaf coffee. Caffeine is probably the most widely used drug in America. It is addictive (if you don't believe it, try going cold turkey from your coffee). It can produce anxiety (haven't you ever found yourself literally walking the walls after too many cups?). Try brewed decaf; it's just as good.

### 10. R & R

*Make sure you get rest and relaxation.* Get plenty of sleep. You really don't function all that well with long periods of two to three hours per night. And get away from studying every once in a while. Go to a party. Read something unrelated to law. Watch T.V. Spend time with your family. Just don't get carried away with it.

### 11. Meditate

*Clear out the cobwebs in your mind on a regular basis.* The process of clearing your mind is called meditation. When they hear the term *meditation*, lawyers conjure images of John, Paul, George, and Ringo sitting around with the Maharishi back in the 60s. In truth, you don't need a mystic guru, incense, or a mantra in order to meditate. All you need is a little bit of quiet time alone each day. Get away from noise, interruption, and distractions. Some people find a peaceful or relaxing setting like a park, a garden, a church, or a quiet comfortable room. Sit down, and begin to breathe slowly and deeply. Shut your eyes, and try to clear out all the mental noise that keeps trying to intrude. "Oh, my God. I have 30 pages of Torts to read for tomorrow." "Will I ever get a job?" "Wow! Did Mr./Ms. X really look good in class today." To help you clear your mind, think of something far away and peaceful, like standing on a tropical beach under the full moon, watching the waves roll in one after another. Or coasting down a lazy river on a comfy raft. Or going out of your body to float among the clouds, removed from the conflicts of life below.

When you have blocked out the intrusive thoughts begin to think about different parts of your body one at a time: your fingers, your arms, your toes, your legs, your stomach, your back. You will find that you can tune in, very acutely, to how each part feels. Then, think to yourself that each part is very relaxed. Let your hands feel heavy. Let the tension in each fade away. When you have been through your entire body, return to your deep breathing, open your eyes, and sit quietly for a few moments returning again to face the world. The whole exercise takes no more than five or ten minutes and can do wonders for your mental well-being. If you have difficulty doing the exercise yourself, you may buy a tape from Professor Peter Kutulakis at Dickinson Law School, Carlisle, PA 17013, which you may play to invoke this relaxation response.

## 12. Help

*Don't let your problems get too big.* This is what the late T. J. Gibson, for many years associate dean at the University of Texas School of Law, used to say to each entering class. Too often, people let problems build up until they cannot deal with them. Frequently, law students fail to confront serious problems until it is too late to do something about them. Sometimes students fail to acknowledge the symptoms of stress until their bodies or minds simply revolt. Almost any law school administrator who has been in the business for any length of time can recount one or more suicides among the ranks of former students. So, Dean Gibson's message was, "Talk to someone." You will find people in the law school who are willing to listen and help when you are troubled. They may or may not have formal training as counselors. Some of the most formidable law professors may be the most sympathetic and concerned human beings when one of their students is facing a legitimate crisis. Many universities and some law schools have a formal counseling center equipped to deal with personal problems of law students. Many law students have access to a minister, priest, or rabbi with whom they can share their concerns. There is nothing wrong with getting help. It is better to take a semester off from law school to get your life together than to stay in and flunk out.

None of this is intended to frighten or intimidate you. It is rather an attempt to present some of the negative realities of law school in a way and at a time when you can do something about them. This could be a very stressful time, but you have the potential to not just survive, but to thrive and grow, which is something you must do in order to succeed in law school.


## D. Drugs, Sex, and Rock-and-Roll

### 1. Life in the Fast Lane

Every law school has its share of party animals. As mentioned previously, all work and no play is not the best approach to law school. Conversely, all play and no work is an invitation for academic disaster. Life in the fast lane has a certain allure to a fair proportion of law students. These students enjoy living life on the edge. They play hard. They may even work hard. They have been described as "Type A" personalities. The legal profession seems to attract a large number of such individuals. They seem to love the thrill of being overwhelmed, not knowing whether they will complete their brief by the 5 o'clock deadline, make it to a hearing on time, or survive their unmanageable caseload.

Certain parallels between these hard-living law students and their lawyer counterparts are inevitable. Moreover, practicing lawyers who have problems related to substance abuse frequently developed an identifiable pattern during law school or earlier. Thus, even if life in the fast lane doesn't get you now, eventually it will catch up with you.

### 2. Prognosis for Type A's

What is the prognosis for "Type A" personalities in the practice of law? Even without alcohol or drug problems, the chances of making a critical error, missing an important deadline, or forgetting about a crucial hearing are greater for those who live on the edge. The possibility of exposure to legal malpractice or professional discipline is increased. The likelihood of career upheavals resulting from an inability to work with more stable partners and associates is constant. At home, the prognosis for divorce and personal crises is greater.

Studies have shown, however, that there is a correlation between abuse of alcohol and/or drugs and the incidence of malpractice among lawyers. Many bar associations have developed crisis intervention programs that attempt to place problem lawyers into treatment centers before they can make mistakes that can result in malpractice or disbarment. If the problem were simply one of what you could do to yourself, we might say that if you want to die sooner, it is your choice. However, when your conduct has an impact on clients, it becomes a concern of other lawyers and the courts.

### 3. A Nonreligious Argument for Slowing Down

This section is not meant to sound like a sermon. It is not a moral argument against drugs, alcohol, or wild living. It is simply a statement that many lawyers are prone to these abuses. For many of them, the results will be professionally self-destructive.

For them, being successful in law school means eschewing a lifestyle that is likely to lead to diminished performance. If you see a pattern of abuse in yourself, you should seek treatment now. If you are aware of problems among classmates, you may be able to help them. Slow down. You will live longer, remain happier, and achieve greater success as a law student and lawyer if you do.

## E. The Job Market

Almost anyone will tell you that the job market for lawyers is lousy. Practicing lawyers will tell you (but they do not want the competition). Reporters will tell you (but for them it's just another story). Your classmates will tell you (but they are as nervous about the future as you are). Even the professors will tell you that they are glad they have jobs. Only the placement director will remind you that the vast majority of last year's class found employment.

This scenario could describe the job market in 1995, 1985, 1965, or 1925. It will probably be the same in 2005 and beyond. The job market is always lousy. There are always too many lawyers and not enough jobs. And always, somehow, people with law degrees find jobs. Maybe we are just a more aggressive, adaptable, and employable lot than most. Maybe legal problems (at least in many areas) are not tied to the economic cycle. Maybe it's easier to talk about our problems than our successes. Who knows?

The fact is, if *you* do not have a job, 100 percent of the people who count are unemployed, and as long as you are looking for a job, there is 100 percent unemployment. And when you finally persuade someone to hire you, there will be 100 percent employment (at least in your job market). The fact is, looking for a job is arduous, tedious, terminally fruitless work. Putting yourself on the line and getting shot down repeatedly is not great for the ego. The fact is, during law school you will spend what seems like an inordinate amount of time looking for a job and an excessive amount of psychic energy thinking about what to do with your life after law school. There may be exceptions, but for most of you, this is true.

If you will necessarily spend a great deal of time dealing with career issues during law school, you need to do things right. First, do not let the job market or job search get you down, and do not become so obsessed with getting a job that your academic career falters (such a result is truly unproductive). Other parts of this book deal with time management, attitude, and organizational skills, and that advice certainly applies to job hunting.

Second, start to deal with career issues early in law school (now is not too early). Many students think that they have made their career decision when they decided to attend law school, though, actually, that is just the first of many career decisions. Talk to your placement director about your career plans. Read about the career planning process. *The Legal Career Guide: From Law Student to Lawyer*, by Gary A. Munneke, and *Nonlegal Careers for Lawyers*, by Gary A. Munneke and William D. Henslee, both published by the American Bar Association, as well as *Careers in Law*, also by Gary A. Munneke, published by VGM Professional Career Series, offer a range of information on legal careers and specific advice on the career planning and job search processes.

Finally, get involved with lawyers and the legal profession. Join student sections of bar associations. Attend programs for lawyers and law students at school and off campus. Look for legally related work during law school, including clerking for law firms, agencies, and courts, researching for professors, and volunteering for community service activities with legal overtones. Begin now to develop a network of contacts and to become an integral part of the legal profession. It is always easier to find work as an insider than as a newcomer in any line of work; law is no exception. And no amount of reading or counseling can substitute for firsthand knowledge gained through personal experience.

Unless you are one of those rare individuals who never plan to work as a lawyer, or intend to use a law degree in some other field, the job market is something you just have to deal with. Make the best of your opportunities, and be ready for whatever comes along. Be patient, and wait for the right choice to come your way. Remember that your career is a path and not a destination. In short, the job market can be a major pitfall in law school, but only if you let it.

# Diverse Students

The bulk of this book has dealt with problems of "typical" law students. Yet, law school student bodies are far from homogenous. They are a mix of ethnic backgrounds, sexes, socioeconomic statuses, and ages. Many of these students have unique concerns that can hinder their chances for success in law school.

## A. Women

Since the early 1960s, when only a handful of women attended law schools, the number of women students has grown to 40 percent of the American law school population. At some schools, the percentage exceeds 50 percent. Women have entered a profession that traditionally was male-dominated and seemingly determined to stay so. Whereas the attitude toward women and opportunities for employment in the profession have changed drastically in the past 20 years, many women students still find vestiges of the old patterns of behavior. Today, large numbers of women are confronted with the dilemma of having to choose between career advancement and family. Many complain that male students, professors, and professional colleagues place more attention on stereotypical factors, such as their looks and dress, than they do for their male counterparts.

In law school, a large percentage of women have children and primary child care responsibilities. Although there are exceptions, many husbands do little to support their wives in this regard. Nor do the law schools help in terms of providing day care, flexible scheduling, or other accommodations. Women have tended to seek out other classmates in similar situations to find both sympathy and solutions.

One of the major causes of stress for law student moms (and in many cases dads) is child care. Although it might make some sense to wait until the kids are themselves in school to begin a legal education, many young parents do not choose to wait. Even older children impose their own demands. With older children, particularly teenagers, it is important to get them on board to support your educational goals. Unsupportive children can be as much of a headache as an unsupportive spouse. For young children, the problem is likely to be reliable babysitters. Get someone you can depend on, or you will end up in a perpetual state of crisis.

## B. Diversity Students

Blacks, Hispanics, Asian Americans, American Indians, and other ethnic groups have not always had the same representation in legal education as Anglo students. Without going into the historical reasons, it is enough to say that despite the fact that law schools have opened their doors to minority students, the atmosphere in many law schools is still less than favorable. Although faculty and administrators try to be responsive to diversity students' needs, channels of communication are not always as good as they could be. Many students have special problems that affect their law school academic progress. Some attended weak inner-city schools as children and still are trying to catch up. Some consider English a second language. Others are economically disadvantaged and must work just to stay in school. Obviously, some nondiverse students have these problems too. And some diversity students come from wealthy families and the best schools. However, more diversity students face difficulties such as these in law school. And like women, they will graduate into a profession in which their group is at best, benignly underrepresented and, at worst, is actively excluded. If you have special problems, go to faculty members for help before exams. Take advantage of university and/or law school programs. Talk to administrators such as the financial aid officer and placement officer regularly about your needs and concerns; seek out other students in similar situations for support.

## C. Second Career Students

A growing contingent in law school is the student returning to law school after another career. In recent years, the median age of law students has increased. There are more post-thirty students today than ever before. These students often have special concerns about their careers. They go to school in an environment populated by twenty-five-year-olds. Many of them have been out of the educational world for years (even decades), and discover that the transition back into academia is not a smooth one. They may have greater financial needs than young, single postcollege students. Although most schools have few programs to assist them, many older students are imbued by experience with the ability to take care of themselves. They find it easier to discuss problems with faculty members and administrators who are their chronological contemporaries. If you are a second career student, use your maturity to the best advantage. Get remedial help to ease your return to school. Reading this book is a good start.

### D. Physically Challenged Students

A small number of law students have sight or hearing impairment, chronic illness, wheelchair confinement, and even learning disorders such as dyslexia. At one time many of these individuals could not dream of going to law school; or perhaps it would be better to say that at one time most law schools would not dream of educating these students. This is no longer the case. Although impediments often remain, law schools today are attempting to create opportunities for physically challenged students. In addition to a variety of state laws providing benefits to physically challenged individuals, the Americans with Disabilities Act (ADA) now mandates that institutions make reasonable efforts to accommodate people protected under the act. You should discuss with relevant government agencies the type and level of support you will be able to receive while you attend law school. Sometimes the school must construct special programs and facilities to aid physically challenged students. If you have a condition, consult with the Admissions Office to work out a plan to tackle law school successfully.

# After the First Year

Ultimately, success in law school is predicated on more than one year's performance. To suggest that this race will be won on the basis of first year achievement is as misleading as assuming the mile being won by the runner leading the race at the end of the first lap. To be sure, first year grades are important. Many law school awards and honors are determined on the basis of first year grades. Many law firms make permanent employment decisions during the fall semester following the first year, with only those grades to review. Psychologically, success in the first year gives many students an edge that they exploit throughout law school.

On the other hand, it is possible to recover from even a disastrous first year. It is sometimes easier to find a job if your grades have improved steadily throughout law school than if they tapered off each semester. If your first year record was impressive, you will want to keep it that way; if less than memorable, you will want to find ways to improve.

## A. Academics

### 1. Class Rank

Many law schools publish class rankings after the first year. These rankings establish your place in class either as a number (e.g., 15 out of 150) or as a percentile (e.g., top 10 percent). These class rankings are often used in the hiring process by legal employers who have difficulty evaluating differences in the meaning of grades from school to school. Not only do different schools use different grading systems, but the same grade may not mean the same thing at different schools with externally similar systems. In this sense, your employability is defined at least in part by comparing you to your classmates. On a different level, employers also compare law schools. They may consider candidates from the top 50 percent of one law school, well known to them, and only the top 5 percent from another.

Some schools that consider themselves "prestigious" have eliminated class rankings or devised grading systems that make it extremely difficult for employers to rank their students (e.g., "high pass," "low pass," "fail"). These schools operate on the theory that all their graduates are good and rankings would create artificial distinctions among the students. In practice, however, only a handful of institutions can enforce such policies.

It is possible to be so obsessed with class rank that you forget about education. Some students take only courses they consider easy in order to maintain or improve their grade point average, usually to their long-term detriment.

### 2. Classroom

The classroom experience is usually quite different in the second, third, and fourth years. Fear of the professors is replaced by guarded respect. Students in class are more likely to challenge the professor if they believe she is wrong or disagree with her point of view. The level of participation in many classes will wane, as many students withdraw from what they view as intellectual game playing. Classes are frequently smaller and, because the students have chosen to be there, there probably will be a core of students in every class who are both highly motivated and possess special skills and experience in that area. Professors in upper level courses are more likely to tell you the law as they see it rather than hide the ball. You may be exposed to other kinds of teaching methods, such as clinical instruction, simulation, research, drafting, and oral presentation. It is perhaps an overly broad generalization to say that the first year of law school is spent learning to think like a lawyer, the second year learning the substantive law, and the third year preparing for the practice of law by applying the knowledge gained during the first two years in practical settings. If you are a night student, you can add another year of learning the law in the middle.

During fall semesters, classroom participation may drop off in proportion to the level of student participation in on-campus interviews with law firms. Absenteeism often increases as students pursue part-time jobs, student activities, and other interests. It is important to remember that the classroom experience remains integral to the learning process. Ideally, outside activities should supplement rather than supplant classroom learning.

### 3. Course Selections

Students at many schools have a wide range of choices of courses to take after the first year. Most schools have a limited number of upper division required courses. Thus, students have considerable freedom in course selection. Course selection definitely plays a part in law school success. There is no one right way to select courses. Individual choices may be influenced by the school's lottery registration system, friends, work schedules, or other extra variables. However, there are a number of general approaches.

You can choose courses on the basis of substantive interest. If you have strong interests in a particular area of law (e.g., tax), you may want to take as many courses as possible in that area. If you are uncertain about your career plans, you may want to try to take a variety of survey courses to help you make career decisions. If you were thinking about starting a solo practice or going into a job where you will have immediate responsibility for your own caseload, you may want to choose courses that have a practical orientation. This approach presupposes that you can actually get a feel for what kind of law you will like to practice from a law school course, which may or may not be the case.

A variation of the substantive course selection theme is the bar review approach. If you know what courses the bar examiners in your state test, you can try to take courses in those subjects. Although a steady diet of esoteric courses (e.g., "post-Marxist Bosnian Civil Rights Law") may have a certain appeal, a curriculum that totally ignores core legal subjects is often unsatisfying in the end. On the other hand, students who choose their classes solely because the subject will be tested on the bar exam may miss unusual academic opportunities.

Some students make course selections for pragmatic considerations. They may hear that the grades in a particular course are high. They may take classes that give them a favorable final examination schedule. Or they may take courses that require a take-home exam or paper or no examination at all.

Perhaps the best way to choose courses is to take them from professors you enjoy and from whom you will learn. If you find a particular professor boring, you are unlikely to learn much in that course. If you harbor some antagonism for the professor, you may find it difficult to learn. Chances are good that you will do better in courses you enjoy. And taking courses that are stimulating and challenging is the best defense against upper division ennui. If you miss one or two courses that are tested on the bar exam, you will still have an opportunity to pick up the information during a bar review course after graduation.

## B. Student Activities

Remember those tables set up at first year orientation? By the second year of law school, you will have a better idea of organizations that interest you and how much time you can afford to devote to student activities. Many law school activities have an educational component, an intrinsic pedagogical value.

### 1. Law Review

The quintessential law school activity is law review. The tradition of student-edited journals in law is unique in American education. Law review membership looks good on your resumé. Traditionally, law review members were selected on the basis of grades from the first year class. Today, at most schools, grades represent only a portion of the selection criteria. Students are required also to participate in a writing competition or other form of review. Aside from the aura that often attaches to law school participation, law review experience is generally a valuable educational one. Legal research and writing skills learned during the first year are enhanced by editorial training unparalleled anywhere in the law school. In addition, law review members learn discipline and attention to detail. Editors hone their organization and leadership abilities. Many schools have not only *the* law review, but one or more specialized law reviews as well. And there usually is some pecking order of prestige among these journals. Doing law review well requires a significant commitment of time, but the rewards far outweigh the cost of investment.

## 2. Moot Court

The second traditional cocurricular activity in law school is moot court. Most law schools require every law student to participate in some form of moot court experience during the first year. For many students that is quite enough oral argument to satisfy them. Other students, however, thrive on these competitions. It is possible to participate in a variety of different moot court, mock trial, client counseling, negotiation, and other competitions after the first year of law school. Some of these are school sponsored for their own students; others are interscholastic, bringing teams from law schools all over the country to compete for prizes. These events may be very prestigious, attracting prominent jurists as judges. A moot court board analogous to the law review editorial board is responsible for coordinating these various competitions, and its membership is often comprised largely of the student representatives on the various interschool teams.

## 3. Student Government

The law school has its own student government, called the Student Bar Association, or SBA. The function of the SBA may vary from school to school. At some schools it may sponsor social events, speakers, and other activities. At many schools the SBA is responsible for student appointments to faculty committees. At some schools the SBA is responsible for allocating budgetary funds to all student organizations. One indication that the sun is in its heaven and all is right with the world will be the fact that the same girl who was always running for student council in your fifth grade class will be running for SBA rep in law school, and 20 years from now for U.S. senator.

## 4. Special Interest Groups

Because law schools themselves are insulated from much of the undergraduate university student life, law school activities have evolved independently of their undergraduate counterparts. In addition to student government, many law schools have their own newspapers, yearbooks, intramural programs, and other organizations. You will find legal fraternities, honorary organizations, and special interest groups. Some of these include organizations devoted to a particular substantive area of law (e.g., real estate, health law, international law, environmental law), outside interests (e.g., film forums, literature study groups), and activities that advocate various political, economic, and social points of view. At most law schools, there exist organizations of women students, minority students, gay and lesbian students, older students, and others. You can probably find some group of students that has your same interests and concerns. During the first year, your friendships with other students were linked to your class schedule, particularly the smaller sections such as legal research and writing. In the second year and beyond, many students find a "home" in a student organization where they feel compatible with the other members.

## C. Other Learning Experiences

Post first year legal education offers a wide variety of other learning experiences for students. The boon as well as the bane of the curriculum at many law schools is its flexibility. In addition, many of the cocurricular and extra-curricular activities contribute to your development as a lawyer. It is a little like visiting a cafeteria without your parents when you were a kid. You can get all desserts if you want to or you can select a well-balanced meal. The wise student will take advantage of this flexibility to make selections of courses and activities consistent with his or her career objectives. One important opportunity you should not pass up is the chance to develop your legal research and writing skills.

### *1. Scholarly Writing*

Although some law schools require an upper division writing experience, many do not. On the other hand, even if you were not selected to write for your school's journal, there are plenty of alternatives. You can enroll in one or more upper division seminars that require a paper in lieu of a final examination. Seminars are usually limited to a small enrollment because of the demands on faculty members to work individually with each student. It may also be possible to arrange for independent study with a professor in a subject area that interests you. Many schools give academic credit for papers produced in such a one-on-one setting. Independent study usually works best if you go to the professor with a specific idea for a paper. If you look around your school, you will notice posters advertising various legal essay contests, some offering fairly substantial monetary prizes. You may be able to conduct your scholarly research in one of these areas.

### 2. Research Assistants

A different approach to scholarly research is to get a job as a research assistant for one of your professors. Law schools usually have funds to cover student research assistants for professors. In such a position, you will do background research, drafting, and cite-checking for your professor's article or book. Instead of producing a finished product of your own, your satisfaction will derive from a small monthly paycheck and a footnote acknowledging your assistance in the professor's final work.

### 3. Nonlaw Courses

In some instances, you may find that the law school curriculum does not offer courses in a field of interest to you. At many law schools, it is possible to take graduate level courses at the affiliated university. It usually is necessary to obtain permission to take such courses, but you may find the experience a welcome respite from the Socratic dialogue.

### 4. Clinical Education

Every law school today has some form of clinical legal education program. In a clinic, students work with actual clients and real problems under the supervision of a faculty member who directs the clinic. The substantive areas covered will vary from school to school and program to program. However, the lawyering skills one can develop have wide applications after graduation. Unfortunately, most schools do not have enough seats in their clinical program to allow all students to participate. Be sure to investigate the clinical offerings at your school to determine how and when to enroll.

### 5. Skills Training

Law schools also offer skills training courses in such areas as trial advocacy, client interviewing and counseling, negotiation, instrument drafting, and law practice management. These courses often use simulated situations, "learning by doing" problems, and computer modeling, as learning devices. For instance, in a trial advocacy course you may be required to make motions and present arguments to the court concerning a hypothetical fact situation. In client interviewing and counseling, you may be asked to interview someone role-playing a client coming to you with a problem.

A recent American Bar Association report, *The Report of the Task Force on Law Schools and the Profession: Narrowing the Gap*, has declared what many critics of legal education have said for a long time: law schools do not prepare students to practice law. The report urges schools to offer more skills and clinical courses, and many schools are rethinking their entire curriculum in light of this suggestion. While you should not expect to see wholesale abandonment of traditional legal education any time soon, you can anticipate that at most schools there will be more opportunities than in the past to develop the practice skills you will use as a lawyer.

### 6. Summer School

Whether or not your law school offers a summer session, many law schools do. Summer school offers law students scheduling options sometimes not apparent immediately. The most obvious rationale for going to summer school is to accelerate graduation, or to lighten the course load the following year. Some students use summer school to take courses either at their law school or another law school that would not be available during the academic year. Summer school abroad, offered by numerous law schools, may be of special interest to many students. The summer session may be an opportunity to enroll in a difficult course, work on a paper, or enroll in a clinic.

### 7. Foreign Study

Many law schools offer programs of legal study in a foreign country. Most of these are held during the summer, but some are given during the regular school year. Generally, the program will be associated with a foreign law school or university, although the classes will be taught in English, usually by American professors. Foreign law study presents an alternative to the routine of law school at home. Since you will receive credit for your coursework abroad, you should not delay your graduation by attending one of these programs, although before enrolling you should make sure that your law school approves the specific courses you take.

### 8. Specialization

Some law schools offer special programs of course concentration in areas like tax, environmental law, trial practice, and others. A few grant certification in these programs. Many schools sponsor joint degree programs (e.g., J.D./M.B.A.). You may want to investigate these specialized offerings if you have a particular career interest. For a more complete listing of specialty and graduate law programs, you should consult *Barron's Guide to Law Schools.*

### 9. Work Experience

After you finish the first year, most of you will consider obtaining legal work experience. A full discussion of placement opportunities is beyond the scope of this book. Take some time to visit your placement officer to discuss career plans before the end of your first year. See also the section on "The Job Market" in Chapter 6, page 136.

Law students work in a wide variety of part-time and summer jobs for law firms, corporations, government agencies, and other organizations. Except in the largest firms and corporations, the pay may not be great. But the experience will help you to learn about the practical side of law. Unfortunately, the quality of clerkships varies widely; there are good and bad lawyers as well as ethical and unethical ones. Generally, however, the experiences of law students are positive ones, supplementing their classroom education and helping them to make sound career decisions based on personal experience. If you do work after the first year, don't forget about your education. It is possible for the practical and the theoretical to go hand in hand.

### D. Problems

After the first year, law school will seem much easier. You will know more about what you need to do to succeed. You will have solved many of the problems that plagued your first year. But, two new upper division problems will confront you.

### *1. Waning Interest*

The first of these derives from waning interest in law school itself. As you move into your final semesters, this problem may become acute. If you decide that you have learned all you can (or want to) from your professors, that work or student organizations are more important than school, or that the result is not worth the effort in terms of grades, you will miss out on an important part of legal education.

After the first year, learning can be fun if you throw yourself into it. Seek out professors and classes that intrigue you. Fight the temptation to coast into graduation. Once you leave law school, it is unlikely that you will have the opportunity to pursue problems that interest you at your own pace. You will have your clients' problems and their deadlines. You will face partners' demands and judges' orders. The day will come when you will look back longingly on the leisurely days of law school. Enjoy it now. You only go around once.

### *2. Self-fulfilling Prophecy*

The second problem involves the tendency of many students to perform at the level of their first year grades. If you did well, this may be fine. If your grades were not as high as you would have liked, you may have to struggle to avoid letting your first year record become a self-fulfilling prophecy. For one thing, you will have to go back and reassess your whole approach to study and exams. Schedule appointments with your professors to discuss your exams, focusing on what you could do differently. Look honestly at your study habits to see if they could be improved. Take steps to remedy weaknesses such as issue spotting, writing, and analysis. You are not destined to mediocrity but you may need to do more work than other students to get ahead. Reevaluate your schedule to make enough room to study. Some students will become lazy after the first year, so there is always room to move up.

# CHAPTER *9*

# Conclusions—What Is Success?

This book started with the question, "What is success?" That is a good place to end. Much of the text has offered specific suggestions to help you make the best of your law school career. Underlying these recommendations is an assumption that you will maximize your opportunities if you maximize your potential. Stated another way, doing the best you can is the surest guarantee to the most career options possible. And doing your best does not mean just trying hard. You can work very hard in law school and get very little to show for it. You need to work hard *and* work smart. This book has provided some hints on how to work smart. The rest is up to you.

In a larger sense, success cannot be measured over the short term. You may win a battle here or there but still lose the war. The long-term view is ultimately what counts. And furthermore, the only one whose opinion matters is you. The world may declare you a winner, but if you perceive yourself to be a loser, a loser you will be. And vice versa. Law school is just one step in building a successful career.

When you cut away all the complexities and trappings, success is happiness. It is satisfaction with who you are and the choices you have made. It is realizing that enjoyment is not found at some destination, it is encountered in the ride. To be sure, we all have our ups and downs, but if we can make the most out of every day, we will be happy and successful.

What makes us happy? Professionally, we are happy doing what we do well. Ideally, there should be a convergence of work and play in our lives. We should get paid to play. Maybe professional athletes approach this ideal. But they frequently have to pay with pain, and most of them can't do it until they die. So if you really love what you do as a lawyer you really can get paid to have fun.

Unfortunately, many lawyers are not happy. For whatever reasons, work is not play. Despite earning substantial incomes they are not satisfied with their lives. These lawyers often do not feel successful, and surveys suggest that many actually leave the legal profession each year to pursue other interests.

There is a definite link between career satisfaction and commitment. In his book *Working*, author Studs Terkel paints a bleak picture of workers in all walks of life who just put in their time. He also describes a minority who enjoy what they do. The one thing that seems to differentiate the satisfied from the rest is commitment to their work.

I remember visiting France some years ago and observing that the waiters in restaurants seemed genuinely proud of their work. Unlike many waiters in this country, who seem to be passing time in their present occupations until something better comes along, their French counterparts were proud of their work, and it usually showed.

Maybe the American dream sets us up for failure. Maybe we can never succeed because there is always something else to achieve. Maybe we have lost sight of the importance of the simple notion of commitment to doing our jobs well. Maybe it is too easy in our affluent world to slide down the slippery slope of least resistance.

What steps can someone entering law school take to assure success? For starters, if you don't like law, get out now. If you decide to stay, give it all you have. There is an incredible burden of work in law school. The preceding pages describe it in detail; they also give you a formula for managing the load. Nowhere has it been suggested that there exists a shortcut to hard work and commitment to the task ahead.

You can also help yourself by making timely, informed decisions. Throughout law school and beyond, you will make innumerable decisions about your career. Every day, you will make countless choices between excellence and mediocrity. If you have a direction in life, it will be easier to identify the courses of action best for you.

The following story, told by Robert Bruce White, a partner in Lucas, Bishop, Bowker and White, Edmonton, Alberta, at a meeting of the American Bar Association Law Practice Management Section, illustrates the point.

A visitor to the Ile de la Cité came upon a marble quarry. In the quarry he found a man with a chisel chipping marble. The visitor asked the man what he was doing. The answer was, "I'm hacking marble. Isn't that obvious?" The visitor went on, and soon came upon another man, also chipping marble. "What are you doing?" asked the visitor. This man answered with a smile, "I'm earning one franc per week." The visitor walked on until he encountered a third man chiseling marble. When asked what it was he was doing, this man responded with tears in his eyes, "I'm building the cathedral of Notre Dame."

Law is a profession that offers many rewards for those willing to make the commitment. And success in law school as well as practice is not hard to achieve when viewed in this light.

# APPENDIX A

Suggested Reading

## On Law School

*Barron's Guide to Law Schools.* New York: Barron's, 1994.

Calamari, John D. and Joseph M. Perillo. *How to Thrive in Law School.* Pelham Manor, NY: Hook Mountain Press, 1984.

Carter, Lief H. *Reason in Law.* 3rd ed. Boston: Little, Brown and Co., 1987.

Ehrlich, Thomas C. and Geoffrey Hayard. *Going to Law School: Readings on Legal Career.* Boston: Little, Brown and Co., 1975.

Law School Admission Council. *Financing Your Law School Education.* Newton, PA: Law School Admission Services, 1986.

Llewellyn, Karl. *The Bramble Bush.* New York: Oceana Press, 1960.

Munneke, Gary A., *Careers in Law.* Chicago: VGM Professional Career Series, 1992.

Munneke, Gary A. *The Legal Career Guide: From Law Student to Lawyer.* Chicago: American Bar Association, 1992.

Munneke, Gary A. *Opportunity in Law Careers.* Chicago: VGM Career Horizons, 1993.

Osborne, John Jay. *The Paper Chase.* New York: Warner Books, 1983.

Research Associates. *Write the "A" Law Exam Answer.* Swampscott, MA: Research Associates, 1980.

Schaffer, Thomas L. and Robert S. Redmont. *Lawyers, Law Students and People.* Colorado Springs: Shepards, Inc., 1977.

Turow, Scott. *One L.* New York: Penguin Books, 1977.

Ward, Kevin P. *Not the Official Lawyers' Handbook.* New York: New American Library, 1984.

Wydik, Richard C. *Plain English for Lawyers.* Durham, NC: Carolina Academic Press, 1979.

## On Lawyering

Auchincloss, Louis. *The Partners.* New York: Warner Books, 1975.

Carlin, Jerome. *Lawyers on Their Own.* New Brunswick, NJ: Rutgers University Press, 1962.

Dickens, Charles. *Bleak House.*

Epstein, Cynthia Fuchs. *Women in Law.* New York: Anchor Books, 1983.

Freud, James C. *Lawyering: A Realistic Approach to Private Practice.* New York: Law Journal Seminars Press, 1979.

Johnston, Quintin and Dan Hopson, Jr. *Lawyers and Their Work.* Indianapolis: Bobbs-Merrill, 1967.

Kanter, Arnold. *The Secret Files of Stanley J. Fairweather.* Chicago: Swallow Press, 1980.

Lewis, Anthony. *Gideon's Trumpet.* New York: Random House, 1964.

Mayer, Martin. *The Lawyers.* New York: Harper & Row, 1966.

Munneke, Gary A. *The Legal Career Guide: From Law Student to Lawyer.* Chicago: American Bar Association, 1992.

Munneke, Gary A. and William D. Henslee. *Non-Legal Careers for Lawyers.* Chicago: American Bar Association, 1994.

Osborne, John Jay. *The Associates.* Boston: Houghton Mifflin, 1979.

Woodward, Bob and Scott Armstrong. *The Brethren: Inside the Supreme Court.* New York: Simon & Schuster, 1979.

# APPENDIX B

Resource Materials
on Intent and Battery

*Prosser & Keeton on Torts*

Prosser & Keeton

# INTENTIONAL INTERFERENCE WITH THE PERSON

## § 8.  Meaning of Intent

In a loose and general sense, the meaning of "intent" is easy to grasp.  As Holmes observed, even a dog knows the difference between being tripped over and being kicked.[1] This is also the key distinction between two major divisions of legal liability—negligence and intentional torts—and it plays a key role in criminal law,[2] and elsewhere.[3] It is one of the most basic, organizing concepts of legal thinking.

"Intent" is also one of the most often misunderstood legal concepts.  The distinction between intentional and unintentional invasions draws a bright line of separation among shadings of almost infinitely varied human experiences.  As might be expected, authoritative definitions that purport to specify exactly where this bright line is to be drawn are not entirely in accord.  There is even some conflict between the two major pronouncements on the subject by the American Law Institute—one in the Restatement—now the Second Restatement—of Torts [4] and the other in the Model Penal

§ 8

1. Of course, a cunning tripper might fool the dog—once, at least.

2. See, e.g., ALI Model Penal Code, 1962, § 2.02(2) (a), (b), defining "purposely" and "knowingly."  The contrasting meanings of "recklessly" and "negligently" are defined, id. at (c), (d).

See also Sandstrom v. Montana, 1979, 442 U.S. 510, 99 S.Ct. 2450, 61 L.Ed.2d 39, condemning an instruction to the jury in a criminal case that "the law presumes that a person intends the ordinary consequences of his voluntary acts."  Clearly distinguishable, however, is an instruction that "it is ordinarily reasonable [for the factfinder] to infer that a person intends the natural and probable consequences of acts."  Hardy v. United States, 1st Cir. 1982, 691 F.2d 39.  For further development of this distinction, see infra this section.

3. See infra, §§ 107, 113.  See also, e.g., R. Keeton Insurance Law Basic Text, 1971, §§ 5.2–5.4, 7.6, 7.7; ALI Federal Securities Code, 1980, § 202(61)(C).

4. See §§ 8A, 13, 16, 18, 20.  For an analysis of the Second Restatement's provisions on intent, with identification of some variations, in form at least, from the

Code.[5]   Still more variations appear in the great mass of statutory and judicial usages, sometimes in explicit definitions and more often among the meanings discovered as implicit when one closely examines the contexts in which statements about intent are made.

The Restatement aims at applying a single, consistent concept of intent throughout. Since the drafters were attempting to "restate" the law of torts, they were aiming for a concept consistent with the most common usage in judicial opinions in tort cases, and it seems a fair assessment that they achieved this aim. Thus, in examining the Restatement concept, we are also examining the most common, though not the only, sense in which courts use "intent" in tort cases.

The three most basic elements of this most common usage of "intent" are that (1) it is a *state of mind* (2) about *consequences* of an act (or omission)[6] and not about the act itself, and (3) it extends not only to having in the mind a purpose (or desire) to bring about given consequences but also to having in mind a belief (or knowledge) that given consequences are substantially certain[7] to result from the act. It is also essential that the state of mind of intent exist when the act occurs. Additional elements of the concept concern the extent to which the intent may relate to different persons[8] or different consequences from those at issue.[9]

Much of the confusion surrounding application of the legal requirement of intent arises from lack of a clear understanding of the relationship among act, intent, and motive.[10]

One prerequisite of liability is that the defendant act (or fail to act when there is a legal duty to act). An involuntary muscular movement of a sleeping or otherwise incapacitated person will not support liability.[11] But an "act," as that term is ordinarily used, is a voluntary contraction of the muscles, and nothing more.[12] An act is to be distinguished from its consequences.

"Thus, if the actor, having pointed a pistol at another, pulls the trigger, the act is the pulling of the trigger and not the impingement of the bullet upon the other's person."[13]

first Restatement, see R. Keeton, Computer-Aided and Workbook Exercises in Tort Law, 1976, 1.14–1.23.

5.   See § 2.02. Note, for example, that in the usage of the Model Penal Code a person "acts knowingly" with respect to a result of his conduct if "he is aware that it is practically certain that his conduct will cause such a result," § 2.02(2)(b), and that a requirement of knowledge is satisfied "if a person is aware of a high probability of its existence, unless he actually believes that it does not exist." § 2.02(7).

6.   The Restatement speaks only of an act (not of an omission) in defining intent, in § 8A, and requires an act, as distinguished from inaction, for battery, in § 14 and comment *c* thereto. Also, the Restatement takes the position that purposely failing to act when there is a legal duty to act is negligence. Scope Note preceding § 13, at 24 ("failure to perform [a duty to act for the protection of others against bodily harm] constitutes negligence * * *, irrespective of whether his failure is or is not deliberate and done for the very purpose of causing the other to suffer the bodily harm from which it was the actor's duty to protect him"). This curious usage is confounding, since there is as clear a distinction (1) between purposely failing to act, in order to produce a desired consequence, and failing to act without adverting to that consequence, as (2) between purposely acting to produce a desired consequence and acting without adverting to that consequence. The confusion is aggravated by the assertion

that an act is required for false imprisonment (§ 35) and that "refusal" to provide a means of escape when there is a duty to do so is a sufficient "act of confinement" (§ 45).

7.   The Model Penal Code uses the phrase "practically certain," § 2.02(2)(b), in contrast with the Restatement's "substantially certain," § 8A. It seems doubtful, however, that any substantive difference was intended by the drafters or by the American Law Institute. See also supra, n. 5, as to differences that are more likely to be substantive.

8.   See the discussion of "transferred intent," infra, this section.

9.   For example, one who intends only to cause a harmful physical contact but succeeds only in causing apprehension that such a contact is imminent is subject to liability for assault; see infra, § 10.

10.   See also supra § 5, concerning motive.

11.   Slattery v. Haley, [1923] 3 Dom.L.Rep. 156, 25 Ont.L.Rep. 95; Stokes v. Carlson, 1951, 362 Mo. 93, 240 S.W.2d 132; Wishone v. Yellow Cab Co., 1936, 20 Tenn. App. 229, 97 S.W.2d 452.

12.   Holmes, The Common Law, 1881, 91; Cook, Act, Intention and Motive in the Criminal Law, 1917, 26 Yale L.J. 644; Second Restatement of Torts, § 2.

13.   Second Restatement of Torts, § 2, Comment *c*.

When "act" is used in this sense, it is tautological to speak of a "voluntary act," and self-contradictory to speak of an "involuntary act," since every act is voluntary. Nevertheless, the phrases "voluntary act" and "involuntary act" do appear in legal prose.[14] Moreover, differences may be deeper than merely a choice of terminology; one who uses the phrase "voluntary act" may be using "act" to mean something different from a mere voluntary contraction of the muscles; sometimes the phrase "voluntary act" is used to mean something closer to the concept of intent (as defined in the Restatement and in common usage), which focuses not upon the mere "act" (in the narrower sense, defined in the Restatement and in common usage) but upon volition in relation to consequences as well as volition in relation to the muscular contraction. The movement of the finger which fires a gun is the same, whether it takes place in a crowded city, or in the solitude of the Mojave Desert, and regardless of the actor's state of mind about the consequences. But the legal outcome will depend on the actor's surroundings and the actor's state of mind. The actor may move the muscles of the finger for the purpose of pulling the trigger, for the purpose of causing the bullet to strike another, for the purpose of killing the other, for the purpose of revenge, of defense of country, or of self-protection against attack. "Intent" is the word commonly used to describe the purpose to bring about *stated physical conse-*

quences;[15] the more remote objective which inspires the act and the intent is called "motive."[16] Both intent and motive are steps removed from volition to move the muscles of the finger. Intent is concerned with consequences of that movement; motive, with reasons for desiring certain consequences. Intent is thus less removed from act than is motive. Each has its own importance in the law of torts, and a justifiable motive, such as that of self-defense, may avoid liability for the intent to kill.

Both intent and motive are states of mind. Act is a combination of muscular movement and the state of mind of volition to make that movement.

As already noted, however, intent is broader than a desire or purpose to bring about physical results. It extends not only to those consequences which are desired, but also to those which the actor believes are substantially certain to follow from what the actor does. The actor who fires a bullet into a dense crowd may fervently pray that the bullet will hit no one, but if the actor knows that it is unavoidable that the bullet will hit someone, the actor intends that consequence.

Another source of great confusion is failure to distinguish between (1) the factual elements essential to a finding of intent and (2) the elements of proof and argument that advocates and factfinders may bring to bear in addressing the question whether those

---

14. Even courts citing and following the Restatement definition of "act" have sometimes lapsed, in other passages, into using phrases such as "voluntary act" and "conscious act." See, e.g., Stokes v. Carlson, 1951, 362 Mo. 93, 240 S.W.2d 132.

Moreover, other courts and writers simply do not accept the Restatement of Torts usage. An example is the ALI Model Penal Code, § 2.01, which uses "voluntary act" and defines it in a way that appears to be very nearly if not precisely identical in meaning with "act" as defined in the Restatement of Torts.

15. See Second Restatement of Torts, § 8A, comment *a*. For a more detailed explanation of this concept, and for discussion of the failure to apply it correctly as a source of error in application of the concept of intent, see R. Keeton, Computer-Aided and Workbook Exercises in Tort Law, 1976, 1.1–1.23. One common source of confusion is failure to focus precisely on

*what consequence* must be intended to meet the requirements of the legal theory at issue. In Garratt v. Dailey, 1955, 46 Wn.2d 197, 279 P.2d 1091, second appeal, 1956, 49 Wn.2d 499, 304 P.2d 681, a boy who pulled away a chair just as plaintiff was about to sit down was held liable for battery because he knew that she was substantially certain "to sit in the place where the chair had been," which, without satisfactory explanation, the court treated as the equivalent of knowing that she was substantially certain to suffer a harmful or offensive bodily contact with the ground. Might the boy not believe that she would not be hurt and that she would think it was all good fun?

16. Cook, Act, Intention and Motive in the Criminal Law, 1917, 26 Yale L.J. 644; Walton, Motive as an Element in Torts in the Common and in the Civil Law, 1909, 22 Harv.L.Rev. 501.

factual elements are present in a given case. The factfinder need not credit the actor's assertion that the actor did not intend the result in question. One of the common lines of argument against crediting the actor's assertion is (1) that, given the circumstances disclosed in the evidence, a reasonable person in the actor's position would have known that the consequence in question was substantially certain to follow the act, (2) that the evidence shows that the actor was even brighter and shrewder than most others, and (3) that the inference is therefore compelling that the actor knew even though testifying otherwise. If the factfinder credits inference (1) but not inferences (2) and (3), the finding is negligence. But if the factfinder credits all three inferences, the finding is intent to produce the consequence in question. Expressed another way the point is this: Since intent is a state of mind, it is plainly incorrect for a court to instruct a jury that an actor is presumed to intend the natural and probable consequences of the actor's conduct; but it is correct to tell the jury that, relying on circumstantial evidence, they may infer that the actor's state of mind was the same as a reasonable person's state of mind would have been.[17] Thus, when the driver who whips up horses with a loud yell while passing a neighbor's team denies intent to cause a runaway, the factfinder may discredit the driver's testimony;[18] and the

defendant on a bicycle who rides down a person in full view on a sidewalk where there is ample room to pass •may learn that the factfinder (judge or jury) is unwilling to credit the statement, "I didn't mean to do it."[19]

On the other hand, the mere knowledge and appreciation of a risk—something short of substantial certainty—is not intent. The defendant who acts in the belief or consciousness that the act is causing an appreciable risk of harm to another may be negligent, and if the risk is great the conduct may be characterized as reckless or wanton,[20] but it is not an intentional wrong. In such cases the distinction between intent and negligence obviously is a matter of degree. The line has been drawn by the courts at the point where the known danger ceases to be only a foreseeable risk which a reasonable person would avoid, and becomes in the mind of the actor a substantial certainty.[21]

The intent with which tort liability is concerned is not necessarily a hostile intent, or a desire to do any harm.[22] Rather it is an intent to bring about a result which will invade the interests of another in a way that the law forbids. The defendant may be liable although intending nothing more than a good-natured practical joke,[23] or honestly believing that the act would not injure the

17. Sandstrom v. Montana, 1979, 442 U.S. 510, 99 S.Ct. 2450, 61 L.Ed.2d 39; Hardy v. United States, 1st Cir. 1982, 691 F.2d 39.

18. Lambrecht v. Schreyer, 1915, 129 Minn. 271, 152 N.W. 645. See also Land v. Bachman, 1921, 223 Ill. App. 473.

19. Mercer v. Corbin, 1889, 117 Ind. 450, 20 N.E. 132. Cf. Commonwealth v. Raspa, 1939, 138 Pa.Super. 26, 9 A.2d 925.

20. See infra, § 34.

21. Hackenberger v. Travelers Mutual Casualty Co., 1936, 144 Kan. 607, 62 P.2d 545; Cook v. Kinzua Pine Mills Co., 1956, 207 Or. 34, 293 P.2d 717. See Second Restatement of Torts, § 13, Comment d; Note, 1962, 34 Rock Mt.L.Rev. 268; De Muth, A Comparison of the Conduct Required in Trespass to Chattels and Negligence, 1961, 33 Rocky Mt.L.Rev. 323.

Compare the following statement, which is somewhat at odds with the Restatement definition of "intent":

"If the manifest probability of harm is very great, and the harm follows, we say that it is done maliciously or intentionally; if not so great, but still considerable, we say that the harm is done negligently; if there is no apparent danger, we call it mischance." Holmes, Privilege, Malice and Intent, 1894, 8 Harv.L. Rev. 1.

22. Baldinger v. Banks, 1960, 26 Misc.2d 1086, 201 N.Y.S.2d 629; Restatement of Torts, § 13, Comment e.

23. Reynolds v. Pierson, 1902, 29 Ind.App. 273, 64 N.E. 484; State v. Monroe, 1897, 121 N.C. 677, 28 S.E. 547.

plaintiff,[24] or even though seeking the plaintiff's own good.[25]

## More Extensive Liability for Intent

There is a definite tendency to impose greater responsibility upon a defendant whose conduct was intended to do harm, or was morally wrong.[26] More liberal rules are applied as to the consequences for which the defendant will be held liable,[27] the certainty of proof required,[28] and the type of damage for which recovery is to be permitted,[29] as well as the measure of compensation.[30] The defendant's interests have been accorded substantially less weight in opposition to the plaintiff's claim to protection when moral iniquity is thrown into the balance. Apparently the courts have more or less unconsciously worked out an irregular and poorly defined sliding scale, by which the defendant's liability is least where the conduct is merely inadvertent, greater for acts in disregard of consequences increasingly likely to follow, greater still for intentionally invading the rights of another under a mistaken belief of committing no wrong, and greatest of all where the motive is a malevolent desire to do harm.

## "Transferred" Intent

One definite area in which there is more extensive liability for intent than for negligence is that covered by the curious surviving fiction of "transferred intent." The defendant who shoots or strikes at A, intending to wound or kill A, and unforeseeably hits B instead, is held liable to B for an intentional tort.[31] The intent to commit a battery upon A is pieced together with the resulting injury to B; it is "transferred" from A to B. "The intention follows the bullet." [32]

This peculiar idea appeared first in criminal cases [33] at a time when tort and crime were still merged in the old trespass form of action. It represents an established rule of the criminal law, in cases in which shooting, striking, throwing a missile or poisoning has resulted in unexpected injury to the wrong person.[34]

24. Vosburg v. Putney, 1891, 80 Wis. 523, 50 N.W. 403; Craker v. Chicago & Northwestern Railway Co., 1875, 36 Wis. 657.

25. Clayton v. New Dreamland Roller Skating Rink, 1951, 14 N.J.Super. 390, 82 A.2d 458 (plaintiff fell and broke her arm; over her protest defendant proceeded to manipulate the arm in order to set it); Johnson v. McConnel, N.Y.1878, 15 Hun 293 (defendant intervened in a scuffle to protect plaintiff and broke plaintiff's leg); Maxwell v. Maxwell, 1920, 189 Iowa 7, 177 N.W. 541, (arrest of insane person for his own protection).

26. Bauer, The Degree of Moral Fault as Affecting Defendant's Liability, 1933, 81 U.Pa.L.Rev. 586; Note, 1962, 14 Stan.L.Rev. 362.

27. "For an intended injury the law is astute to discover even very remote causation. For one which the defendant merely ought to have anticipated it has often stopped at an earlier stage of the investigation of causal connection. And as to those where there was neither knowledge nor duty to foresee, it has usually limited accountability to direct and immediate results. This is not because the defendant's act was a more immediate cause in one case than in the others, but because it has been felt to be just and reasonable that liability should extend to results further removed when certain elements of fault are present." Derosier v. New England Telephone & Telegraph Co., 1925, 81 N.H. 451, 463, 130 A. 145, 152. See infra, § 43.

See Green, Rationale of Proximate Cause, 1925, 170 ff.

28. Cases are Collected in Bauer, The Degree of Moral Fault as Affecting Defendant's Liability, 1933, 81 U.Pa.L.Rev. 586, 592–596.

29. Thus damages for mental disturbance, whether or not it results in physical injury, are more readily held to be recoverable where the wrong is intentional. See infra, §§ 12, 54.

30. Cases are collected in Bauer, The Degree of Defendant's Fault as Affecting the Administration of Law of Excessive Compensatory Damages, 1934, 82 U.Pa.L.Rev. 583. See for example the rules applied to innocent and wilful trespassers who remove timber or minerals from land, as to the value of the property converted "in place" or after removal. McCormick, Damages, 1935, 492–496.

31. Prosser, Transferred Intent, 1967, 45 Tex.L. Rev. 650.

32. State v. Batson, 1936, 339 Mo. 298, 305, 96 S.W.2d 384, 389.

33. Regina v. Salisbury, 1553, 1 Plowd. 100, 75 Eng. Rep. 158; Queen v. Saunders and Archer, 1576, 2 Plowd. 473, 75 Eng.Rep. 706.

34. Dunaway v. People, 1884, 110 Ill. 333; State v. Williams, 1904, 122 Iowa 115, 97 N.W. 992; State v. Ochoa, 1956, 61 N.M. 225, 297 P.2d 1053; People v. Aranda, 1938, 12 Cal.2d 307, 83 P.2d 928; Coston v. State, 1939, 139 Fla. 250, 190 So. 520.

*Restatement (Second) of Torts*

## § 8 A. Intent

The word "intent" is used throughout the Restatement of this Subject to denote that the actor desires to cause consequences of his act, or that he believes that the consequences are substantially certain to result from it.

**Comment:**                    See Reporter's Notes.

*a.* "Intent," as it is used throughout the Restatement of Torts, has reference to the consequences of an act rather than the act itself. When an actor fires a gun in the midst of the Mojave Desert, he intends to pull the trigger; but when the bullet hits a person who is present in the desert without the actor's knowledge, he does not intend that result. "Intent" is limited, wherever it is used, to the consequences of the act.

*b.* All consequences which the actor desires to bring about are intended, as the word is used in this Restatement. Intent is not, however, limited to consequences which are desired. If the actor knows that the consequences are certain, or substantially certain, to result from his act, and still goes ahead, he is treated by the law as if he had in fact desired to produce the result. As the probability that the consequences will follow decreases, and becomes less than substantial certainty, the actor's conduct loses the character of intent, and becomes mere recklessness, as defined in § 500. As the probability decreases further, and amounts only to a risk that the result will follow, it becomes ordinary negligence, as defined in § 282. All three have their important place in the law of torts, but the liability attached to them will differ.

**Illustrations:**

1. A throws a bomb into B's office for the purpose of killing B. A knows that C, B's stenographer, is in the office. A has no desire to injure C, but knows that his act is substantially certain to do so. C is injured by the explosion. A is subject to liability to C for an intentional tort.

2. On a curve in a narrow highway A, without any desire to injure B, or belief that he is substantially certain to do so, recklessly drives his automobile in an attempt to pass B's car. As a result of this recklessness, A crashes into B's car, injuring B. A is subject to liability to B for his reckless conduct, but is not liable to B for any intentional tort.

Reprinted from *Torts in a Nutshell: Injuries to Persons and Property,* by Edward J. Kionka, © copyright 1977, with permission of the West Publishing Corporation.

# CHAPTER 6

## LIABILITY FOR INTENTIONAL MISCONDUCT

### § 6—1.  Intent

As we have seen (§ 1—3), the early English law of wrongs was not much concerned with the wrongdoer's intent.  If his act was voluntary and the resulting physical harm direct, liability usually followed.

Gradually, the actions of trespass and case evolved such that, so far as physical harm is concerned, the distinction between them was no longer whether the harm was direct or indirect, but rather whether the tort could be classified within the confines of the traditional trespass actions—battery, assault, false imprisonment, trespass to land and chattels—or whether the wrong involved mere negligence, for which case was the usual remedy.  At the same time the courts came to require fault as a condition to trespass liability —that is, some sort of wrongful intent.  Thus, the trespass actions became what we now call the intentional torts.

Morally, greater blame attaches to intentional misconduct than to lesser degrees of fault, and this is reflected in the law of intentional torts. In general, to establish a prima facie case, plaintiff need only prove that defendant intentionally invaded a protected interest.  The burden then shifts to defendant to show some justification or excuse. And, unlike negligence actions, actual damages need not be proved. If plaintiff cannot establish any actual harm (tangible or intangible), nominal damages can be awarded.

Traditionally, the intentional torts are those named and discussed in the sections which follow. However, there has come to be recognized a general principle of intentional tort liability, analogous to the general principle of negligence liability (see § 3—1), sometimes called "prima facie tort," which may be invoked when no particular intentional tort applies. Section 870 of the Restatement (Second) as tentatively approved provides:

> One who intentionally causes injury to another is subject to liability to the other for the actual harm incurred, if his conduct is culpable and not justifiable. This liability may be imposed despite the fact that the actor's conduct does not come within one of the traditional categories of tort liability.

For a discussion of the elements and limits of this liability, see the Comments to this section; for authorities supporting it, see the Reporter's Notes. A recent case discussing this doctrine is Nees v. Hocks (Or.1975) (wrongful discharge). Of course, it must not be inferred from this that all unjustified intentional wrongs are actionable. But in a proper case, the courts need not and do not consider themselves bound by the traditional intentional tort pigeon-holes.

An intentional tort is an act committed (or omitted) with a particular state of mind. How is the actor's state of mind to be proved? Direct evidence—the actor's own statement of his actual intent—is rarely available. Indeed, after the fact he may claim to have had the best of intentions. Thus, as in all other cases where one's state of mind must be shown, it is usually proved by circumstantial evidence. His conduct, in the context of his surroundings and what he presumably knew and perceived, is evidence from which his intent may be inferred. The law presumes that one intends the natural and probable consequences of his acts in light of the surrounding circumstances of which he may be assumed to be aware.

Intent, in the sense required here, must be distinguished from motive. *Intent* is usually defined as the desire to cause certain immediate consequences. One who throws a rock with great force against a glass window obviously intends that it will be broken. One who points a loaded gun at another and pulls the trigger surely intends that the bullet will strike and injure him. The actor's *motive* for his conduct—revenge, protest, punishment, theft, self-defense, or even a desire to be of help (e.g. the surgeon who operates without consent)—may, in certain cases, aggravate, mitigate or excuse the wrong. For example, malice may permit assessment of punitive damages; self-defense may be a complete defense to tort liability. But to establish a prima facie case, all that need be shown is the defendant's conduct, the invasion of a legally protected interest of the plaintiff, and the requisite intent.

Since intent is a desire to cause certain immediate consequences, very young children may be held liable for intentional torts though so young as to be incapable of negligence.

Intent is a state of mind, a subjective matter. But the law's definition of intent is objective to this extent: an actor is deemed to intend the consequences of his act which he knows are substantially certain to result, irrespective of his actual intent. R. § 8A. Thus, *A* throws a bomb into a room in which *B* and *C* are present for the purpose of killing *B*. *A* knows that *C* is present, but has no desire to hurt *C*, and in fact fervently hopes that *C* will not be injured. Nevertheless, since he knew that physical harm to *C* was substantially certain, he is held to have intended that harm.

Thus, certainty of the harmful consequences is the basis on which we distinguish intentional torts from negligent or reckless ("wilful and wanton") ones. If the result is intended or substantially certain to occur, the tort is intentional. But if the actor's conduct merely creates a foreseeable *risk* of harm, which may or may not be realized, then the conduct is negligent or reckless depending upon the magnitude of the risk.

Unique to the intentional torts, borrowed from the criminal law, the doctrine of "transferred intent" reflects the greater blame which attaches to intentional misconduct. In effect, it is a broadened rule of proximate cause. Thus, where $A$ acts with the intent to injure $B$, but at the same time or instead injures $C$, his intent to injure $B$ "transfers" to $C$ and $A$ is deemed to have committed an intentional tort upon $C$, even though he was completely unaware of $C$'s existence or of any risk of harm to $C$. For example, $A$ shoots at $B$ and wounds or misses him. The bullet strikes $C$ who was hidden from view and not known to be in the vicinity. $A$ may be liable to $C$ in battery. In addition, the intent transfers among the five progeny of the parent trespass action—battery, assault, false imprisonment, trespass to land and trespass to chattels—so long as the harm is direct and immediate. For example, $A$'s intent to commit only an assault upon $B$ such as by shooting in his direction to frighten him may support liability for a battery to $C$ who is unexpectedly struck by the bullet.

Often the same act is both a tort and a crime. This is especially true with respect to the intentional torts. But despite their common origins, tort and criminal law rules are now more different than similar, and analogies and comparisons between torts and crimes of the same name or having similar bases in conduct should be made only with the greatest caution.

Both a civil tort action and a criminal prosecution may be brought for the same wrongful conduct. The remedies are concurrent, and either a successful or an unsuccessful result in one is ordinarily not a bar to the other. However, since the most common intentional torts are more often committed by judgment-proof persons, and intentional torts are frequently uninsured and in some cases uninsurable, intentional tort litigation is of relatively minor significance in the day-to-day work of lawyers and courts.

## § 6—2.  Battery

Battery is the remedy for an intentional and unpermitted physical contact with plaintiff's person by defendant or (now that the distinction be tween trespass and case has disappeared) by an agency defendant has set in motion. It reflects the basic right to have one's body left alone by others. Secondarily, it seeks to deter relatively minor but offensive contacts which can precipitate breaches of the peace.

Plaintiff's "person" is held to include his body and those things in contact or closely connected to it and identified with it, such as clothing, an object held in his hand, or an object so associated or identified with plaintiff that, considering the nature of the contact, a normal person would deem it an offense against his person.

The tort is the contact, and thus plaintiff need not have been aware of it at the time.

Two forms of contact are actionable. First and foremost are those which cause some *physical harm,* broadly defined to include any physical impairment of the condition of the body (such as a cut, a bruise, a burn, etc., however slight), even if beneficial; illness; and physical (but not emotional) pain. R. § 15. Second, battery also encompasses contacts which do not cause physical harm but are hostile, offensive, or insulting, such as poking with a finger in anger, angrily knocking off one's hat, dousing one with water, spitting in one's face, cutting hair, and even an unwanted kiss. R. §§ 18, 19. The gist of the action is contact without consent, resulting in harm to plaintiff's person or dignity.

The contact must have been intended (unless the doctrine of transferred intent applies); otherwise the action if any lies in negligence. But defendant need not have intended any harm. It is no defense that defendant intended only a joke or a compliment, or even to render assistance. Thus, where a doctor performs surgery without the patient's consent, a battery has been committed.

If plaintiff consents to the contact, defendant is privileged to make it and there is no tort. This is generally true of all torts. See § 7—2. So far as battery is concerned, consent may sometimes be assumed.

*Legalines, Torts adaptable to Prosser casebook*

*Legalines* are published by Harcourt Brace Legal & Professional Publications, Inc. (1-800-787-8717)

## II. INTENTIONAL INTERFERENCE WITH PERSON OR PROPERTY
### A.   INTENT

1. **Introduction.** One of the major classifications of tort liability is liability based on the intent of the defendant. It is the intent to bring about certain consequences that is important, not merely the intent to do an act. Intent includes not only the desire to bring about the physical results, but also the knowledge or belief that certain results are substantially certain to follow from the actor's conduct.

   a. **Need not be malicious.** The intent forming the basis of tort liability need not be immoral, malicious, or hostile; instead, it need only be an intent to affect a legally protected interest in a way that will not be permitted by law.

   b. **Objective standard.** The actor's subjective knowledge or belief that certain results are substantially certain to follow from his conduct is determined on an objective rather than a subjective basis. That is, actual knowledge or belief, or lack thereof, on the part of the defendant is immaterial if a reasonable person in the position of the defendant would have believed that certain results were substantially certain to follow from the conduct of the defendant. Of course, the external, objective standard must have certain subjective inputs based upon the position of the defendant; i.e., age, physical abilities, mental capacity, special skills, etc. It is on the basis of the theoretical reasonable person who possesses these same characteristics of the defendant that knowledge or belief for purposes of tort liability is determined.

   c. **Intentional acts by children.** Children are charged with what is expected of them considering age, experience, intelligence, etc. They are liable only for what they are capable of, considering the foregoing factors. If they are capable of knowledge of the consequences of an act, they may be liable for these consequences.

Garratt v. Dailey

2. **Substantial Certainty--Garratt v. Dailey,** 279 P.2d 1091 (Wash. 1955).

   a. **Facts.** Garratt (P) alleged that Dailey (D) had *deliberately* pulled a chair out from under her as she was sitting down, causing her to fall and fracture her hip. D, five years old, claimed that he had moved the chair so that he could sit in it himself, and, upon noticing that P was about to sit down, tried in vain to move the chair back in time. On remand, the court found that when D moved the chair, he knew with substantial certainty that P would attempt to sit down where the chair had been. Appeal from a decision denying P recovery of damages for an alleged assault and battery.

b. **Issue.** In an action for assault and battery, may defendant be held liable if he did not subjectively intend to cause the resultant harm but knew with substantial certainty that his actions would likely cause it?

c. **Held.** Yes. Judgment reversed and remanded for clarification.

   1) Battery is the intentional infliction of a harmful or offensive bodily contact upon another.

   2) An "act" is deemed to be intentional if it is done either with the subjective purpose of causing the contact or the apprehension thereof, or with the knowledge that such contact or apprehension is *substantially certain to result* therefrom.

   3) When a minor has committed a tort with force, he is just as subject to suit as any other person would be.

d. **Remand.** On remand, the court found that D knew with substantial certainty that P would attempt to sit where the chair had been located. Based on this finding that D had the requisite intent to be liable for battery, the court awarded P $11,000. This verdict was upheld on appeal. [Garratt v. Dailey, 304 P.2d 681 (Wash. 1956)]

e. **Comment.** Intentional conduct is an act that a reasonable person in D's position would know is substantially certain to lead to the damage of another's legally protected interests.

3. **Distinguishing Intent from Negligence--Spivey v. Battaglia,** 258 So. 2d 815 (Fla. 1972).

Spivey v. Battaglia

a. **Facts.** Spivey (P) and Battaglia (D) worked for the Battaglia Fruit Co. During a lunch break, D teased P by putting his arm around her and pulling her head toward him. The movement caused a sharp pain in P's neck and paralyzed her on the left side of her face and mouth. More than two years later, P sued for negligence and assault and battery. The trial court granted D summary judgment on the assault and battery allegation because the two-year statute of limitations for intentional torts had run. The trial court also granted summary judgment on the negligence allegation on the ground that D's conduct constituted assault and battery, which is not negligence. P appeals.

b. **Issue.** If a person intends to do an act that produces harm, but does not intend to cause the harm, may the person be liable for negligence?

    **c.**    **Held.** Yes. Judgment reversed.

        1)    Liability for intentional torts does not necessarily rest on a hostile intent or a desire to do harm. It is sufficient if a reasonable person would believe that a particular result was substantially certain to follow. Knowledge and appreciation of a risk short of substantial certainty, however, is not equivalent to intent.

        2)    The line between negligence and intent is drawn where the known danger ceases to be only a foreseeable risk which a reasonable person would avoid, and becomes a substantial certainty. In this case, the harm suffered by P was not substantially certain to follow from D's conduct. D did not have the intent to cause P's paralysis, and thus did not act intentionally for purposes of tort liability.

        3)    D may be liable for the unanticipated injury to P if he was negligent. This depends on whether the consequences of his acts were reasonably foreseeable, even though the exact result was not contemplated. The jury should decide this case after being instructed on the elements of negligence.

    **d.**    **Comment.** The court contrasted a case in which the defendant had embraced and kissed the plaintiff. During the plaintiff's struggle to resist, she struck her face on an object and suffered injury. That case was an assault and battery and not negligence, because the injury was substantially certain to follow from the defendant's conduct. In this case, by contrast, the injury was a bizarre result.

**4.**    **Mistake.**

    **a.**    **General rule.** Normally, good faith mistake is not a defense to a tort suit. Under certain circumstances, however, it may justify assertion of privilege, as when a defendant acted out of a mistaken but reasonable belief that he was being attacked when he injured the plaintiff in self-defense.

anson v.
itner    **b.**    **Application--Ranson v. Kitner,** 31 Ill. App. 241 (1888).

        1)    **Facts.** Defendants, while hunting wolves, shot plaintiff's dog, mistaking it for a wolf. Defendants acted in good faith, believing the dog to be a wolf. The jury gave a verdict to plaintiff for damages equal to the value of the dog.

        2)    **Issue.** Is a good faith mistake a defense to an intentional tort?

        3)    **Held.** No. Judgment affirmed.

## *Gilbert Law Summaries on Torts* by Marc Franklin

*Gilbert Law Summaries* are published by Harcourt Brace Legal & Professional Publications, Inc. (1-800-787-8717)

### A. TORTS TO THE PERSON

1. **Battery:** [§1]   Prima facie case:

> *Act by Defendant*
> *Intent*
> *Harmful or Offensive Touching*
> *Causation*
> *(Lack of Consent—discussed as a defense, see infra, §§80 et seq.)*

    a. **Act by defendant:** [§2]   The word "act" as used in intentional torts means an external manifestation of the actor's will; it refers to some *volitional movement* by the actor of some part of his body. Thus, if D intentionally drove his automobile into P, the "act" complained of would not be the driving of the automobile, but rather the movement by D of his *arms and legs* in setting the automobile into motion and directing it at P. [Restatement (Second) of Torts ("Rest. 2d") §2 (1965)]

    (1) **Unconscious acts:** [§3]   Because of the requirement of a "volitional" movement, the movements of persons having an epileptic seizure or of persons asleep or under the influence of drugs are not generally sufficient "acts" for the purpose of establishing liability for intentional torts. [Lobert v. Pack, 9 A.2d 365 (Pa. 1939)]

    (2) **Reflex actions:** [§4]   On the other hand, a muscular reaction by a person in command of his senses is always an "act" unless it is purely a reflex action in which the mind and will have no share. Thus, the blinking of eyelids in defense against an approaching missile is not an "act" because it is purely reflexive. But if someone, finding himself about to fall, stretches his hand out to save himself, the stretching out of his hand *is* an "act"; his mind has grasped the situation and dictated a muscular contraction in an effort to prevent the fall.

    (3) **Acts by incompetents:** [§5]   Persons who are not legally competent are still capable of volitional conduct; *i.e.*, insane persons or minors may be held liable for their acts. [McGuire v. Almy, 8 N.E.2d 760 (Mass. 1937); Goff v. Taylor, 708 S.W.2d 113 (Ky. 1986)]

    b. **Intent:** [§6]   The defendant must have done the "act" with the intent *to inflict a harmful or offensive touching* on the plaintiff or a third person. [Rest. 2d §13(a)]

    (1) **Test—desire or belief in substantial certainty:** [§7]   Whether the defendant had the requisite intent is measured by whether he acted with the *desire* to cause the result *or believed that the result was substantially certain* to occur; *i.e.*, the defendant must have desired a harmful or offensive touching *or* believed that such a touching was substantially certain to result from his act. [Garratt v. Dailey, 279 P.2d 1091 (Wash. 1955); Frey v. Kouf, 484 N.W.2d 864 (S.D. 1992)]

(a)    **Example:** D shoved P, a young child, to get her out of the area in which some boys were playing. P fell and broke her elbow; D has committed a battery. Even if D did not desire the result, he believed that an offensive (if not harmful) touching was substantially certain to occur. [Baldinger v. Banks, 26 Misc. 2d 1086 (1960)]

(b)    **Test is subjective:** [§8]    The issues of "desire" and what the defendant "believed" to be substantially certain to occur turn on the subjective consideration of what was in the defendant's mind when he acted. Although juries may make inferences about the defendant's state of mind from objective facts, the basic question is *not* what a reasonable person would have desired or believed, but what the defendant *in fact* desired or believed.

(2)  **Motives immaterial:** [§9]    The same distinction must be made between "malice" and "intent" in tort law as is drawn in criminal law. (*See* Criminal Law Summary.) "Malice" refers to the defendant's *motives* (*why* defendant acted as he did), and motives are generally immaterial. Tort law is concerned only with whether the defendant had the requisite *intent* under the "desire or belief in substantial certainty" test, above.

(a)    **But note:** If "malice" (intent to injure) exists, the defendant may be held liable for *punitive* damages (*see* below).

(3)  **Transferred intent doctrine:** [§10]    The old common law form of action called "trespass" gave rise to five modern actions: battery, assault, false imprisonment, trespass to land, and trespass to chattels. Under the doctrine of transferred intent, if the defendant acts intending to cause one of these harms to a person, the defendant will be liable on an intentional tort theory if *any* of the five harms occurs to that person or even to *the plaintiff*—even though plaintiff is unexpected and the harm is unexpected.

(a)    **Example:** D attempted to strike X, who ducked. The blow hit P, who had unexpectedly appeared. *Held:* D committed a battery on P. [Carnes v. Thompson, 48 S.W.2d 903 (Mo. 1932)]

(b)    **Example:** D unlawfully shot at X's dog and hit P. Even though D had no reason to know that anyone might be in the area, D committed a battery on P. [Corn v. Shepard, 229 N.W. 869 (Minn. 1930); Altieri v. Colasso, 362 A.2d 798 (Conn. 1975)—attempted assault on X led to battery on P]

(c)    **Comment:** Although phrased as involving "intent," the better explanation for the doctrine is that the courts are imposing strict liability on D because of his serious misbehavior in directing the initial act against X.

# APPENDIX C

Cases and Materials on
Strict Liability

*Cases*

## Chapter XIV

## STRICT LIABILITY

When a court imposes "strict liability" on a defendant, it is saying that he must pay damages although he neither intentionally injured plaintiff nor failed to live up to the objective standard of reasonable care that traditionally has been at the root of negligence law. Some courts and textwriters call this process "absolute liability." This description is misleading because there are numerous defenses to an action for strict liability. Some other textwriters and courts group the cases in this chapter under the rubric "liability without fault." This description is over-inclusive; there are many examples of imposition of liability without fault under the negligence and intentional tort bases of liability.

As Dean Prosser observed: "Once the legal concept of 'fault' is divorced, as it has been from the personal standard of moral wrongdoing, there is a sense in which liability with or without 'fault' must beg its own conclusion. The term requires such extensive definition, that it seems better not to make use of it at all, and to refer instead to strict liability, apart from either wrongful intent or negligence." Torts (4th ed. 1971) 496.

For an overview see Calabresi and Hirschoff, Toward a Test for Strict Liability in Torts (1972) 81 Yale L.J. 1055; Malone, This Brave New World—A Review of Negligence Without Fault (1951) 25 So.Calif.L.Rev. 14; Fletcher, Fairness and Utility in Tort Theory (1972) 85 Harv.L.Rev. 537; Gregory, Trespass to Negligence to Absolute Liability (1951) 37 Va.L.Rev. 359; Kalven, Torts: The Quest for Appropriate Standards (1965) 53 Calif.L.Rev. 189; Keeton, Conditional Fault in the Law of Torts (1959) 72 Harv.L.Rev. 401; Morris, Hazardous Enterprises and Risk Bearing Capacity (1952) 61 Yale L.J. 1172; Peck, Negligence and Liability Without Fault in Tort Law (1971) 46 Wash.L.Rev. 225; Posner, Strict Liability: A Comment (1973) 2 J. Legal Studies 205; Wade, The Continuing Development of Strict Liability in Tort (1968) 22 Ark.L.Rev. 233; Shavell, Strict Liability Versus Negligence (1980) 9 J.Leg.Stud. 1.

### 1.   ANIMALS

*Trespassing Animals.* Somewhere around the middle of the fourteenth century the courts began to recognize a rule making the owner of cattle liable when his animals trespassed upon the plaintiff's land. The origin of the rule is somewhat obscure. It has been attributed to a fiction that the trespass of the animals was to be attributed to the owner, because he was in some way identified with them, and responsible for what they did. According to Glanville Williams, Liability for Animals (1939) 127–134, there was no such fiction, and the early cases were those in which the owner intentionally put his cattle upon the land of the plaintiff. Liability for mere escape originated as a deliberate extension designed to remedy a gap in the law; and because it came before the full development of the action on the case, it was identified with trespass, although the invasion was an indirect one. Out of this there developed the rule that the owner of animals of a kind likely to roam and do damage is strictly liable for their trespasses.

The kinds of animals for whose trespasses their owner would be liable were limited, and they had a definite barnyard pattern. They included cattle, horses, sheep, hogs and goats, as well as such common errant fowl as turkeys, in McPherson v. James (1896) 69 Ill.App. 337, and chickens, in Adams Bros. v. Clark (1920) 189 Ky. 279, 224 S.W. 1046, or even pigeons, in Taylor v. Granger (1896) 19 R.I. 410, 34 A. 153, 37 A. 13.

On the other hand, such household favorites as dogs were not included. Olson v. Pederson (1939) 206 Minn. 415, 288 N.W. 856; McDonald v. Castle (1925) 116 Okl. 46, 243 P. 215. The same is true of cats. Buckle v. Holmes [1926] 2 K.B. 125; Bischoff v. Cheney (1914) 89 Conn. 1, 92 A. 660. The reason formerly given was that dogs and cats were of no value, which is of course clearly wrong; and that their trespasses were likely to be trivial and do no serious harm. This last, of course, is unlikely to appeal to the owners of flowerbeds and poultry. A better explanation may be that of Glanville Williams, Liability for Animals (1939) 145–146, that dogs and cats are very difficult to confine or restrain, and the general custom of the community has permitted them to roam at large. In other words, the keeping of these household pets is so far sanctioned by general usage that an exception is made in their favor. Cf. Baker v. Howard County Hunt (1936) 171 Md. 159, 188 A. 223 (trespass rule applied to pack of hunting dogs).

An early and well established exception to the rule of strict liability for trespassing cattle and the like was the case of animals straying from a highway on which they were lawfully being driven. Tillett v. Ward [1882] L.R. 10 Q.B. 17. This obviously arose out of the necessity of getting the animals to market. It was explained as in the nature of a servitude to which owners of lands adjoining the highway were subject; and it did not apply to other lands. Thus there was strict liability when cattle strayed from the lands of A, and thence onto the land of B, removed from the highway. Wood v. Snider (1907) 187 N.Y. 28, 79 N.E. 858.

In the United States the rule as to strict liability for animal trespass has had something of a checkered history. In the early days many of the courts, particularly in the western part of the country where cattle were customarily permitted to graze at large on open range, rejected the common law rule, as not suitable to the conditions of the country and established local custom. See for example Delaney v. Errickson (1880) 10 Neb. 492, 6 N.W. 600; Beinhorn v. Griswold (1902) 27 Mont. 79, 69 P. 557. These animals cases are among the leading authorities for the proposition that, under state reception statutes, the common law of England is to be followed only when it is suitable and appropriate.

As the country became more settled, these states began to enact "fencing out" statutes, which provided that if the plaintiff fenced his land properly there was strict liability when the animals broke through the fence, but otherwise there was liability only if their owner was at fault. See for example Buford v. Houtz (1890) 133 U.S. 320; Garcia v. Sumrall (1942) 58 Ariz. 526, 121 P.2d 640.

As the country became still more settled, the conflict between the grazing interests and developing agricultural interests—or in other words, as the motion pictures would have it, between the range men and the "nesters" along the creek bed—resulted in many states in "fencing in" statutes, which required the owner of the animals to fence them in or otherwise restrain them, and made him strictly liable if he did not do so. See for example Ariz.Code Ann. § 50–606.

Finally, some states, particularly in the eastern part of the country, have fully returned to the common law rule. See King v. Blue Mountain Forest Ass'n (1956) 100 N.H. 212, 123 A.2d 151.

A common type of statute today permits a county to choose the rule it wishes to apply. Thus in some states animals are permitted to run at large unless a county adopts a "fencing in" or a "fencing out" ordinance. Others permit counties to employ the fiction of designating the boundary lines of lots or tracts as lawful fences, which automatically results in a rule of strict liability. There are states in which all four variants of the rule—strict liability, fencing out, fencing in, and no liability without fault—can be found in different counties.

*Dangerous Animals.* Under the common law of England the owner or possessor of a nondomesticated animal (collectively referred to by courts as "wild animals" or animals *"ferae naturae"*) was subject to strict liability if the animal attacked a person. See May v. Burdett [1846] 9 Q.B. 101 (monkey bite); Filburn v. People's Palace and Aquarium Co., Ltd. [1890] 25 Q.B.Div. 258 (C.A.) (attacking elephant). On the other hand the owner of a domestic animal such as a cat, dog, sheep, or horse was subject to strict liability only if the owner knew or had reason to know that the animal had vicious propensities.

This led to interesting problems of classification. Obviously lions, tigers, leopards, and bears were deemed "wild animals." What about deer? Congress & Empire Spring Co. v. Edgar (1879) 99 U.S. 645; Briley v. Mitchell (1959) 238 La. 551, 115 So.2d 851. A pet raccoon? Andrew v. Kilgour (1910) 19 Man.L.Rep. 544. A hive of bees? Ammons v. Kellogg (1925) 137 Miss. 551, 102 So. 562. Annot. (1978) 86 A.L.R.3d 829. A boar? Marshall v. Ranne (Tex.1974) 511 S.W.2d 255. A bird able to open his own cage and startle people? See Neagle v. Morgan (1971) 360 Mass. 864, 277 N.E.2d 482.

The customs of the community apparently enter in. In Burma an elephant is regarded as a domesticated animal, for which there is no strict liability. Maung Kayn Dun v. Ma Kyian (1900) 2 Upper Burma Rulings, Civ. 570. Suppose a Burma elephant is brought to England to perform in a circus. Behrens v. Bertram Mills Circus, Ltd., [1957] 2 Q.B. 1. How about a camel, which is now domesticated virtually everywhere it is found? McQuaker v. Goddard, [1940] 1 K.B. 687.

The majority American position has followed the rule of strict liability in regard to wild animals. See Isaacs v. Powell (Fla.App. 1972) 267 So.2d 864 (chimpanzee); Franken v. City of Sioux Center (Iowa 1978) 272 N.W.2d 422 (tiger); Whitefield v. Stewart (Okl. 1978) 577 P.2d 1295 (monkey).

But some courts have moved away from strict liability to a negligence standard with regard to the liability of persons who display wild animals to the public, although the standard of care is often changed to one of extreme caution. See Hansen v. Brogan (1965) 145 Mont. 224, 440 P.2d 265 (buffalo); Vaughan v. Miller Bros. "101" Ranch Wild West Show (1931) 109 W.Va. 170, 153 S.E. 289 (ape). The trend is more pronounced with regard to public zoos, although some of the decisions are based on the fact that the legislature authorized the activity. See, e.g., City and County of Denver v. Kennedy (1970) 29 Colo.App. 15, 476 P.2d 762. Contra: City of Mangum v. Brownlee (1938) 181 Okla. 515, 75 P.2d 174. See generally, McNeely, A Footnote on Dangerous Animals (1939) 37 Mich.L.Rev. 1181; Note (1975) 49 Tulane L.Rev. 719; Annot. (1968) 21 A.L.R.3d 603.

As for domestic animals the canard is often repeated that the common law rule is that a domestic animal such as a dog (or cat) is entitled to one bite. The cases do not bear this out. If the owner knows or has reason to know (scienter) that a domestic animal has vicious propensities, this is sufficient to classify that animal with wild ones and strict liability is imposed. See Andrews v. Smith (1936) 324 Pa. 455, 188 A. 146; Barger v. Jimerson (1954) 130 Colo. 459, 276 P.2d 744; Harris v. Williams (1932) 160 Okl. 103, 15 P.2d 580. Many of the cases show interesting and imaginative efforts on the part of plaintiff's counsel to prove that the animal had such a temperament and that the owner was aware of it. See, e.g., Zarek v. Fredericks (3 Cir. 1943) 138 F.2d 689 (dog snarled at guests and was almost always accompanied by his owners); Frederickson v. Kepner (1947) 82 Cal.App.2d 905, 187 P.2d 800; and Perkins v. Drury (1953) 57 N.M. 269, 258 P.2d 379 (children warned to stay away from dog); Hill v. Moseley (1941) 220 N.C. 485, 17 S.E.2d 676 (dog had bad reputation in the neighborhood). Compare the valiant but unsuccessful attempt to have German shepherds classified as "vicious by nature" in Rolen v. Maryland Casualty Co. (La.App.1970) 240 So. 2d 42.

In many states the common law regarding liability for dog bites has been changed by statute. These statutes usually do away with the necessity of plaintiff's proving scienter in order to recover. The statutes may also list defenses—e.g., plaintiff committing a trespass or warning sign posted.

Liability is also affected by statutory provisions requiring dogs to be muzzled or leashed. If a person is injured due to the failure of the owner to comply with the ordinance, the owner becomes "negligent per se" and so liable for the damages. Wistafka v. Grotowski (1917) 205 Ill.App. 529. However, if the muzzling of the dog would not have prevented the injury, as where the dog does not bite the plaintiff but knocks him down, there is no causal connection, and the common law rule applies. Kennet v. Sossnitz (1940) 260 App.Div. 759, 23 N.Y.S.2d 961, affirmed in (1941) 286 N.Y. 623, 36 N.E.2d 459.

## 2.    ABNORMALLY DANGEROUS ACTIVITIES

### RYLANDS v. FLETCHER

In the Exchequer, 1865.  3 H. & C. 774, 159 Eng.Rep. 737.
In the Exchequer Chamber, 1866.  L.R. 1 Ex. 265.
In the House of Lords, 1868.  L.R. 3 H.L. 330.

[Action brought in 1861 and tried at the Liverpool Summer Assizes (1862).  A verdict was found for the plaintiff subject to the award of an arbitrator, who was afterwards empowered by a court order to state a special case instead of making an award.  The material facts in the special case stated by the arbitrator were as follows:

The defendants were the owners of a mill; in order to supply it with water they constructed upon the nearby land of Lord Wilton, with his permission, a reservoir.  The plaintiff under lease from Lord Wilton was working certain coal mines under lands close to but not adjoining the premises on which the reservoir was constructed.  They worked their mine in the direction of the reservoir until they came upon certain old workings, part of which at least had been made and abandoned at a time beyond living memory.  They consisted of horizontal passages and vertical shafts, the latter apparently filled with rubbish and marl similar to that of the solid earth surrounding them. The defendant employed a competent engineer and competent contractors to plan and construct the reservoir and it was so planned and constructed solely by them upon a site, in the choice of which the defendants were guilty of no personal fault, though in fact the old mine workings lay beneath it and, continuing under the intermediate lands, communicated, at the point to which the plaintiff had pushed its workings in that direction, with the workings of the plaintiff. The contractors in excavating for the bed of the reservoir came upon five of the above mentioned vertical shafts; the sides or walls of these were of timber, but, being filled with soil of the same kind as that composing the surrounding ground, neither the contractors nor the defendants suspected that they were abandoned mine shafts. The arbitrator found that the defendants were guilty of no personal negligence or fault, but that the engineer and contractors had not in fact exercised proper care, with reference to the shafts discovered, to provide for the sufficiency of the reservoir to bear the pressure that it was designed to bear when in use.

The reservoir was completed in December, 1860, and the defendants had it partly filled. Within a few days, one of the shafts that had been met while excavating gave way and burst downward, letting the water into the old abandoned workings beneath, through which it flowed, through the communications that the plaintiffs in working their mine had made between the two, into the plaintiffs' workings, flooding their mine.

The question for the opinion of the Court was whether the plaintiff was entitled to recover damages from the defendant by reason of the matters thus stated by the arbitrator.

In the Exchequer, judgment was given for the defendants by a 2-to-1 vote. Martin, B., said there was no trespass, because the damage was not "immediate," but "mediate or consequential." There was no nuisance, because the defendants were doing a lawful and reasonable act. The same rule must be applied to real property as to personal property, that there must be negligence on the part of the defendant to make him responsible. The plaintiff brought error to the Exchequer Chamber.]

BLACKBURN, J. * * * It appears from the statement in the case, that the plaintiff was damaged by his property being flooded by water which, without any fault on his part, broke out of a reservoir constructed on the defendants' land by the defendants' orders, and maintained by the defendants. * * *

The plaintiff, though free from all blame on his part, must bear the loss, unless he can establish that it was the consequence of some default for which the defendants are responsible. The question of law therefore arises, what is the obligation which the law casts on a person who, like the defendants, lawfully brings on his land something which though harmless whilst it remains there, will naturally do mischief if it escape out of his land. It is agreed on all hands that he must take care to keep in that which he has brought on the land and keeps there, in order that it may not escape and damage his neighbors; but the question arises whether the duty which the law casts upon him, under such circumstances, is an absolute duty to keep it in at his peril, or is, as the majority of the Court of Exchequer have thought, merely a duty to take all reasonable and prudent precautions, in order to keep it in, but no more. If the first be the law, the person who has brought on his land and kept there something dangerous, and failed to keep it in, is responsible for all the natural consequences of its escape. If the second be the limit of his duty, he would not be answerable except on proof of negligence, and consequently would not be answerable for escape arising from any latent defect which ordinary prudence and skill could not detect. * * *

We think that the true rule of law is that the person who for his own purposes brings on his lands and collects and keeps there any thing likely to do mischief if it escapes, must keep it in at his peril, and if he does not do so, is prima facie answerable for all the damage which is the natural consequence of its escape. He can excuse himself by showing that the escape was owing to the plaintiff's default; or perhaps that the escape was the consequence of vis major, or the act of God; but as nothing of this sort exists here, it is unnecessary to inquire what excuse would be sufficient. The general rule, as above stated, seems on principle just. The person whose grass or corn is eaten down by the escaping cattle of his neighbor, or whose mine is flooded by the water from his neighbor's reservoir, or whose cellar is invaded by the filth of his neighbor's privy, or whose habitation is made unhealthy by the fumes and noisome vapors of his neighbor's alkali works, is damnified without any fault of his own; and it seems but reasonable and just that the neighbor, who has brought something on his own property which was not naturally there, harmless to others so long as it is confined to his own property, but which he knows to be mischievous if it gets on his neighbor's, should be obliged to make good the damage which ensues if he does not succeed in confining it to his own property. But for his act in bringing it there no mischief could have accrued, and it seems but just that he should at his peril keep it there, so that no mischief may accrue, or answer for the natural and anticipated consequences.  And upon authority, this we think is established to be the law, whether the things so brought be beasts, or water, or filth, or stenches.

The case that has most commonly occurred and which is most frequently to be found in the books, is as to the obligation of the owner of cattle which he has brought on his land to prevent their escaping and doing mischief.  The law as to them seems to be perfectly settled from early times;  the owner must keep them in at his peril, or he will be answerable for the natural consequences of their escape;  that is, with regard to tame beasts, for the grass they eat and trample upon, though not for an injury to the person of others, for our ancestors have settled that it is not the general nature of horses to kick, or bulls to gore;  but if the owner knows that the beast has a vicious propensity to attack man, he will be answerable for that too.
\*   \*   \*

Judgment for the plaintiff.

Rylands and Horrocks brought error to the House of Lords against the judgment of the Exchequer Chamber, which had reversed the judgment of the Court of Exchequer.

THE LORD CHANCELLOR (Lord CAIRNS).  \*   \*   \*  My Lords, the principles in which this case must be determined appear to me to be extremely simple.  The defendants, treating them as the owner or occupiers of the close on which the reservoir was constructed, might lawfully have used that close for any purpose for which it might in the ordinary course of the enjoyment of land be used;  and if, in what I may term the natural user of that land, there had been any accumulation of water, either on the surface or underground, and if, by the operation of the laws of nature, that accumulation of water had passed off into the close occupied by the plaintiff, the plaintiff could not have complained that that result had taken place.  If he had desired to guard himself against it, it would have been lain upon him to have done so, by leaving, or by interposing, some barrier between his close and the close of the defendants in order to have prevented that operation of the laws of nature.

As an illustration of that principle, I may refer to a case which was cited in the argument before your Lordships, the case of Smith v. Kendrick, in the Court of Common Pleas, 7 C.B. 515.

On the other hand, if the defendants, not stopping at the natural use of their close, had desired to use it for any purpose which I may term a non-natural use, for the purpose of introducing into the close that which in its natural condition was not in or upon it, for the purpose of introducing water either above or below ground in quantities and in a manner not the result of any work or operation on or under the land; and if in consequence of their doing so, or in consequence of any imperfection in the mode of their doing so, the water came to escape and to pass off into the close of the plaintiff, then it appears to me that that which the defendants were doing they were doing at their own peril; and, if in the course of their doing it the evil arose to which I have referred, the evil, namely, of the escape of the water and its passing away to the close of the plaintiff and injuring the plaintiff, then for the consequence of that, in my opinion, the defendants would be liable. As the case of Smith v. Kendrick is an illustration of the first principle to which I have referred, so also the second principle to which I have referred is well illustrated by another case in the same Court, the case of Baird v. Williamson, 15 C.B.N.S. 317, which was also cited in the argument at the bar.    *   *   *

Judgment of the Court of Exchequer Chamber affirmed.

[The concurring opinion of Lord CRANWORTH is omitted.]

---

1. Why not liability simply for trespass to land? Or nuisance? The contractor who did the work was negligent in not discovering the abandoned mine shafts and blocking them up. Why was defendant not liable for the negligence of the person he employed? Would he be liable today? Was defendant negligent in having the reservoir at all? If not negligent was he still at fault? See Keeton, Conditional Fault in the Law of Torts (1959) 72 Harv.L.Rev. 401.

2. The reservoir in this case was located in a part of Lancashire devoted to coal mining. The American equivalent would be a reservoir in the immediate vicinity of Scranton, Pa. Has this any significance?

3. Professor Bohlen, The Rule in Rylands v. Fletcher (1911) 59 U.Pa. L.Rev. 298, first advanced a "materialistic" explanation of the principal case, to the effect that the judges who wrote the opinions belonged to the landed gentry, and were seeking to protect that class against the encroachments of industry. This was refuted by the painstaking biographies of the judges in Molloy, Fletcher v. Rylands: A Re-examination of Juristic Origins (1942) 9 U.Chi.L.Rev. 266. Nevertheless it continues to be repeated. See, for example, C. Morris, Torts (1953) 246–7.

4. How far does the opinion of Lord Cairns limit that of Blackburn? What does he mean by a "natural use" of land? Something like trees, in a state of nature? Note that he relies on Smith v. Kendrick [1849] 7 C.B. 515, 137 Eng.Rep. 205, where defendant's normal and usual mining operations resulted in the flow of percolating water from springs into plaintiff's adjoining mine, and defendant was held not liable. A parallel case is Zampos v. United States Smelting R. & M. Co. (10 Cir. 1953) 206 F.2d 171. He relies also upon Baird v. Williamson [1863] 15 C.B. (N.S.) 376, 143 Eng. Rep. 831, where defendant pumped the water from his mine to a higher level, from which it flowed into plaintiff's mine and he was held liable.

5. Subsequent decisions in England have followed the distinction between "natural" and "nonnatural" uses of land made by Lord Cairns. In determining what is a nonnatural use, the English courts have looked not only to the character of the thing or activity in question, but also to the place in which it is maintained, and its relation to its surroundings. Thus water collected in large tanks in dangerous proximity to plaintiff's land has been held to be a matter for strict liability; but water in a cistern, in household pipes, in a water closet, or in a barnyard tank supplying cattle, has not. Fire in a fireplace, or in an authorized railway engine is a natural use; but a traction engine shooting out sparks on the highway is not. Although the automobile is dangerous, and fatal to thousands annually, it is held to be "natural"; but a ten ton traction engine or a steam roller which crushes conduits under the street is not. See Stallybrass, Dangerous Things and the Non-Natural User of Land (1929) 3 Camb.L.J. 376; Fleming, Torts (4th ed. 1971) 280; Newark, Non-Natural Use and Rylands v. Fletcher (1961) 24 Mod.L.Rev. 447. How would you state the English rule?

6. In Read v. J. Lyons & Co. Ltd. [1947] A.C. 156, where a government inspector was injured by an explosion in defendant's munitions plant, the court further limited Rylands v. Fletcher by holding that the rule would apply only when something "escaped" from defendant's land. The case might perhaps be justified on the ground that plaintiff had assumed the risk. Cf. E. I. Du Pont de Nemours & Co. v. Cudd (10 Cir. 1949) 176 F.2d 855, where this was held as to an employee working around a highly dangerous activity. The Read Case was, however, followed in Barrette v. Franki Compressed Pile Co. [1955] 2 Dom.L.Rep. 665, where it was held that vibration from pile driving that damaged plaintiff's building did not involve the "escape" of anything. Is the distinction sound?

7. In the United States, Rylands v. Fletcher started out with approval in Ball v. Nye (1868) 99 Mass. 582, 97 Am.Dec. 56 (percolation of filthy water), and Cahill v. Eastman (1871) 18 Minn. 324, 10 Am.Rep. 184 (water escaping from a tunnel). The case then was rejected in its entirety by three leading American courts in three years. Losee v. Buchanan (1873) 51 N.Y. 476, 10 Am.Rep. 623; Marshall v. Welwood (1876) 38 N.J.L. 339, 20 Am.Rep. 394; Brown v. Collins (1873) 53 N.H. 442, 16 Am.Rep. 372. The first two of these involved the explosion of ordinary steam boilers, and the third a runaway horse. They were clearly cases of customary, natural uses, to which the English courts would certainly never have applied the rule. Cf. Howard v. Furness Houlder Argentine Lines [1936] 2 All Eng.Rep. 781. In each case the attack was directed at Blackburn's broad statement in the intermediate court, and the decision in the House of Lords was given little

or no attention. Rylands v. Fletcher was treated as holding that the defendant is absolutely liable whenever anything whatever escapes from his control and causes damage. In other words, the rule of the case was misstated, and as misstated was rejected, in cases in which it had no proper application in the first place.

8. These decisions gave Rylands v. Fletcher a bad name, and it was rejected in other jurisdictions, such as Kentucky, Pennsylvania, Rhode Island and Washington. For a time a majority of the courts that considered the case by name rejected it. In recent years the American trend has been very much in favor of approval of the case, and a substantial majority now favor the case.

9. Many of the courts rejecting Rylands v. Fletcher by name have accomplished much the same result in many cases by calling the defendant's activity or condition an "absolute nuisance." See infra pages 861–862. Also Prosser, Nuisance Without Fault (1942) 20 Tex.L.Rev. 399.

10. Rylands v. Fletcher has been a favorite topic of legal writers. See Bohlen, The Rule in Rylands v. Fletcher (1911) 59 U.Pa.L.Rev. 298; Thayer, Liability Without Fault (1916) 29 Harv.L.Rev. 801; Morris, Hazardous Enterprises and Risk-Bearing Capacity (1952) 61 Yale L.J. 1172; Stallybrass, Dangerous Things and the Non-Natural User of Land (1929) 3 Camb.L.J. 376; Carpenter, The Doctrine of Green v. General Petroleum Corp. (1932) 5 So.Cal.L.Rev. 263; Prosser, The Principle of Rylands v. Fletcher, in Selected Topics on the Law of Torts (1953) 135; Baker, An Eclipse of Fault Liability (1954) 40 Va.L.Rev. 273; Note, The Rylands v. Fletcher Doctrine in America: Abnormally Dangerous, Ultrahazardous or Absolute Nuisance, 1978 Ariz.St.L.J. 99.

## YUKON EQUIPMENT, INC. v. FIREMAN'S FUND INS. CO.

Supreme Court of Alaska, 1978.
585 P.2d 1206.

MATTHEWS, Justice. A large explosion occurred at 2:47 a. m. on December 7, 1973, in the suburbs north of the city of Anchorage. The explosion originated at a storage magazine for explosives under lease from the federal government to petitioner E. I. du Pont de Nemours and Company, which was operated by petitioner Yukon Equipment, Inc. The storage magazine is located on a 1,870 acre tract of federal land which had been withdrawn by the Department of the Interior for the use of the Alaska Railroad for explosive storage purposes by separate orders in 1950 and 1961. The magazine which exploded was located 3,820 feet from the nearest building not used to store explosives and 4,330 feet from the nearest public highway. At the time of the explosion it contained approximately 80,000 pounds of explosives. The blast damaged dwellings and other buildings within a two mile radius of the magazine and, in some instances, beyond a two mile radius. The ground concussion it caused registered 1.8 on the Richter scale at the earthquake observation station in Palmer, some 30 miles away.

The explosion was caused by thieves. Four young men had driven onto the tract where the magazine was located, broken into the storage magazine, set a prepared charge, and fled. They apparently did so in an effort to conceal the fact that they had stolen explosives from the site a day or two earlier.

This consolidated lawsuit was brought to recover for property damage caused by the explosion. Cross-motions for partial summary judgment were filed, and summary judgment on the issue of liability was granted in favor of the respondents. * * *

The leading case on liability for the storage of explosives is Exner v. Sherman Power Const. Co., 54 F.2d 510 (2d Cir. 1931). There dynamite stored by the defendant exploded causing personal injury and property damage to the plaintiffs who resided some 935 feet away from the storage site. A distinguished panel of the Circuit Court of Appeals for the Second Circuit held the defendant liable regardless of fault:

"Dynamite is of the class of elements which one who stores or uses in such a locality, or under such circumstances as to cause likelihood of risk to others, stores or uses at his peril. He is an insurer, and is absolutely liable if damage results to third persons, either from the direct impact of rocks thrown out by the explosion (which would be a common law trespass) or from concussion." Id. at 512–13.

The court pointed out that while the general principle of absolute liability expressed in the English case of Rylands v. Fletcher had been accorded a mixed reception at best in United States courts, there had been no such reluctance to impose absolute liability in blasting cases. The court then noted that some authorities had made a distinction between damage done by rocks or debris hurled by an explosion, as to which there would be absolute liability, and damage caused by a concussion, as to which a negligence standard applied. The court concluded that such a distinction was without a logical basis and rejected it. Id. at 514. The court also determined that there was no reason for attaching different legal consequences to the results of an explosion "whether the dynamite explodes when stored or when employed in blasting." The court expressed the policy behind the rule of absolute liability as follows:

"The extent to which one man in the lawful conduct of his business is liable for injuries to another involves an adjustment of conflicting interests. * * * When, as here, the defendant, though without fault, has engaged in the perilous activity of storing large quantities of a dangerous explosive for use in his business, we think there is no justification for relieving it of liability, and that the owner of the business, rather than a third party who has no relation to the explosion, other than that of injury, should bear the loss." Id. at 514.

*Exner* has been widely followed, and was based on many earlier authorities imposing absolute liability for explosions.

As *Exner* reflects, the particular rule of absolute liability for blasting damage received earlier and more general acceptance in the United States than the generalized rule of absolute liability for unusually dangerous activity which has its antecedents in Rylands v. Fletcher. The generalized rule gained added currency in the United States following its adoption by the American Law Institute as sections 519–524 of the Restatement of Torts (1938). Under the Restatement § 519, a rule of absolute liability for "ultra-hazardous" activity was imposed. Section 520 defined an activity as ultra-hazardous if it "(a) necessarily involves a risk of serious harm to the person, land or chattels of others which cannot be eliminated by the exercise of the utmost care, and (b) is not a matter of common usage."

Comments (c) and (e) to that section make it clear that the storage of explosives is *per se* ultra-hazardous. Comment (c) states in part:

"The storage and transportation of explosive substances are ultrahazardous activities because no precautions and care can make it reasonably certain that they will not explode and because the harm resulting from their explosion is almost certain to be serious."

Comment (e) addresses the question of common usage, stating: "While blasting is recognized as a proper means of clearing woodlands for cultivating and of excavating for building purposes, the conditions which require its use are usually of brief duration. It is generally required because of the peculiar character of the land and it is not a part of the customary processes of farming or of building operations. Likewise, the manufacture, storage, transportation and use of high explosives, although necessary to the construction of many public and private works, are carried on by a comparatively small number of persons and, therefore, are not matters of common usage."

Thus the particular rule of *Exner,* absolute liability for damage caused by the storage of explosives, was preserved by the Restatement and a general rule, inferred from *Exner* and the authorities on which it was based, and from Rylands v. Fletcher and its antecedents, was stated which imposed absolute liability on any other activity which met the definition of ultra-hazardous.

The Restatement (Second) of Torts (1977), adopted by the ALI after the explosion in this case, does not reflect a *per se* rule of liability for the storage of explosives. Instead it lists six factors to be considered in determining whether an activity is "abnormally dangerous" and therefore subject to the rule of absolute liability. * * *

[The Court quotes § 520 and discusses the application of these factors to the fact situation. The section is treated in the next case.]

Since five of the six factors required by section 520 of the Restatement (Second) are met and the sixth is debatable, we would impose absolute liability here if we were to use that approach.

However, we do not believe that the Restatement (Second) approach should be used in cases involving the use or storage of explosives. Instead, we adhere to the rule of Exner v. Sherman Power Constr. Co. and its progeny imposing absolute liability in such cases. The Restatement (Second) approach requires an analysis of degrees of risk and harm, difficulty of eliminating risk, and appropriateness of place, before absolute liability may be imposed. Such factors suggest a negligence standard.[10] The six factor analysis may well be necessary where damage is caused by unique hazards and the question is whether the general rule of absolute liability applies, but in cases involving the storage and use of explosives we take that question to have been resolved by more than a century of judicial decisions.

The reasons for imposing absolute liability on those who have created a grave risk of harm to others by storing or using explosives are largely independent of considerations of locational appropriateness. We see no reason for making a distinction between the right of a homesteader to recover when his property has been damaged by a blast set off in a remote corner of the state, and the right to compensation of an urban resident whose home is destroyed by an explosion originating in a settled area. In each case, the loss is properly to be regarded as a cost of the business of storing or using explosives. Every incentive remains to conduct such activities in locations which are as safe as possible, because there the damages resulting from an accident will be kept to a minimum.

The next question is whether the intentional detonation of the storage magazine was a superseding cause relieving petitioners from liability.   *   *   *

Prior to the explosion in question the petitioners' magazines had been illegally broken into at least six times. Most of these entries involved the theft of explosives. Petitioners had knowledge of all of this. [The court found the intentional detonation not to be a superseding cause.]

The partial summary judgment is affirmed.

RABINOWITZ, Justice, concurring. Although I concur in the result reached by the court, I disagree with its adoption of the approach of Exner v. Sherman Power Construction Co., 54 F.2d 510 (2d Cir. 1931), which imposes absolute or strict liability in all cases involving the use or storage of explosives. I am persuaded that sections 519 and 520 of the Restatement (Second) of Torts (1977) em-

---

**10.** In the analogous area of strict liability for defective products we have rejected the approach of § 402(a) of the Restatement (Second) of Torts which requires proof that a product is "unreasonably dangerous." "It represents a step backwards in the development of products liability cases. The purpose of strict liability is to overcome the difficulty of proof inherent in negligent and warranty theories, thereby insuring that the costs of physical injuries are borne by those who market defective products." Butaud v. Suburban Marine & Sporting Goods, Inc., 543 P.2d 209, 214 (Alaska 1975).

body a sounder rule of law. On balance, I think it is preferable that the court, in making the determination whether an activity is "abnormally dangerous" and therefore subject to absolute liability, employ the criteria articulated in section 520 to analyze the particular acts and circumstances of the case. In my view, consideration of these criteria offers a rational solution to the problem of determining whether a particular activity is abnormally dangerous.

Despite the foregoing, I can agree with the court's overall disposition of this appeal since application of section 520 to the facts of the case leads to the conclusion that the activity in question was abnormally dangerous. Thus absolute liability was properly imposed.

---

1. This storage location was essentially in the suburbs of Anchorage. Should that make a difference? Consider also the quantity of explosives stored. Suppose a hardware store in a small town keeps with all due care a small amount of dynamite for sale to farmers blasting stumps. Should the same rule apply? Cf. Barnes v. Zettlemoyer (1901) 25 Tex.Civ.App. 468, 62 S.W. 111.

2. Is the Alaska court laying down a special rule for the use and storage of explosives, or is it laying down a broad general rule for activities that are to be classed as ultrahazardous or abnormally dangerous?

3. A majority of the courts impose strict liability for blasting if it is done in an urban area. In the principal case the court cites authorities from 14 jurisdictions following the holding in the Exner case and numerous others prior to *Exner*. Some, however, state that the location is important in controlling whether the activity is ultrahazardous. See Liber v. Flor (1966) 160 Colo. 7, 415 P.2d 332; Otero v. Burgess (1973) 84 N.M. 575, 505 P.2d 1251; cf. Chavez v. Southern Pac. Transp. Co. (D.C.Cal.1976) 413 F.Supp. 1203 (keeping 18 bomb-loaded box cars in railroad yard near town). And still others, stressing the comparative safety with which it can be carried on by the exercise of due care, hold that there is liability only for negligence. Reynolds v. W. H. Hinman Co. (1956) 145 Me. 343, 75 A.2d 831; Wadleigh v. City of Manchester (1956) 100 N.H. 277, 123 A.2d 831. Sometimes strict liability is accomplished by calling the activity a nuisance, as in Gossett v. Southern R. Co. (1905) 115 Tenn. 376, 89 S.W. 737.

See, generally, Smith, Liability for Substantial Physical Damage to Land by Blasting (1920) 33 Harv.L.Rev. 542 & 667; McNeal, Use of Explosives and Liability Questions Involved (1956) 23 Ins.Coun.J. 125; Note (1971) 37 Mo.L.Rev. 121; Annots. (1951) 20 A.L.R.2d 1372, (1971) 35 A. L.R.3d 1177, (1974) 56 A.L.R.3d 1077.

## LANGAN v. VALICOPTERS, INC.

Supreme Court of Washington, 1977.
88 Wash.2d 855, 567 P.2d 218.

DOLLIVER, Associate Justice. This is an appeal from a judgment against appellants for damages resulting from their crop spraying activities. \* \* \* The Langans are organic farmers: that is, they use no nonorganic fertilizers, insecticides or herbicides to aid them in their farming but rely on natural fertilizers and natural pest control agents. They had planned to can and sell their produce to organic food buyers.

Valicopters, Inc., is a Washington corporation which engages in the aerial application of agricultural pesticides. \* \* \* The Thalheimers, doing business as Thalheimer Farms, owned and farmed the land adjoining that of the respondents. It was their land that was being sprayed by Valicopters. \* \* \*

On June 3, 1973, Bepple sprayed for Colorado Beetle infestation on the Thalheimer farm with a chemical pesticide known as Thiodan. \* \* \* Patrick Langan testified that, during one spraying pass, the helicopter began spraying while it was over his property [and] \* \* \* that the spray settled on the entire length of their tomato, bean, garlic, cucumber and Jerusalem artichoke rows. \* \* \*

[The Northwest Organic Food Producers' Association (NOFPA) decertified the property of the Langans after laboratory tests showed the crops had a residue higher than allowable under its by-laws.]

After a jury trial, a judgment in the amount of $5,500 was entered against appellants. They appealed to the Court of Appeals, Division Three. That court certified the case to this court and we accepted certification. \* \* \*

The next issue is whether the trial court erred by instructing the jury that appellants would be strictly liable for damage that was proximately caused by their aerial spraying. The trial judge gave the following instruction:

"If you find that defendants' chemicals fell upon plaintiffs' crops, you are instructed that as a matter of law the defendants are liable for such damage to plaintiffs' crops, if any, as you find was proximately caused by defendants' spray application."

Liability for damage caused by crop dusting or spraying generally is imposed on the basis of either negligence or strict liability. See generally Liability for Injury Caused by Spraying or Dusting of Crops, Annot., 37 A.L.R.2d 833 (1971). The courts in most jurisdictions that have held crop dusters liable have used the theory of negligence. [Citations] However, other opinions which have ostensibly relied upon the principles of negligence have been criticized by legal writers because the reasoning is not clear or more nearly resembles strict liability. [Citations]

Three jurisdictions have held crop dusting to be an activity to which the principles of strict liability apply. [Citations] In Loe v. Lenhardt, [227 Or. 242, 362 P.2d 312 (1961)] Justice Goodwin, writing for the majority, noted that the dangers of spraying agricultural chemicals by aircraft has been the subject of considerable legislative attention nationwide, citing the laws of 29 states. These laws, he concluded, were evidence of the dangerous character of aerial spraying. The court recognized the activity was one capable of inflicting damage notwithstanding the exercise of utmost care by the applicator, and that the damage was within the scope of the risk created by spraying an adjoining field. The court cited Bedell v. Goulter, 199 Or. 344, 362–63, 261 P.2d 842 (1953), a case involving strict liability for blasting, in which it stated:

" * * * Basic to the problem is 'an adjustment of conflicting interests', * * * of the right of the blaster, on the one hand, to pursue a lawful occupation and the right of an owner of land, on the other, to its peaceful enjoyment and possession. Where damage is sustained by the latter through the nonculpable activities of the former, who should bear the loss—the man who caused it or a 'third person', as Judge Hand says, 'who has no relation to the explosion, other than that of injury'?" Loe v. Lenhardt, supra, 227 Or. at 253, 362 P.2d at 318.

In Washington, this court has adopted the Restatement (Second) of Torts §§ 519, 520. Section 519 of the Restatement provides: *

"(1) One who carries on an abnormally dangerous activity is subject to liability for harm to the person, land or chattels of another resulting from the activity, although he has exercised the utmost care to prevent the harm.

"(2) This strict liability is limited to the kind of harm, the possibility of which makes the activity abnormally dangerous."

Section 520 lists the factors to be used when determining what constitutes an abnormally dangerous activity:

"In determining whether an activity is abnormally dangerous, the following factors are to be considered:

"(a) existence of a high degree of risk of some harm to the person, land or chattels of others;

"(b) likelihood that the harm that results from it will be great;

"(c) inability to eliminate the risk by the exercise of reasonable care;

"(d) extent to which the activity is not a matter of common usage;

"(e) inappropriateness of the activity to the place where it is carried on; and

"(f) extent to which its value to the community is outweighed by its dangerous attributes."

* The opinion quotes §§ 519 and 520, and their comments as they appeared in Tentative Draft No. 10 (1964). There were some minor changes in diction in the final volume, appearing in 1977. The language of the final volume is substituted here.—[Ed.]

Whether an activity is abnormally dangerous is a question of law for the court to decide.   Siegler v. Kuhlman [81 Wash.2d 448, 502 P. 2d 1181 (1972)]; Restatement (Second) of Torts § 520, comment (*l*). In making this determination, we have considered each of the factors listed in the Restatement, § 520.   We note that not all of the elements listed in § 520 must weigh equally in favor of characterizing an activity as abnormally dangerous in order that we may so find it to be.

"In determining whether the danger is abnormal, the factors listed in Clauses (a) to (f) of this Section are all to be considered, and are all of importance.   Any one of them is not necessarily sufficient of itself in a particular case, and ordinarily several of them will be required for strict liability.   On the other hand, it is not necessary that each of them be present, especially if others weigh heavily. Because of the interplay of these various factors, it is not possible to reduce abnormally dangerous activities to any exact definition.   The essential question is whether the risk created is so unusual, either because of its magnitude or because of the circumstances surrounding it, as to justify the imposition of strict liability for the harm which results from it, even though it is carried on with all reasonable care." Restatement (Second) of Torts § 520, comment (f).   [Citation] However, in this case, each test of the Restatement is met.

§ 520(a): *Existence of a High Degree of Risk of Some Harm to the Person, Land or Chattels of Others.*   It is undisputed among the authorities cited to us that crop dusting involves an element of risk of harm.   In Note, Crop Dusting: Legal Problems in a New Industry, 6 Stan.L.Rev. at 72–75, the author points out that the drift of chemicals is virtually unpredictable due to three "uncertain and uncontrollable factors: (1) the size of the dust or spray particles; (2) the air disturbances created by the [applicating aircraft]; and (3) natural atmospheric forces."   The author discusses these three factors in detail and notes: "In the opinion of leading scientists who are working to alleviate the dangers of crop dusting, it is impossible to eliminate drift with present knowledge and equipment.   Experience bears this out."   6 Stan.L.Rev. at 75.   The author states further that the problem of drift is reduced but not eliminated by the use of helicopters.   Subsequent commentators have made the same observations about the uncontrollability of drift.   [Citation]   In this case, there is no evidence that it is possible to eliminate the risk of drift in crop spraying.

§ 520(b): *Likelihood That the Harm That Results from It Will Be Great.*   Whether there will be great harm depends upon what adjoining property owners do with their land.   For example, one property owner may grow wheat (a narrow-leafed crop) and his neighbor may grow peas (a broad-leafed crop).   The wheat farmer may wish to spray his crop with the chemical herbicide (weed killer) 2,4–D, which kills only broad-leafed plants. If the 2,4–D drifts onto the pea farmer's property, his entire crop could be destroyed since peas are broad-leafed plants. Frear, Chemistry of Insecticides, Fungicides and Herbicides 316 (2d ed. 1948). The reported cases are illustrative of the many possible fact situations which indicate that neighboring property may be sensitive to and damaged by the spraying activity of an adjoining landowner. See Comment, Crop Dusting: Two Theories of Liability?, 19 Hastings L.J. 476, 479, n. 38. The cases cited in that note include the following situations: Gerrard Co. v. Fricker, 42 Ariz. 503, 27 P.2d 678 (1933) (bees killed by insecticide Dutox No. 20); Bynum Cooperage Co. v. Coulter, 219 Ark. 818, 244 S.W.2d 955 (1952) (cotton damaged by 2,4–D); McPherson v. Billington, 399 S. W.2d 186 (Tex.Civ.App.1965) (hogs killed by arsenical). The extent of damage can be very high. See, e.g., Crouse v. Wilbur-Ellis Co., 77 Ariz. 359, 272 P.2d 352 (1954) (plaintiff recovered $10,000 when his cantaloupe crop was damaged by insecticide containing sulphur); Sanders v. Beckwith, 79 Ariz. 67, 283 P.2d 235 (1955) (plaintiff recovered $10,000 when his dairy herd was injured by DDT and benzene hexachloride).

As the present case illustrates, it is economically damaging for an organic farmer who is a member of NOFPA to apply nonorganic materials to his crops because he would lose the association's certification. There was substantial evidence before the trial court that, once an organic farmer loses his certification, it is highly unlikely that he will be able to sell his crops on the regular commercial market due to his failure to enter into contracts with commercial produce buyers before the season begins, and, even if he could sell his crops to a commercial produce buyer, the farmer would be unable to command as high a price for his goods as he could on the organic market.

§ 520(c): *Inability to Eliminate the Risk by the Exercise of Reasonable Care.* The same elements that produce a high degree of risk of harm, namely the uncontrollability of dust or spray drift (§ 520(a) above), also cannot be eliminated by the exercise of reasonable care. [Citation]

§ 520(d): *Extent to Which the Activity is not a Matter of Common Usage.* The Restatement (Second) of Torts, § 520(i), observes "An activity is a matter of common usage if it is customarily carried on by the great mass of mankind, or by many people in the community." Although we recognize the prevalence of crop dusting and acknowledge that it is ordinarily done in large portions of the Yakima Valley, it is carried on by only a comparatively small number of persons (approximately 287 aircraft were used in 1975) and is not a matter of common usage.

§ 520(e): *Inappropriateness of the Activity to the Place Where It Is Carried on.* Given the nature of organic farming, the use of pesticides adjacent to such an area must be considered an activity conducted in an inappropriate place.

§ 520(f): *Extent to Which Its Value to the Community Is Outweighed by Its Dangerous Attributes.* As a criterion for determining strict liability, this factor has received some criticism among legal writers. In 2 Harper & James, Law of Torts, Comment to § 14.4 (Supp.1968), the authors suggest that § 520(f) is not a true element of strict liability: "The justification for strict liability, in other words, is that useful but dangerous activities must pay their own way." [Citation]

There is no doubt that pesticides are socially valuable in the control of insects, weeds and other pests. They may benefit society by increasing production. Whether strict liability or negligence principles should be applied amounts to a balancing of conflicting social interest—the risk of harm versus the utility of the activity. In balancing these interests, we must ask who should bear the loss caused by the pesticides. [Citation]

In the present case, the Langans were eliminated from the organic food market for 1973 through no fault of their own. If crop dusting continues on the adjoining property, the Langans may never be able to sell their crops to organic food buyers. Appellants, on the other hand, will all profit from the continued application of pesticides. Under these circumstances, there can be an equitable balancing of social interests only if appellants are made to pay for the consequences of their acts.

We realize that farmers are statutorily bound to prevent the spread of insects, pests, noxious weeds and diseases. RCW 15.08.030 and RCW 17.10.140-.150. But the fulfillment of that duty does not mean the ability of an organic farmer to produce organic crops must be destroyed without compensation.

Thus, for the reasons mentioned above, we find that the trial court did not err by instructing the jury on strict liability. * * *

There is no reversible error; the judgment of the trial court is affirmed.

---

1. What significant differences exist between the ultrahazardous-activity approach of the First Restatement and the abnormally-dangerous approach of the Second Restatement?

2. Some other activities held subject to strict liability:

A. *Inflammable liquids* stored in quantity in an urban area. Zero Wholesale Gas Co. v. Stroud (1978) 264 Ark. 27, 571 S.W.2d 74 (propane gas); MacKenzie v. Fitchburg Paper Co. (1966) 351 Mass. 292, 218 N.E.2d 579; cf. Yommer v. McKenzie (1969) 255 Md. 220, 257 A.2d 138 (seepage into well); Siegler v. Kuhlman (1972) 91 Wash.2d 448, 502 P.2d 1181 (transporting gasoline in large tank truck). Contra: Hudson v. Peavey Oil Co. (1977) 279 Or. 3, 566 P.2d 175 (filling stations common in residential areas).

B. *Pile driving,* setting up excessive vibration. Caporale v. C. W. Blakeslee & Sons, Inc. (1961) 149 Conn. 79, 175 A.2d 561; Lowry Hill Properties v. Ashbach Constr. Co. (1971) 291 Minn. 429, 194 N.W.2d 767; Vern J. Oja & Associates v. Washington Park Towers, Inc. (1977) 89 Wash.2d 72, 569 P.2d 1141.

C. *Crop Dusting.* In addition to the principal case, see Gotreaux v. Gary (1957) 232 La. 373, 94 So.2d 293; Young v. Darter (Okl.1961) 363 P. 2d 829; Loe v. Lenhardt (1961) 227 Or. 242, 362 P.2d 312. Contra, requiring negligence: S. A. Gerrard Co. v. Fricker (1933) 42 Ariz. 503, 27 P.2d 678; Miles v. A. Arena & Co., (1937) 23 Cal.App.2d 680, 73 P.2d 1260. Lawler v. Skelton (1961) 241 Miss. 274, 130 So.2d 565. See Notes, 9 Gonzaga L.Rev. 816 (1974), 19 Hast.L.J. 476 (1968), 40 Texas L.Rev. 527 (1962), 49 Iowa L.Rev. 135 (1963).

D. *Poisonous Gases.* Luthringer v. Moore (1948) 31 Cal.2d 489, 190 P.2d 1 (fumigation); Langlois v. Allied Chemical Corp. (1971) 258 La. 1067, 249 So.2d 133. Contra: Fritz v. DuPont de Nemours & Co. (1950) 45 Del. 427, 75 A.2d 256.

E. *Rockets.* Defendants testing rocket fuel have been held subject to strict liability in Smith v. Lockheed Propulsion Co. (1967) 247 Cal.App.2d 774, 56 Cal.Rptr. 128; and Berg v. Reaction Motors Div. (1962) 37 N.J. 396, 181 A.2d 487.

F. *Hazardous Waste Disposal Site.* Cf. Village of Wilsonville v. SCA Services, Inc. (1981) 86 Ill.2d 1, 55 Ill.Dec. 499, 426 N.E.2d 824; Bauer, Love Canal: Common Law Approaches to a Modern Tragedy, 11 Env.L. Nw.U. 133 (1980); Hurley-Bruno, The Development of a Strict Liability Cause of Action for Personal Injuries Resulting from Hazardous Waste, 16 N.Eng.L.Rev. 543 (1981); Notes, 69 Geo.L.J. 1047 (1981), 64 Minn.L.Rev. 949 (1980).

G. *Oil Wells.* Green v. General Petroleum Corp. (1928) 215 Cal. 328, 270 P. 952. Contra: Turner v. Big Lake Oil Co. (1936) 128 Tex. 155, 96 S.W.2d 221 (salt water reservoir).

H. *Water Escape.* Clark-Aiken Co. v. Cromwell-Wright Co. (1975) 367 Mass. 70, 323 N.E.2d 876; Smith v. Board of County Comm'rs (1966) 5 Mich.App. 370, 146 N.W.2d 702; Thorsen v. City of Minot (N.D.1967) 153 N.W.2d 764; cf. Doundoulakis v. Town of Hempstead (1977) 42 N.Y.2d 440, 368 N.E.2d 24, 398 N.Y.S.2d 401 (hydraulic landfill); Cities Service Co. v. State (Fla.App.1975) 312 So.2d 799 (settling pond for sludge). Not so with water pipes. McDaid v. City of Pendleton (1970) 5 Or.App. 380, 428 P.2d 643; Pacific N. W. Bell Tel. Co. v. Port of Seattle (1971) 80 Wash.2d 59, 491 P.2d 1037.

3. *Aviation—Ground Damage.* In early stages of commercial aviation, airlines were held strictly liable for ground damage resulting from a crash. This view is no longer justified by the character of the planes and their accident records if the basis is an ultrahazardous or abnormally dangerous activity; and a number of courts have retreated to a negligence standard. See Wood v. United Air Lines, Inc. (1961) 32 Misc.2d 955, 223 N.Y.S.2d 692, affirmed memorandum 16 A.D.2d 659, 226 N.Y.S.2d 1022, appeal dismissed 11 N.Y.2d 1053, 230 N.Y.S.2d 207, 184 N.E.2d 180; Southern Cal. Edison Co. v. Coleman (1957) 150 Cal.App.2d Supp. 829, 310 P.2d 504; Vrazel v. Bieri (Tex.Civ.App.1956) 294 S.W.2d 148; In re Kinsey's Estate

(1949) 152 Neb. 95, 40 N.W.2d 526, 531. Does it make sense that as an industry becomes stronger economically or technologically it is shifted to a less stringent basis of liability? The law review discussions do not deal directly with this point. Compare articles advocating a negligence standard—Orr, Is Aviation Ultra-Hazardous (1954) 21 Ins. Counsel J. 48; Symposium: Airplanes and Liability (1961) 28 Tenn.L.Rev. 117; Whitehead, Liability of Owners and Operators of Planes (1963) 15 Syr.L.Rev. 1—with those supporting strict liability, Schmidt, Piercing the Aluminum Overcast (1974) 9 Linc.L.Rev. 37; Vold, Strict Liability for Airplane Crashes (1953) 5 Hast.L.J. 1; Note (1971) 23 Stan.L.Rev. 569. After considerable wavering by the American Law Institute, a rule of strict liability was adopted in § 520A of the Second Restatement. Is there any other basis on which strict liability can be justified?

4. *"Matter of Common Usage."* Automobile accidents kill and injure more people and damage more property than any other. Why is driving an automobile not an abnormally dangerous activity subject to strict liability?

See also Beck v. Bel Air Properties, Inc. (1955) 134 Cal.App.2d 834, 286 P.2d 503 (earth moving operations incident to subdividing and grading hills and slopes with residential building sites); Rodgers v. City of Lovington (1977) 91 N.M. 306, 573 P.2d 240 (burning dead leaves and grass); Insurance Co. of North America v. Sheinbern (Okl.1971) 488 P.2d 1273 (same); cf. Zero Wholesale Gas Co. v. Stroud (1978) 264 Ark. 27, 571 S.W.2d 74 (propane gas storage—defendant failed to raise properly the issue of common usage).

5. *"Inappropriate for the Location."* Many of the differences in the cases cited in Note 2, supra, can be explained on the basis of the location. See also the Reporter's Note to § 520 of the Restatement, classifying the cases according to the location of the activity.

Professor Seavey suggested that a nuclear reactor would be a nonnatural use of land no matter where it was located. See Seavey, Torts and Atoms, 46 Calif.L.Rev. 3, 9 (1958). Compare Carolina Environmental Study Group, Inc. v. United States Atomic Energy Comm'n (D.C.N.C.1977) 431 F.Supp. 203, reversed sub nom. Duke Power Co. v. Carolina Study Group, Inc. (1978) 438 U.S. 59.

6. *Policy Behind the Imposition of Strict Liability.* Strict liability is "founded upon a policy of the law that imposes upon anyone who for his own purposes creates an abnormal risk of harm to his neighbors, the responsibility of relieving against that harm when it does in fact occur. The defendant's enterprise, in other words, is required to pay its way by compensating for the harm it causes because of its special, abnormal and dangerous character." Restatement, Second, Torts § 519, Comment d. The liability "is applicable to an activity that is carried on with all reasonable care, and that is of such utility that the risk involved in it cannot be regarded as so great or so unreasonable as to make it negligence merely to carry it on." Id., § 520, Comment b. Observe also, that the decision of whether an activity is subject to strict liability is for the court, not the jury, to make. § 520, Comment b.

In other words, this liability is analogous to negligence per se, but it is not called negligence because its value to the community is sufficiently great that the mere participation in the activity is not to be stigmatized as wrongdoing in the negligence sense. It is simply required to pay its own way, without that stigma. Of course, one who carries on an abnormally dangerous activity may also be negligent in the way in which he conducts it and therefore subject to liability on both bases.

If this analysis is accurate, why did the court hold that contributory negligence is a defense to a negligent action but not to one based on strict liability. Is there an explanation? Is it a valid reason?

### 3.   LIMITATIONS ON STRICT LIABILITY

#### FOSTER v. PRESTON MILL CO.

Supreme Court of Washington, 1954.
44 Wash.2d 440, 268 P.2d 645.

HAMLEY, Justice.   Blasting operations conducted by Preston Mill Company frightened mother mink owned by B. W. Foster, and caused the mink to kill their kittens. Foster brought this action against the company to recover damages. His second amended complaint, upon which the case was tried, sets forth a cause of action on the theory of absolute liability   *   *   *

After a trial to the court without a jury, judgment was rendered for plaintiff in the sum of $1,953.68. The theory adopted by the court was that, after defendant received notice of the effect which its blasting operations were having upon the mink, it was absolutely liable for all damages of that nature thereafter sustained.   *   *   *

The primary question presented by appellant's assignments of error is whether, on these facts, the judgment against appellant is sustainable on the theory of absolute liability.

[The court pointed out that in Washington there is strict liability in blasting cases whether the damage is caused by trespassory or non-trespassory invasions.]

However the authorities may be divided on the point just discussed, they appear to be agreed that strict liability should be confined to consequences which lie within the extraordinary risk whose existence calls for such responsibility. [Citations] This limitation on the doctrine is indicated in the italicized portions of the rule as set forth in Restatement of Torts, § 519:

"Except as stated in §§ 521–4, one who carries on an ultrahazardous activity is liable to another whose person, land or chattels the actor should recognize as likely to be harmed by the unpreventable miscarriage of the activity for harm resulting thereto *from that which makes the activity ultrahazardous,* although the utmost care is exercised to prevent the harm." (Italics supplied.)

This restriction which has been placed upon the application of the doctrine of absolute liability is based upon considerations of policy.   *   *   *   "*   *   * It is one thing to say that a dangerous enterprise must pay its way within reasonable limits, and quite another to say that it must bear responsibility for every extreme of harm that it may cause.   The same practical necessity for the restriction of liability within some reasonable bounds, which arises in connection with problems of 'proximate cause' in negligence cases, demands here that some limit be set.  *  *  *  This limitation has been expressed by saying that the defendant's duty to insure safety extends only to certain consequences.   More commonly, it is said that the defendant's conduct is not the 'proximate cause' of the damage.   But ordinarily in such cases no question of causation is involved, and the limitation is one of the policy underlying liability."   Prosser on Torts, 457, § 60.

Applying this principle to the case before us, the question comes down to this:  Is the risk that any unusual vibration or noise may cause wild animals, which are being raised for commercial purposes, to kill their young, one of the things which make the activity of blasting ultrahazardous?

We have found nothing in the decisional law which would support an affirmative answer to this question.   The decided cases, as well as common experience, indicate that the thing which makes blasting ultrahazardous is the risk that property or persons may be damaged or injured by coming into direct contact with flying debris, or by being directly affected by vibrations of the earth or concussions of the air.  *  *  *

The relatively moderate vibration and noise which appellant's blasting produced at a distance of two and a quarter miles was no more than a usual incident of the ordinary life of the community. See 3 Restatement of Torts, 48, § 522, comment a.   The trial court specifically found that the blasting did not unreasonably interfere with the enjoyment of their property by nearby landowners, except in the case of respondent's mink ranch.

It is the exceedingly nervous disposition of mink, rather than the normal risks inherent in blasting operations, which therefore must, as a matter of sound policy, bear the responsibility for the loss here sustained.   We subscribe to the view expressed by Professor Harper (30 Mich.L.Rev. 1001, 1006, supra) that the policy of the law does not impose the rule of strict liability to protect against harms incident to the plaintiff's extraordinary and unusual use of land.   This is perhaps but an application of the principle that the extent to which one man in the lawful conduct of his business is liable for injuries to another involves an adjustment of conflicting interests.  *  *  *

It is our conclusion that the risk of causing harm of the kind here experienced, as a result of the relatively minor vibration, concussion, and noise from distance blasting, is not the kind of risk which makes the activity of blasting ultrahazardous.   The doctrine of absolute liability is therefore inapplicable under the facts of this case, and respondent is not entitled to recover damages.

The judgment is reversed.

1.  Suppose defendant had been found negligent in making unnecessary noise with heavy equipment, knowing of the possibility that plaintiff's mink might be frightened and kill their kittens.  Should defendant be held liable?  See Summit View, Inc. v. W. W. Clyde & Co. (1965) 17 Utah 2d 26, 403 P.2d 919.  Suppose the defendant could postpone his blasting activity until the one-month-danger period for the mink (whelping season) was over.  Under the rationale of the principal case, should that make a difference?  What about liability in negligence?  See MacGibbon v. Robinson, [1953] 2 D.L.R. 689; Mason v. Grandel [1952] 1 D.L.R. 516.  Should it make any difference that these cases arose in a portion of Canada where the raising of mink was an important part of the economy?

2.  In accord with the principal case, upon similar facts, are Madsen v. East Jordan Irrigation Co. (1942) 101 Utah 552, 125 P.2d 794, and Gronn v. Rogers Constructors, Inc. (1960) 221 Or. 226, 350 P.2d 1086.  Compare Uvalde Const. Co. v. Hill (1943) 142 Tex. 19, 175 S.W.2d 247, where the blasting frightened a cow, which bounded against a milkmaid.

3.  Without any negligence on the part of the defendant, his cow trespasses in plaintiff's garden.  Plaintiff tries to drive the cow out, and the cow attacks and injures her.  Strict liability?  Troth v. Wills (1897) 8 Pa.Super. 1; Nixon v. Harris (1968) 15 Ohio St.2d 105, 238 N.E.2d 785.  What about the miscegenation of the scrub bull and the pedigreed heifer?  The court had some fun with this in Kopplin v. Quade (1911) 145 Wis. 454, 130 N.W. 511.  What if the cow wanders into plaintiff's barn and breaks through a rotten place in the floor; and plaintiff, entering the barn in the dark falls into the hole and is injured?  Hollenbeck v. Johnson (1894) 79 Hun 499, 29 N.Y.S. 945.

4.  Defendant parades his circus elephants through the streets of a city.  Plaintiff's skittish horse, seeing a large object pass at a distance of a city block, takes fright and runs away, and plaintiff is injured.  Is there strict liability?  Schribner v. Kelly (1862) 32 Barb. (N.Y.) 14; Bostock-Ferrari Amusement Co. v. Brocksmith (1875) 34 Ind.App. 566, 73 N.E. 281.

5.  Defendant keeps a vicious dog that he knows has in the past attacked human beings.  This dog, trotting peacefully down the street accidentally runs into plaintiff and knocks him down.  Strict liability?  Koetting v. Conroy (1936) 223 Wis. 550, 270 N.W. 625, 271 N.W. 369.  What if the dog's owner knows that the animal has attacked other dogs and fought with them but it has never attacked a human being?  Is there strict liability when it does so?  Cf. Ewing v. Prince (Ky.1968) 425 S.W.2d 732.  See also Martinez v. Modenbach (La.App.1981) 396 So.2d 471 (chasing dog away, plaintiff slips on the wet grass and falls).

6.  In Behrens v. Bertram Mills Circus Ltd. [1957] 2 Q.B. 1, defendant's elephant became frightened by a dog and knocked over a tent that was inhabited by two midgets.  One occupant was injured and the other was frightened.  Under English precedent, elephants were deemed hazardous because they attacked man.  Should it make any difference that this elephant had no desire to attack but only to avoid the fearsome canine?

## GOLDEN v. AMORY

Supreme Judicial Court of Massachusetts, 1952.
329 Mass. 484, 109 N.E.2d 131.

LUMMUS, Justice. The defendants owned a hydroelectric plant in Ludlow in the Red Bridge area. As a result of the hurricane of September 21, 1938, the Chicopee River overflowed and damaged the real estate of the several plaintiffs. In these actions of tort the first count of the several declarations alleged that no permit or decree or approval of the county commissioners was secured by the defendants for the construction, maintenance, and operation of the Alden Street dike. The second count alleged negligence in the maintenance of that dike. The judge directed verdicts for the defendants on the first count, and on the second count, after verdicts for the plaintiffs, entered verdicts for the defendants under leave reserved. To that action, as well as to the exclusion of certain evidence offered by the plaintiffs, the plaintiffs excepted.

The plaintiffs rely upon the rule stated in Fletcher v. Rylands, L.R., 1 Ex. 265, 279, and affirmed in Rylands v. Fletcher, L.R., 3 H.L. 330, 339–340, that "the person who for his own purposes brings on his lands and collects and keeps there anything likely to do mischief if it escapes, must keep it in at his peril, and, if he does not do so, is prima facie answerable for all the damage which is the natural consequence of its escape." That rule is the law of this Commonwealth. [Citations] But that rule does not apply where the injury results from "vis major, the act of God * * *, which the owner had no reason to anticipate." Gorham v. Gross, 125 Mass. 232, 238; Bratton v. Rudnick, 283 Mass. 556, 560–561, 186 N.E. 669. In the present case the flood, as disclosed by the evidence, was plainly beyond the capacity of any one to anticipate, and was clearly an act of God. [Citation] For this reason the rule under discussion does not apply, and the defendants cannot be held liable for injury caused by the flood waters.

Upon the whole case, we find no error, either in the rulings of the judge or in his exclusion of evidence offered by the plaintiffs.

Exceptions overruled.

----

1. In accord are Nichols v. Marsland [1876] L.R. 2 Ex.Div. 1 (dam washed out by extraordinary rainfall); Bratton v. Rudnick (1933) 283 Mass. 556, 186 N.E. 669 (same); Murphy v. Gillum (1898) 73 Mo.App. 487 (seepage from dam embankment caused by unprecedented frost). Cf. Carstairs v. Taylor [1871] L.R. 6 Ex. 217 (rat gnawed a hole in defendant's water box).

2. What if defendant's reservoir overflows because the owner of another reservoir upstream releases suddenly a large quantity of water? Box v. Jubb [1879] 4 Ex.Div. 76. Cf. Rickards v. Lothian [1913] A.C. 263

(malicious third person plugged up defendant's lavatory basin and turned the water on full); Kaufman v. Boston Dye House (1932) 280 Mass. 161, 182 N.E. 297 (petroleum product ignited by third person's gasoline engine); Perry v. Kendricks Transport, Ltd. [1956] 1 W.L.R. 85 (petrol in automobile tank, held to fall within Rylands v. Fletcher, exploded when boys deliberately threw lighted matches into it); Kleebauer v. Western Fuse & Explosives Co. (1903) 138 Cal. 497, 71 P. 617 (alleged murderer, pursued by police, took refuge in defendant's powder magazine and committed suicide by blowing it up). Cf. Baker v. Snell [1908] 2 K.B. 352, 825. Defendant, the owner of a dog that he knew to be vicious, entrusted it to his servant. The servant deliberately incited it to attack the plaintiff. Two of the judges, with a third dissenting, thought there would be strict liability even if the servant were not acting within the scope of his employment. And see Yukon Equipment, Inc. v. Firemen's Fund Ins. Co., supra page 717.

3. See Harper, Liability Without Fault and Proximate Cause (1932), 30 Mich.L.Rev. 1001. On the effect of an intervening act of God or of a third party, compare the provisions in Restatement, Second, Torts §§ 504(3)(c) (livestock), 510 (wild or dangerous animals) and 522 (abnormally dangerous activities). Why the difference?

## SANDY v. BUSHEY

Supreme Judicial Court of Maine, 1925.
124 Me. 320, 128 A. 513.

STURGIS, J.   In the summer of 1923, the plaintiff turned his mare and colt out in the pasture of a neighbor. Other horses occupied the pasture during the season, including the defendant's three-year old colt. On July 14, 1923, the plaintiff went to the pasture to grain his mare, and, while so doing, was kicked by the defendant's horse and seriously injured. This action on the case is brought to recover damages for such injuries and, after verdict for the plaintiff, is before this court on a general motion.

By the common law the owners or keepers of domestic animals are not answerable for an injury done by them in a place where they have a right to be, unless the animals in fact, and to the owners' knowledge, are vicious. If, however, a person keeps a vicious or dangerous animal which he knows is accustomed to attack and injure mankind, he assumes the obligation of an insurer against injury by such animal, and no measure of care in its keeping will excuse him. His liability is founded upon the keeping of such an animal when he has knowledge of its vicious propensities, and his care or negligence is immaterial. In an action for an injury caused by such an animal, the plaintiff has only to allege and prove the keeping, the vicious propensities, and the scienter. Negligence is not the ground of liability, and need not be alleged or proved. This rule of liability of keepers of domestic animals finds its origin in the ancient common law and, except as modified by statute in case of injuries by dogs, is retained as the rule of law in this class of cases in this state. [Citations]

A careful consideration of the evidence discloses facts which fairly tend to establish that the defendant's horse had exhibited a vicious and ugly disposition at various times prior to the day on which the plaintiff was injured, and notice of the animal's vicious propensities had been brought home to the defendant. Upon these issues the jury's verdict in favor of the plaintiff was fully warranted.

The defendant, however, says that the plaintiff was guilty of contributory negligence and cannot, therefore, recover in this action. We are unable to sustain this contention under the rule of liability adopted by this court. In those jurisdictions which have departed from the ancient common-law rule and declared negligence to be the ground of liability in actions for injuries by animals, the defense of contributory negligence has been recognized, and the injured party's failure to exercise due care will defeat his action. [Citations] In this state, however, the negligence doctrine has not been accepted, and contributory negligence in the strict sense of that term cannot be held to constitute a defense to the action. Exclusion of negligence as the basis of liability forbids the inclusion of contributory negligence as a defense. Something more than slight negligence or want of due care on the part of the injured party must be shown in order to relieve the keeper of a vicious domestic animal known to be such from his liability as an insurer.

In Muller v. McKesson, 73 N.Y. 195, 29 Am.Rep. 123, which may be fairly accepted as the leading case in this country upon the question of contributory negligence as a defense to an action of this character, Church, C.J., in stating the opinion of the court, says:

"If a person with full knowledge of the evil propensities of an animal wantonly excites him, or voluntarily and unnecessarily puts himself in the say of such an animal, he would be adjudged to have brought the injury upon himself, and ought not to be entitled to recover. In such a case it cannot be said, in a legal sense, that the keeping of the animal, which is the gravamen of the offense, produced the injury. * * * But as the owner is held to a rigorous rule of liability on account of the danger to human life and limb, by harboring and keeping such animals, it follows that he ought not to be relieved from it by slight negligence or want of ordinary care. To enable an owner of such an animal to interpose this defense, acts should be proved with notice of the character of the animal, which would establish that the person injured voluntarily brought the calamity upon himself." * * *

We are convinced that the principle announced by Chief Justice Church correctly defines the degree of responsibility which must be fixed upon the injured party in order to relieve the keeper of a known vicious animal from his liability as an insurer with which he is charged in this state. The fact must be established that the injury is attributable, not to the keeping of the animal, but to the injured party's unnecessarily and voluntarily putting himself in a way to be hurt knowing the probable consequences of his act, so that he may fairly be deemed to have brought the injury upon himself.

Applying this rule to the facts in the case before us, we are of the opinion that the prima facie case against the defendant, established by the evidence, is not rebutted by the plaintiff's acts or omissions. The plaintiff led his mare away from the other horses in the pasture and started to grain her, when the defendant's horse approached in a threatening manner. The plaintiff drove him away and turned to continue feeding the mare. The colt's return was silent and swift and his attack unexpected. It cannot be said that the plaintiff voluntarily put himself in a way to be injured by the defendant's horse, knowing the probable consequences of his act. The defendant is liable, as found by the jury.

Motion overruled.

------

1. A recent application of the rule in this case is Marshall v. Ranne (Tex.1974) 511 S.W.2d 255 where plaintiff was taunted and tormented periodically by his neighbor's wild boar. One day the boar made good on his threats and bit plaintiff.

2. The Restatement, Second, Torts has also adopted the rule for both wild animals and abnormally dangerous activities. See §§ 515, 523, 524. Is this a logical rule? If ordinary contributory negligence is a defense when defendant is negligent, why is it not a defense when he is not even negligent? How should these rules apply in a comparative negligence state?

3. Defendant keeps a bear in a cage at a circus. Plaintiff crawls under the rope in front of the cage and goes within six inches of the bars. The bear slaps at him through the bars hitting him in the face and putting out his eye. Is defendant liable? Cf. Ervin v. Woodruff (1907) 119 App. Div. 603, 103 N.Y.S. 1051; Heideman v. Wheaton (1948) 72 S.D. 375, 34 N.W.2d 492. A customer at a service station put his hand in an unlocked box of snakes kept for public display at a service station. He was bitten by a rattlesnake. Is his claim barred? See Keyser v. Phillips Petroleum Co. (Fla.App.1973) 287 So.2d 364. Compare the case of a person who came within range of a bull known to be vicious. Anderson v. Anderson (1961) 259 Minn. 412, 107 N.W.2d 647. See, also, Franken v. City of Sioux Center (Iowa 1979) 272 N.W.2d 422; Whitefield v. Stewart (Okl.1978) 577 P.2d 1295.

4. Defendant is conducting blasting operations in dangerous proximity to a highway. He stations a flagman to stop traffic when a blast is about to be set off. Plaintiff drives past the flagman, and is injured by the blast. Should it make any difference whether plaintiff does not see the flagman because he is not looking, or sees him and deliberately drives past? See Worth v. Dunn (1922) 98 Conn. 51, 62, 118 A. 467, 471; Wells v. Knight (1911) 32 R.I. 432, 80 A. 16.

5. *Immunity Created by Legal Sanction.* Statutory sanction for defendant's conduct has frequently been held to confer immunity from strict

liability, on the ground that the defendant cannot be held liable for merely doing properly what the law has authorized him to do, although he will still of course be liable for any negligence. Thus the custodian of a public zoo may be held not subject to strict liability for harm done by the animals kept in it. Jackson v. Baker (1904) 24 App.D.C. 100; Guzzi v. New York Zoological Society (1920) 192 App.Div. 263, 182 N.Y.S. 257, affirmed (1922) 233 N.Y. 511, 135 N.E. 897. This has been held to be true for gas or electric conduits laid in the street under legislative authority. Green v. Chelsea Waterworks Co. [1894] 70 L.T. 457; Gould v. Winona Gas Co. (1907) 100 Minn. 258, 111 N.W. 254. Also for common carriers required by law to ship wild animals or explosives. Stamp v. Eighty-Sixth St. Amusement Co. (1916) 95 Misc. 599, 159 N.Y.S. 683; Actiesselskabet Ingrid v. Central R. Co. of N. J. (2 Cir. 1914) 216 F. 72; Pope v. Edward M. Rude Carrier Corp. (1953) 138 W.Va. 218, 75 S.E.2d 584.

The rule has also been extended to a contractor doing such work as blasting for the state. Nelson v. McKenzie-Hague Co. (1934) 192 Minn. 180, 256 N.W. 96; Pumphrey v. J. A. Jones Const. Co. (1959) 250 Iowa 559, 94 N.W.2d 737. There has been a strong challenge to the proposition that a government contract alone should shield the contractor from strict liability. While it is true that such a privilege may result in lower costs to government, that saving is acquired at the expenditure of denying recovery to an innocent victim. In light of the abrogation of governmental immunity itself, modern courts may be inclined to give more consideration to the injured party and impose strict liability on the contractor who engages in an abnormally dangerous activity. There is a good discussion in Smith v. Lockheed Propulsion Co. (1967) 247 Cal.App.2d 744, 56 Cal.Rptr. 128, 139–142. See Comment (1979) 67 Ky.L.J. 441.

# APPENDIX D

Cases and Materials
on Statutory Violation

*Sample Cases*

## 6. VIOLATION OF STATUTE

### OSBORNE v. McMASTERS

Supreme Court of Minnesota, 1889.
40 Minn. 103, 41 N.W. 543.

Action for damages by M. Osborne, administrator, against S. R. McMasters, for the death of plaintiff's intestate, resulting from the use of poison sold without a label by defendant's clerk in the course of his employment. Judgment for plaintiff, and defendant appeals

MITCHELL, J. Upon the record in this case it must be taken as the facts that defendant's clerk in his drug-store, in the course of his employment as such, sold to plaintiff's intestate a deadly poison without labeling it "Poison," as required by statute; that she, in ignorance of its deadly qualities, partook of the poison which caused her death. * * * It is now well settled, certainly in this state, that where a statute or municipal ordinance imposes upon any person a specific duty for the protection or benefit of others, if he neglects to perform that duty he is liable to those for whose protection or benefit it was imposed for any injuries of the character which the statute or ordinance was designed to prevent, and which were proximately produced by such neglect. * * * It is immaterial whether the duty is one imposed by the rule of common law requiring the exercise of ordinary care not to injure another, or is imposed by a statute designed for the protection of others. In either case the failure to perform the duty constitutes negligence, and renders the party liable for injuries resulting from it. The only difference is that in the one case the measure of legal duty is to be determined upon common-law principles, while in the other the statute fixes it, so that the violation of the statute constitutes conclusive evidence of negligence, or, in other words, negligence *per se*. The action in the latter case is not a statutory one, nor does the statute give the right of action in any other sense, except that it makes an act negligent which otherwise might not be such, or at least only evidence of negligence. All that the statute does is to establish a fixed standard by which the fact of negligence may be determined. The gist of the action is still negligence, or the non-performance of a legal duty to the person injured. * * *

Judgment affirmed.

1. Compare the remarks of Traynor, J. in Clinkscales v. Carver (1943) 22 Cal.2d 72, 136 P.2d 777: "A statute that provides for a criminal proceeding only does not create a civil liability; if there is no provision for a remedy by civil action to persons injured by a breach of the statute it is because the Legislature did not contemplate one. A suit for damages is based on the theory that the conduct inflicting the injuries is a common-law tort, in this case the failure to exercise the care of a reasonable man at a boulevard stop. The significance of the statute in a civil suit for negligence lies in its formulation of a standard of conduct that the court adopts in the determination of such liability. (See Holmes, The Common Law, 120–129; Morris, The Relation of Criminal Statutes to Tort Liability, 46 Harv.L.Rev. 453.) The decision as to what the civil standard should be still rests with the court, and the standard formulated by a legislative body in a police regulation or criminal statute becomes the standard to determine civil liability only because the court accepts it. In the absence of such a standard the case goes to the jury, which must determine whether the defendant has acted as a reasonably prudent man would act in similar circumstances. The jury then has the burden of deciding not only what the facts are but what the unformulated standard is of reasonable conduct. When a legislative body has generalized a standard from the experience of the community and prohibits conduct that is likely to cause harm, the court accepts the formulated standards and applies them." See also Rudes v. Gottschalk (1959) 159 Tex. 552, 324 S.W.2d 201, 205.

2. Why give any effect at all in a civil action for negligence to a statute which merely specifies a crime, and provides only for a criminal penalty? What about the following arguments?

A. The reasonable person will always obey the criminal law. Is this true? Should it be a question for the jury? What about a statute, such as the legendary one providing that when two railroad trains approach a crossing each shall stop and neither shall move forward until the other has passed by?

B. The legislature intended, or is "presumed" to have intended, a civil remedy for the violation. What is the probability as to the state of mind of the legislature: (1) it did intend to provide a civil remedy, but did not say so; (2) it intended not to provide one and therefore omitted it; (3) it never thought about the matter at all?

C. The statute gives rise to a right. A right without a remedy is useless and the court supplies an appropriate remedy. *Ubi ius ibi remedium.*

D. The court adopts the standard of conduct from the criminal statute and lays it down as a rule of law in the civil action. See the preceding section.

3. Must the court accept the statute as controlling? See the next case. See also Stevens v. Luther (1920) 105 Neb. 184, 180 N.W. 87 (six mile an hour speed limit); Stafford v. Chippewa Valley Electric R. Co. (1901) 110 Wis. 331, 85 N.W. 1036 (requirement that a street bell be rung continuously).

4. What if a criminal statute is invalid, and totally ineffective for criminal prosecutions? For example, an ordinance establishing an arterial stop sign, and requiring drivers to stop under criminal penalty, was never

properly published, as required for the adoption of such ordinances. Does this prevent the court, in a negligence action, from adopting the stop as a required standard of conduct? A number of cases say, no. See Lewis v. City of Miami (1937) 127 Fla. 426, 173 So. 150; Ponca City v. Reed (1925) 115 Okl. 166, 242 P. 164; Clinkscales v. Carver (1943) 22 Cal.2d 72, 136 P. 2d 777.

## STACHNIEWICZ v. MAR–CAM CORP.

Supreme Court of Oregon, 1971.
259 Or. 583, 488 P.2d 436.

HOLMAN, Justice. The patron of a drinking establishment seeks to recover against the operator for personal injuries allegedly inflicted by other customers during a barroom brawl. The jury returned a verdict for defendant. Plaintiff appealed.

From the evidence introduced, the jury could find as follows:

A fight erupted in a bar between a group of persons of American Indian ancestry, who were sitting in a booth, and other customers who were at an adjacent table with plaintiff. One of plaintiff's friends had refused to allow a patron from the booth to dance with the friend's wife because the stranger was intoxicated. Thereafter, such threats as, "Hey, Whitey, how big are you?" were shouted from the booth at plaintiff and his companions. One of the persons at the table, after complaining to the bartender, was warned by him, "Don't start trouble with those guys." Soon thereafter, those individuals who had been sitting in the booth approached the table and one of them knocked down a person who was talking to a member of plaintiff's party. With that, the brawl commenced.

After a short melee, someone shouted "Fuzz!" and those persons who had been sitting in the booth ran out a door and into the parking lot, with one of plaintiff's friends in hot pursuit. Upon reaching the door, the friend discovered plaintiff lying just outside with his feet wedging the door open.

Plaintiff suffered retrograde amnesia and could remember nothing of the events of the evening. No one could testify to plaintiff's whereabouts at the time the [disturbance occurred] or to the cause of the vicious head injuries which plaintiff displayed when the brawl was ended.

The customers in the booth had been drinking in defendant's place of business for approximately two and one-half hours before the affray commenced.

The principal issue is whether, as plaintiff contends, violations of ORS 471.410(3) and of Oregon Liquor Control Regulation No. 10–065(2) constitute negligence as a matter of law. The portion of the statute relied on by plaintiff reads as follows:

212 *How to Succeed in Law School*

"(3) No person shall give or otherwise make available any alcoholic liquor to a person visibly intoxicated * * *."

The portion of the regulation to which plaintiff points provides:

"(2) No licensee shall permit or suffer any loud, noisy, disorderly or boisterous conduct, or any profane or abusive language, in or upon his licensed premises, or permit any visibly intoxicated person to enter or remain upon his licensed premises."

The trial court held that a violation of either the statute or the regulation did not constitute negligence per se. It refused requested instructions and withdrew allegations of negligence which were based on their violation.

A violation of a statute or regulation constitutes negligence as a matter of law when the violation results in injury to a member of the class of persons intended to be protected by the legislation and when the harm is of the kind which the statute or regulation was enacted to prevent. [Citations.] The reason behind the rule is that when a legislative body has generalized a standard from the experience of the community and prohibits conduct that is likely to cause harm, the court accepts the formulation. Justice Traynor in Clinkscales v. Carver, 22 Cal.2d 72, 136 P.2d 777 (1943).

However, in addition, it is proper for the court to examine preliminarily the appropriateness of the standard as a measure of care for civil litigation under the circumstances presented. F. James, Jr., "Statutory Standards and Negligence in Accident Cases," 11 La.L. Rev. 95, 111–12 (1950–51); Restatement (Second) of Torts § 286, comment *d*. (1965). The statute in question prevents making available alcohol to a person who is *already visibly intoxicated.* This makes the standard particularly inappropriate for the awarding of civil damages because of the extreme difficulty, if not impossibility, of determining whether a third party's injuries would have been caused, in any event, by the already inebriated person. Unless we are prepared to say that an alcoholic drink given after visible intoxication is the cause of a third party's injuries as a matter of law, a concept not advanced by anyone, the standard would be one almost impossible of application by a factfinder in most circumstances. * * *

The regulation promulgated by the commission is an altogether different matter. * * *

ORS 471.030, entitled "Purpose of Liquor Control Act," provides, in part, as follows:

"(1) The Liquor Control Act shall be liberally construed so as:

"(a) To prevent the recurrence of abuses associated with saloons or resorts for the consumption of alcoholic beverages." * * *

An examination of the regulation discloses that it concerns matters having a direct relation to the creation of physical disturbances in bars which would, in turn, create a likelihood of injury to customers. A common feature of our western past, now preserved in story and reproduced on the screen hundreds of times, was the carnage of the barroom brawl. No citation of authority is needed to establish that the "abuses associated with saloons," which the Liquor Control Act seeks to prevent, included permitting on the premises profane, abusive conduct and drunken clientele (now prohibited by the regulation) which results in serious personal injuries to customers in breach of the bar owner's duty to protect his patrons from harm. We find it reasonable to assume that the commission, in promulgating the regulation, intended to prevent these abuses, and that they had in mind the safety of patrons of bars as well as the general peace and quietude of the community. In view of the quoted purpose of the Act and of the history of injury to innocent patrons of saloons, we cannot assume otherwise.

In addition, we see no reason why the standard is not an appropriate one for use in the awarding of civil damages. Because plaintiff was within the class of persons intended to be protected by the regulation and the harm caused to him was the kind the statute was intended to prevent, we hold that the trial court erred in not treating the alleged violations of the regulation as negligence as a matter of law. * * *

We believe it would be fair for the jury to infer, in the circumstances set forth in the statement of the facts, that plaintiff was injured by one of the persons in the booth who had created the disturbance and that the injuries would not have occurred except for defendant's violation of the commission's regulation, as alleged.

The judgment of the trial court is reversed and the case is remanded for a new trial.

---

1. What is the basis upon which a court seeks to select or reject a criminal statute as a standard of care in a particular tort suit? This is not a readily solvable problem. The court must determine that:

A. The party seeking to charge the other with violation of the statute is a member of the class the legislature intended to protect. See Thomas v. Baltimore & O. R. Co. (1973) 19 Md.App. 217, 310 A.2d 186 (plaintiff who knew of location of railway crossing not in class to be protected by regulation requiring warning); Erickson v. Kongsli (1952) 40 Wash.2d 79, 240 P.2d 1209 (abutting landowner's property damaged when defendant made an illegal left turn—not in class to be protected).

What result in the principal case if an employee of the drinking establishment had been injured in the melee?

B. The hazard that occurred was one the legislature intended to prevent. The leading case on the "different hazard" is Gorris v. Scott [1874] L.R. 9 Ex. 125, where a contagious diseases act required that animals shipped by boat be kept in pens, to avoid the spread of disease. Plaintiff's sheep were washed overboard from defendant's boat during a storm, because they were not in pens. It was held that the violation of the statute did not make the defendant liable for the loss of the sheep.

What result in the principal case if plaintiff had been injured when an intoxicated person had stumbled and fallen upon him?

2.   The Restatement, Second, Torts spells out in greater detail these requirements in § 287, and it states in § 288:

"The court will not adopt as the standard of conduct of a reasonable man the requirements of a legislative enactment or an administrative regulation whose purpose is found to be exclusively

"(a) to protect the interests of the state or any subdivision of it as such, or

"(b) to secure to individuals the enjoyment of rights or privileges to which they are entitled only as members of the public, or

"(c) to impose upon the actor the performance of a service which the state or any subdivision of it undertakes to give the public, or

"(d) to protect a class of persons other than the one whose interests are invaded, or

"(e) to protect another interest than the one invaded, or

"(f) to protect against other harm than that which has resulted, or

"(g) to protect against any other hazards than that from which the harm has resulted."

3.   Because state legislative history is usually scanty and also difficult to obtain, there may be wide latitude for a court to decide who is in the "class" or what was the "hazard" that the legislature had in mind.  On occasion the court may rely on the title or the preamble of the statute.  Compare Kelly v. Henry Muhs Co. (1904) 71 N.J.Law 358, 59 A. 23 with Drake v. Fenton (1912) 237 Pa. 8, 85 A. 14.

4.   *Federal Legislation.*  There is no "doctrine" of negligence per se in federal laws.  If there is no general federal common law of negligence as a result of Erie R. Co. v. Tompkins (1938) 304 U.S. 64, the federal courts are in no position to adopt a criminal statutory rule of conduct as a civil rule of conduct replacing the general standard of care.  The result is that they find it necessary to "imply" a civil action from the criminal statute, thus placing the responsibility for the action on the Congress.  See infra p. 1211.

5.   The states do have a "doctrine" of negligence per se.  Should violation of a federal statute be a basis for finding negligence per se in a state court?  Surprisingly, there is very little consideration of this problem.  See Steagall v. Dot Mfg. Corp. (1969) 223 Tenn. 428, 446 S.W.2d 515, where the court assumed that violation of the Federal Hazardous Substances Act might be negligence per se but found no proximate cause.  In diversity cases where they are applying state law, federal courts have sometimes assumed, without careful consideration, that the state court would apply negligence per se to a federal statute.  See Orthopedic Equipment Co. v. Eutsler (4 Cir. 1960) 276 F.2d 455 (Federal Food, Drug & Cosmetic Act—Virginia law) ; Gober v. Revlon, Inc. (4 Cir. 1963) 317 F.2d 47 (same—California law).  On the Occupational Safety and Health Act of 1970, see Annots. (1977) 79 A.L.R.3d 962; (1977) 35 A.L.R.Fed. 461.

# NEY v. YELLOW CAB CO.

Illinois Supreme Court, 1954.
2 Ill.2d 74, 117 N.E.2d 74.

MAXWELL, Justice. \* \* \* The Appellate Court here affirmed the trial court's judgment fixing liability on the defendant for violation of a section of the Uniform Traffic Act. The plaintiff charged that defendant, by its servant, negligently permitted its taxicab to remain unattended on a Chicago street without first stopping the engine or locking the ignition or removing the key, contrary to a section of said act. The undisputed facts reveal that a thief stole the taxicab and while in flight ran into plaintiff's vehicle causing property damage. Defendant's motion to dismiss the complaint was based on the theory that the acts or omissions of the defendant did not constitute actionable negligence, nor the proximate cause of the damage. Briefly stated, plaintiff contended that the defendant's violation of the statute was negligence and the proximate cause of the damage.

The statute in question, section 92 of article XIV of the Uniform Traffic Act, provides: "(a) No person driving or in charge of a motor vehicle shall permit it to stand unattended without first stopping the engine, locking the ignition and removing the key, or when standing upon any perceptible grade without effectively setting the brake thereon and turning the front wheels to the curb or side of the highway. (b) No person shall operate or drive a motor vehicle who is under fifteen years of age." Ill.Rev.Stat.1953, chap. 95½, par. 189; Jones Ann.Stat. 85.221.

The defendant takes the position that this particular statute is not an antitheft measure but is a traffic regulation, the violation of which could impose no liability on the owner or operator of the vehicle for the misconduct of a thief, for the reason that, under such circumstances, the violation of the statute is not actionable negligence in that the misconduct is neither negligence with relation to the resulting injury, nor its proximate cause. The plaintiff, on the other hand, contends that the statute is a safety measure for the benefit of the public; that its violation is prima facie evidence of negligence; and that reasonable persons might reasonably foresee that its violation could result in the consequences which occurred here. The plaintiff further contends that irrespective of the statute there would be a common-law liability under the same circumstances, and that in either event the questions of negligence and proximate cause are, under the facts alleged and admitted here, questions of fact and not questions of law.

The First District Appellate Court in Ostergard v. Frisch, 333 Ill.App. 359, 77 N.E.2d 537, held, with one Justice dissenting, that there was a liability under similar circumstances. The Third District Appellate Court in Cockrell v. Sullivan, 344 Ill.App. 620, 101 N.E.2d

878, held there was no liability. Thereafter, in the present case, Ney v. Yellow Cab Co., 348 Ill.App. 161, 108 N.E.2d 508, the First District court again held that liability existed.

A repetitious review of the cases and decisions of the foreign jurisdictions cited in the parties' briefs will serve no good purpose, as our Appellate Courts have already done so in a most scholarly manner. Suffice it to say here that the majority rule seems to hold there is no liability while the minority rule holds there is. Various distinctions, qualifications and limitations have been pointed out by both plaintiff and defendant in criticism of the cited cases. We have carefully studied the reasoning of our Appellate Courts and the courts of the other jurisdictions, in the light of these distinctions, and conclude that the issue presented requires our determination of the following questions: (a) What was the legislative intention? (b) Is the violation of the statute the proximate cause of the injury? (c) Is the act of the thief an intervening, independent, efficient force which breaks the causal connection between the original wrong and the injury?

Labeling of the statute does not solve the problem. Defendant urges that the statute is a traffic regulation and not an antitheft measure, and from this premise reasons to a conclusion of nonliability. It seems to argue that if it were an antitheft measure liability would attach in this case. * * * We think the key to the construction of the statute with regard to the legislative intention appears in the statute itself. The requirement that the brakes be set and the wheels turned to the curb on a grade is no material theft deterrent. The second subparagraph of the section prohibiting persons under fifteen years of age from operating a motor vehicle indicates to us that the legislature was thinking about the danger to the public in permitting persons lacking in experience, judgment, knowledge and maturity to operate such vehicles. We cannot but conclude that this entire section is a public safety measure. This being so, what harm did the legislature foresee and attempt to prevent by prohibiting the leaving of an unattended motor vehicle with the key in the ignition? The motor vehicle with the key in its ignition in itself could obviously do no harm.

Consequently, there enters into our consideration the question of foreseeability as to intervention of outside agencies not under the control of the person in charge of the motor vehicle. The drawing of lines of demarcation in problems of cause and effect is often difficult in the study of formal logic and these difficulties are not minimized in the field of jurisprudence. We cannot say that the legislature intended to distinguish between certain types of outside agencies without expressing such distinction. Such a distinction would be too tenuous a ground to serve as a basis for decision in view of the broad general sweep of the statutory language employed. The legislature has here used clear and express terms making it the duty of persons in charge of motor vehicles to do certain acts upon leaving their vehicles unattended. The motivation of such legislation is not the State's desire to punish but rather its interest in public welfare for protection of life, limb and property by prevention of recognized hazards.

The violation of the statute is prima facie evidence of negligence under the prevailing rule of this State. [Citations] This in itself creates no liability. The injury must have a direct and proximate connection with the violation of the statute before liability will be held to exist. It is the existence of this cause and effect relationship which makes the negligence of the defendant actionable.

Where an independent agency intervenes, the solution of the problem becomes aggravated. * * *

A further problem is presented when the independent agency is an illegal or criminal act. Wrongful acts of independent third persons, not actually intended by the defendant, are not regarded by the law as natural consequences of his wrong, and he is not bound to anticipate the general probability of such acts, any more than a particular act by this or that individual. The rule applies a fortiori to criminal acts. The intervention of a criminal act, however, does not necessarily interrupt the relation of cause and effect between negligence and an injury. If at the time of the negligence, the criminal act might reasonably have been foreseen, the causal chain is not broken by the intervention of such act. * * *

The speed and power of automobiles have increased to the extent that safety experts are now showing keen awareness of their potentials even in the hands of rightful owners and careful operators. Incidents of serious havoc caused by runaway thieves or irresponsible juveniles in stolen or "borrowed" motor vehicles frequently shock the readers of the daily press. With this background must come a recognition of the probable danger of resulting injury consequent to permitting a motor vehicle to become easily available to an unauthorized person through violation of the statute in question. The percentage of cases of this nature or the incidence of injury done where an independent force has intervened after such violation, however, is not the standard or measure of liability. We are here concerned only with the question as to whether or not this intervening force is without or within the range of reasonable anticipation and probability. * * *

* * * [W]e recall the reasoning of Justice Cardozo, that the range of reasonable apprehension is at times for the court, and at times, if varying inferences are possible, a question for the jury. The possibility of varying inferences in a case such as the one before us has been amply demonstrated. * * *

We are in agreement with the court below in our belief that reasonable men might differ on the question where there were special circumstances surrounding the defendant's violation of the statute which may be the proximate cause of the damage that followed. We do not mean to be understood as holding that given a cause similar to the facts in the Palsgraf case we would hold otherwise than in the majority opinion; we do, however, believe that under the circumstances as presented in the case before us we find no persuasive authority and no impelling reasoning for this court to hold, *as a matter of law,* that no actionable negligence can exist.

Questions of negligence, due care and proximate cause are ordinarily questions of fact for a jury to decide. The right of trial by jury is recognized in the Magna Charta, our Declaration of Independence and both our State and Federal constitutions. It is a fundamental right in our democratic judicial system. Questions which are composed of such qualities sufficient to cause reasonable men to arrive at different results should never be determined as matters of law. The debatable quality of issues such as negligence and proximate cause, the fact that fair-minded men might reach different conclusions, emphasize the appropriateness and necessity of leaving such questions to a fact-finding body. The jury is the tribunal under our legal system to decide that type of issue. To withdraw such questions from the jury is to usurp its function. [Citation]

For the foregoing reasons, it is our opinion that the Appellate Court was correct in affirming the judgment of the municipal court of Chicago.

Judgment affirmed.

HERSHEY, J., dissenting.

The majority opinion is contradictory within itself. It first concludes that section 92 of article XIV of the Uniform Traffic Act [Citation] is not an antitheft statute, but is, in fact, a public safety measure. Although the opinion fails to answer in specific fashion its question as to what harm the legislature foresaw and attempted to prevent by the passage of this act, it does ultimately determine that the statute was to prevent accidents caused by a thief in stealing the vehicle. This determination is manifest by the majority's adoption of the Appellate Court determination. The majority thus finds the statute, or at least that part of the statute rendering it unlawful to fail to remove the keys from a parked vehicle, to be an antitheft measure.
*  *  *

The majority concludes that all parts of this statute, except that portion referring to the keys, indicate an intention on the part of the legislature to prevent harm to the public by an inadvertent or negligent movement of a parked vehicle, or through its being driven by a young person devoid of experience, judgment, knowledge, or maturity. It finds that the legislature's purpose in relation to those portions of the statute was not to deter theft. However, the majority then concludes that the portion directing the removal of the keys from the vehicle was to prevent the operation of the vehicle and possible public harm by a thief in flight. The slightest experience renders everyone cognizant of the fact that the removal of automobile ignition keys is only a minor deterrent, if any, to the theft of an automobile and a subsequent flight from detection and pursuit. Consequently, it is only reasonable and logical to construe the legislature's intention in the passage of this portion of the statute in the same light as is attributed to the remainder of the section. One can only conclude, therefore, that the legislature required the removal of the key to prevent a mere negligent or inadvertent starting of the automobile and an ensuing uncontrolled movement thereof. Obviously the legislature could not presume by such legislation to prevent a wilful movement of the vehicle by an unauthorized person. It is generally recognized that one may leave a motor vehicle standing unattended in a public street temporarily, without being guilty of negligence, provided he takes the ordinary precautions of securing it by the appliances with which it is equipped for that purpose, and that if it is thereafter set in motion by the wilful or negligent act of a third person, such wilful or negligent act will be deemed the proximate cause of the accident or injury resulting therefrom and the owner will not be liable. * * *

This section, not being an antitheft measure, and not making the failure to remove the key an absolute act of negligence, cannot constitute the proximate cause of this injury. But for the intervention of the theft the failure to remove the key could not have caused this injury. Moreover, unless the thief was in immediate flight from the scene of his theft, the act of thievery could not even be a factor contributing to the injury. * * *

----

1. The principal case illustrates how much discretion a court may have in determining the purpose of a statute. Was the purpose of this key-in-the-car statute to prevent theft of the car, with resulting loss to the owner and his insurance company and an increased burden on the police? Cf. Anderson v. Theisen (1950) 231 Minn. 369, 43 N.W.2d 272. To prevent the car from being started up by children or other irresponsible people? Cf. Bouldin v. Sategna (1963) 71 N.M. 329, 378 P.2d 370. To prevent joy-riding teenagers from "taking it out for a spree"? To prevent it from being stolen by a tense thief, endangering people in the vicinity while trying to make his get-away?

2. Observe how the two opinions in this case argue for a single purpose. May there not be more than one purpose? Cf. Hines v. Foreman (Tex.Comm.App.1923) 243 S.W. 749. The statute prohibited use of a "cut-out" in the exhaust pipe leading to the muffler, in order to make a zooming or roaring noise. Plaintiff had his cut-out open driving down the streets of a Texas city. He approached a railroad track, and unknown to him because of the noise of the cutout, there was a train coming and he was engaged in a race that ended in a tie. The issue was whether he was contributorily negligent, and he claimed that the statute was irrelevant because its purpose was to prevent harassing noises. Held, it had a double purpose, and one of them was to eliminate noises preventing him from hearing traffic hazards.

3. This statute is part of the Uniform Vehicle Code prepared and revised by the National Committee on Uniform Traffic Laws and Ordinances and continuously monitored and revised. It is in a chapter on safety provisions and committee members have stated that it was intended as a safety measure. Is this relevant? For a strong case holding that the purpose includes a thief making a get-away, with the opinion written by a former torts teacher, see Ross v. Hartman (D.C.Cir. 1943) 139 F.2d 14.

4. Who makes the decision as to the purpose of the statute—judge or jury?

5. How long and how far away should the owner be liable for dangerous driving by the thief? Cf. Liberto v. Holfeldt (1959) 221 Md. 62, 155 A.2d 698 (five days later, considerable distance across city); Wannebo v. Gates (1948) 227 Minn. 194, 34 N.W.2d 695 (get-away only). Suppose the thief intentionally runs into a policeman he thinks is trying to arrest him. Berko v. Freda (1980) 172 N.J.Super. 436, 412 A.2d 821. See Peck, An Exercise Based on Empirical Data: Liability for Harm Caused by Stolen Automobiles, 1969 Wis.L.Rev. 909; Wade, Torts—1961 Tennessee Survey (1962) 15 Vand.L.Rev. 952, 955.

6. Both opinions in the principal case became heavily involved in the problem of proximate cause. There should be no problem of proximate cause if the event is within the hazard that the statute is intended to avert. By deciding the purpose of the statute the court eliminates the proximate cause problem. See Ross v. Hartman, supra n. 3. Is there an element of begging the question by following this procedure? But it may simplify some of the difficulties of proximate cause. Look for it later when the subject of proximate cause is taken up.

7. See Morris, The Role of Criminal Statutes in Negligence Actions (1949) 49 Col.L.Rev. 21, reprinted in Morris, Studies in the Law of Torts (1952) 141 (especially valuable); Morris, The Relation of Criminal Statutes to Tort Liability (1933) 49 Harv.L.Rev. 453; Thayer, Public Wrong and Private Action (1914) 27 Harv.L.Rev. 317. See also James, Statutory Standards and Negligence in Accident Cases (1950) 11 La.L.Rev. 95.

Professors Thayer and Morris have postulated that courts may be reluctant to utilize a statute when it would create a new duty entirely unknown at common law. There is some support for this in the cases. See Brown v. Kelly (1964) 42 N.J. 362, 200 A.2d 781; Fitzwater v. Sunset Empire, Inc. (1972) 263 Or. 276, 502 P.2d 214, both declining to find that ordinances requiring abutting landowners to keep sidewalks in repair and remove snow and ice were enacted for the benefit of pedestrians. Decisions on this issue may have been influenced, at least initially, by the fact that the statute creates an affirmative duty.

8. A statute requires that a seller of a "deadly weapon receive positive identification" of the purchaser from two residents of the state, and keep a record of name, age, address and other details. Defendant sells a gun without complying, and the purchaser uses it on the plaintiff in the course of an armed robbery. Should the defendant be liable? Cf. Hetherton v. Sears, Roebuck & Co. (3 Cir. 1979) 593 F.2d 526, second appeal (3 Cir. 1981) 652 F.2d 1152.

9. Once the statute is declared "out of the case," what issues remain?

10. The effect of the violation of criminal (and other) statutes and regulations on the law of torts is not confined by any means to the tort of

negligence and the doctrine of negligence per se. It has been generally recognized that in furtherance of the purpose of particular legislation and to insure its effectiveness, a court may, despite the absence of a provision to this effect, supply a civil action for damages according relief to a person for whose benefit conduct of another was either proscribed or required by the legislation. Restatement, Second, Torts § 874A. The usual explanation is that the right is "implied" from the legislation. See infra pages 1211–1243.

## BROWN v. SHYNE

Court of Appeals of New York, 1926.
242 N.Y. 176, 151 N.E. 197.

LEHMAN, J. The plaintiff employed the defendant to give chiropractic treatment to her for a disease or physical condition. The defendant had no license to practice medicine, yet, he held himself out as being able to diagnose and treat disease, and, under the provisions of the Public Health Law (Const.Laws, c. 45), he was guilty of a misdemeanor. The plaintiff became paralyzed after she had received nine treatments by the defendant. She claims, and upon this appeal we must assume, that the paralysis was caused by the treatment she received. She has recovered judgment in the sum of $10,000 for the damages caused by said injury. * * *

At the close of the plaintiff's case the plaintiff was permitted to amend the complaint to allege "that in so treating the plaintiff the defendant was engaged in the practice of medicine contrary to and in violation of the provisions of the Public Health Law of the state of New York in such case made and provided, he at the time of so treating plaintiff not being a duly licensed physician or surgeon of the state of New York." Thereafter the trial judge charged the jury that ["from the violation of the statute the jury might infer negligence which produced injury to the plaintiff."] * * *

In so charging the jury * * * the trial justice in my opinion erred.

The provisions of the Public Health Law prohibit the practice of medicine without a license granted upon proof of preliminary training, and after examination intended to show adequate knowledge, are of course intended for the protection of the general public against injury which unskilled and unlearned practitioners might cause. If violation of the statute by the defendant was the proximate cause of the plaintiff's injury, then the plaintiff may recover upon proof of violation. If violation of the statute has no direct bearing on the injury, proof of the violation becomes irrelevant. For injury caused by neglect of duty imposed by the penal law there is civil remedy; but, of course, the injury must follow from the neglect.

Proper formulation of general standards of preliminary education and proper examination of the particular applicant should serve to raise the standards of skill and care generally possessed by members of the profession in this state; but the license to practice medicine confers no additional skill upon the practitioner, nor does it confer immunity from physical injury upon a patient if the practitioner fails to exercise care. Here, injury may have been caused by lack of skill or care; it would not have been obviated if the defendant had possessed a license yet failed to exercise the skill and care required of one practicing medicine. True, if the defendant had not practiced medicine in this state, he could not have injured the plaintiff, but the protection which the statute was intended to provide was against risk of injury by the unskilled or careless practitioner, and, unless the plaintiff's injury was caused by carelessness or lack of skill, the defendant's failure to obtain a license was not connected with the injury. The plaintiff's cause of action is for negligence or malpractice. The defendant undertook to treat the plaintiff for a physical condition which seemed to require remedy. Under our law such treatment may be given only by a duly qualified practitioner who has obtained a license.

The defendant in offering to treat the plaintiff held himself out as qualified to give treatment. He must meet the professional standards of skill and care prevailing among those who do offer treatment lawfully. If injury follows through failure to meet those standards, the plaintiff may recover. The provisions of the Public Health Law may result in the exclusion from practice of some who are unqualified. Even a skilled and learned practitioner who is not licensed commits an offense against the state; but against such practitioners the statute was not intended to protect, for no protection was needed, and neglect to obtain a license results in no injury to the patient and, therefore, no private wrong. The purpose of the statute is to protect the public against unfounded assumption of skill by one who undertakes to prescribe or treat for disease. In order to show that the plaintiff has been injured by defendant's breach of the statutory duty, proof must be given that defendant in such treatment did not exercise the care and skill which would have been exercised by qualified practitioners within the state, and that lack of skill and care caused the injury. Failure to obtain a license as required by law gives rise to no remedy if it has caused no injury. * * *

For these reasons the judgments should be reversed, and a new trial granted, with costs to abide the event.

[The dissenting opinion of CRANE, J., is omitted.]

---

1. Who is more likely to use reasonable care in practicing medicine, the class of persons who are licensed or unlicensed? Should this make any difference in the principal case?

2. In Whipple v. Grandchamp (1927) 261 Mass. 40, 158 N.E. 270, a medical licensing statute was held to establish standards of skill and compe-

tence, and a chiropractor practicing medicine with no license was held negligent as a matter of law. Can the two cases be reconciled?

3. Statutes requiring drivers' licenses for the operation of an automobile have received, in general, the same treatment. New Hampshire used to be an exception. In Johnson v. Boston & Maine R. Co. (1928) 83 N.H. 350, 143 A. 516, it was held that the legislature has made a "positive limitation of right," and for the protection of those on the highway had ruled out even competent drivers. "There is no other practical way to accomplish the desired result. The fit can protect themselves by procuring a license. If they do not, they cannot complain of being classed with the unfit."

Following this, the legislature amended the statute in 1937 to provide that driving without a license "in any civil action shall be prima facie evidence of unfitness to drive." The Johnson case was overruled "in its entirety," and the question is now merely one of whether the driver was in fact competent to drive. Fuller v. Sirois (1951) 97 N.H. 100, 82 A.2d 82.

4. Statutes requiring the registration of automobiles and license plates are commonly held to be merely for purposes of taxation, and to aid the police, and not to give rise to any civil action based upon the violation.

Massachusetts formerly had a unique rule that anyone driving an unregistered car was a "trespasser on the highway," and therefore liable for all injuries he caused, and could not recover himself except for injuries caused intentionally or recklessly. After the Massachusetts court, in Comeau v. Harrington (1955) 333 Mass. 286, 130 N.E.2d 554, had expressed disapproval of the doctrine, but said that any change must be for the legislature, the legislature changed the rule in 1959 by an amendment to the licensing section. It is now provided that the violation shall not be a defense in an action by the violator, but shall be deemed evidence of negligence in an action against him. Mass.Laws 1959, c. 250.

5. See, generally, Gregory, Breach of Criminal Licensing Statutes in Civil Litigation (1951) 36 Corn.L.Q. 622.

## MARTIN v. HERZOG

Court of Appeals of New York, 1920.
228 N.Y. 164, 126 N.E. 814.

Action by Elizabeth Martin, as administratrix of William J. Martin, deceased, against Samuel A. Herzog and another. Judgment for the plaintiff against the named defendant was reversed by the Appellate Division (176 App.Div. 614, 163 N.Y.Supp. 189), and plaintiff appeals.

[Plaintiff's decedent was killed in a collision between the buggy he was driving, and defendant's automobile. It was after dark, and decedent was driving the buggy without lights, in violation of a criminal statute requiring lights. The trial judge refused defendant's request for an instruction that the absence of a light on the plaintiff's vehicle was "prima facie evidence of contributory negligence," and instructed instead that the jury might consider the absence of lights as some evidence of negligence, but that it was not conclusive evidence.

He also granted plaintiff's request for an instruction that "the fact that the plaintiff's intestate was driving without a light is not negligence in itself." The jury returned a verdict for the plaintiff, on which judgment was entered. The Appellate Division reversed for error in the instructions. Plaintiff now appeals to the Court of Appeals.]

CARDOZO, J.   *   *   *   We think the unexcused omission of the statutory signals is more than some evidence of negligence. It is negligence in itself. Lights are intended for the guidance and protection of other travelers on the highway. Highway Law, § 329a. By the very terms of the hypothesis, to omit, willfully or heedlessly, the safeguards prescribed by law for the benefit of another that he may be preserved in life or limb, is to fall short of the standard of diligence to which those who live in organized society are under a duty to conform. That, we think, is now the established rule in this state. [Citations]

In the case at hand, we have an instance of the admitted violation of a statute intended for the protection of travelers on the highway, of whom the defendant at the time was one. Yet the jurors were instructed in effect that they were at liberty in their discretion to treat the omission of lights either as innocent or as culpable. They were allowed to "consider the default as lightly or gravely" as they would (Thomas, J., in the court below). They might as well have been told that they could use a like discretion in holding a master at fault for the omission of a safety appliance prescribed by positive law for the protection of a workman. [Citations] Jurors have no dispensing power, by which they may relax the duty that one traveler on the highways owes under the statute to another. It is error to tell them that they have. The omission of these lights was a wrong, and, being wholly unexcused, was also a negligent wrong. No license should have been conceded to the triers of the facts to find it anything else.

We must be on our guard, however, against confusing the question of negligence with that of the causal connection between the negligence and the injury. A defendant who travels without lights is not to pay damages for his fault, unless the absence of lights is the cause of the disaster. A plaintiff who travels without them is not to forfeit the right to damages, unless the absence of lights is at least a contributing cause of the disaster. To say that conduct is negligence is not to say that it is always contributory negligence. "Proof of negligence in the air, so to speak, will not do." Pollock Torts (10th Ed.) p. 472.

We think, however, that evidence of a collision occurring more than an hour after sundown between a car and an unseen buggy, proceeding without lights, is evidence from which a causal connection may be inferred between the collision and the lack of signals. [Citations] If nothing else is shown to break the connection, we have a case, prima facie sufficient, of negligence contributing to the result.

We are persuaded that the tendency of the charge, and of all the rulings, following it, was to minimize unduly, in the minds of the triers of the facts, the gravity of the decedent's fault. Errors may not be ignored as unsubstantial, when they tend to such an outcome. A statute designed for the protection of human life is not to be brushed aside as a form of words, its commands reduced to the level of cautions, and the duty to obey attenuated into an option to conform.

The order of the Appellate Division should be affirmed, and judgment absolute directed on the stipulation in favor of the defendant, with costs in all courts.

[The dissenting opinion of HOGAN, J., is omitted.]

———

1. The great majority of the courts take the position stated by Cardozo in this case, that when a statute applies to the facts, an unexcused violation is "negligence per se," which must be declared by the court and not left to the jury.

2. California treats such a violation as giving rise to a "presumption" of negligence, which becomes negligence as a matter of law unless the presumption is rebutted. Since it can be rebutted only by showing an excuse for the violation, this appears to come out at much the same place as the "negligence per se" rule. Vermont formerly held the same way, but has apparently swung over to "negligence per se." See Shulins v. New England Ins. Co. (2 Cir. 1966) 360 F.2d 781.

3. A minority of about half a dozen states, such as Massachusetts and New Jersey, hold that the violation is only evidence of negligence, which the jury may accept or reject as it sees fit.

4. The California court had quite a workout on all this in Satterlee v. Orange Glenn School District (1947) 29 Cal.2d 581, 177 P.2d 279, with Traynor, Edmonds and Carter, JJ., each writing an opinion, and taking a different one of the foregoing three positions. Edmonds carried the majority of the court with his "presumption" theory. The case has a good exposition of the arguments.

5. Ordinances, in general, have been treated in the same manner as statutes. A few states, such as New York and Michigan, which hold the violation of a statute to be negligence per se, have treated the violation of an ordinance as only evidence of negligence. Kentucky once made this distinction, in the case of a foolish ordinance providing a speed limit of six miles an hour for railway trains. Louisville & N. R. Co. v. Dalton (1897) 102 Ky. 290, 43 S.W. 431. The case was overruled, and the violation of any ordinance held negligence per se, in Greyhound Terminal v. Thomas (1947) 307 Ky. 44, 209 S.W.2d 478.

6. There is a similar conflict as to the effect of the regulations of administrative bodies, acting under statutory authority. These are sometimes given the effect of negligence per se, sometimes held to be only evidence of

negligence. There is more of a tendency toward the latter position than in the case of statutes. See Hassan v. Stafford (3 Cir. 1973) 472 F.2d 88, noted in 77 Temp.L.Rev. 739; Morris, The Role of Administrative Safety Measures in Negligence Actions (1949) 28 Tex.L.Rev. 143.

7. Advisory safety codes promulgated by governmental authority, industry or voluntary associations may be admissible on the issue of negligence if properly identified and shown through expert testimony to have general acceptance in the industrial community. See Lemery v. O'Shea Dennis, Inc. (1972) 112 N.H. 199, 291 A.2d 616; Philo, Use of Safety Standards, Codes and Practices in Tort Litigation (1965) 41 Notre Dame Law. 1; Comment, Admissibility of Safety Codes, Rules and Standards in Negligence Cases (1970) 37 Tenn.L.Rev. 381. Many jurisdictions reject them, however, on the ground that they are hearsay. See Annot. (1961) 75 A.L.R.2d 778.

8. The fact that a statute is inapplicable, either because it is not intended for the protection of the class of persons in which the plaintiff is included, or because it was not intended for protection against the particular risk, does not necessarily rule it out entirely as evidence bearing on the issue of negligence. Thus in Hansen v. Kemmish (1926) 201 Iowa 1008, 208 N.W. 277, a statute, intended only to prevent the misbreeding of animals, provided that hogs should be confined by fences of specified strength. Defendant fenced his hogs with a fence of less strength; one of them broke through the fence, escaped into the highway, and wrecked plaintiff's car. It was held that, while the statute did not define a standard of conduct to be adopted as a matter of law, the jury could consider it as bearing on the kind of fence necessary for the proper confinement of hogs.

### ZENI v. ANDERSON

Supreme Court of Michigan, 1976.
397 Mich. 117, 243 N.W.2d 270.

WILLIAMS, Justice. * * * The accident which precipitated this action occurred one snowy morning, March 7, 1969, when the temperature was 11° F, the sky was clear and the average snow depth was 21 inches. Plaintiff Eleanor Zeni, then a 56-year-old registered nurse, was walking to her work at the Northern Michigan University Health Center in Marquette. Instead of using the snow-covered sidewalk, which in any event would have required her to walk across the street twice to get to her job, she traveled along a well-used pedestrian snowpath, with her back to oncoming traffic.

Defendant Karen Anderson, a college student, was driving within the speed limit in a steady stream of traffic on the same street. Ms. Anderson testified that she had turned on the defroster in the car and her passenger said she had scraped the windshield. An eyewitness whose deposition was read at trial, however, testified that defendant's windshield was clouded and he doubted that the occupants could see out. He also testified that the car was traveling too close to the curb and that he could tell plaintiff was going to be hit.

Defendant's car struck the plaintiff on the driver's right side. Ms. Anderson testified she first saw the plaintiff between a car parked on the right-hand side of the road and defendant's car, and that she did not hear nor feel her car strike Ms. Zeni. The eyewitness reported seeing plaintiff flip over the fender and hood. He said when he went over to help her his knees were on or inside the white line delineating a parking space. A security officer observed blood stains on the pavement approximately 13 feet from the curb.

Ms. Zeni's injuries were serious and included an intra-cerebral subdural hematoma which required neurosurgery. She has retrograde amnesia and therefore, because she does not remember anything from the time she began walking that morning until sometime after the impact, there is no way to determine whether she knew defendant was behind her. Following an extended period of convalescence, plaintiff, still suffering permanent disability, could return to work on only a part-time basis.

Testimony at trial indicated that it was common for nurses to use the roadway to reach the Health Center, and a security officer testified that in the wintertime it was safer to walk there than on the one sidewalk. Apparently, several days before the accident, Ms. Zeni had indeed fallen on the sidewalk. Although she was not hurt when she fell, the Director of University Security was hospitalized when he fell on the walk.

Defendant, however, maintained that plaintiff's failure to use that sidewalk constituted contributory negligence because, she said, it violated M.C.L.A. § 257.655; M.S.A. § 9.2355, which requires:

"Where sidewalks are provided, it shall be unlawful for pedestrians to walk upon the main traveled portion of the highway. Where sidewalks are not provided, pedestrians shall, when practicable, walk on the left side of the highway facing traffic which passes nearest."

\* \* \*

[There was a jury verdict for plaintiff in the trial court. The court of appeals reversed because of instructions on the subject of last clear chance. Discussion of last clear chance is omitted.]

*A. Violation of Statute as Rebuttable Presumption.* In a growing number of states, the rule concerning the proper role of a penal statute in a civil action for damages is that violation of the statute which has been found to apply to a particular set of facts establishes only a prima facie case of negligence, a presumption which may be rebutted by a showing on the part of the party violating the statute of an adequate excuse under the facts and circumstances of the case. The excuses may not necessarily be applicable in a criminal action, since, in the absence of legislatively-mandated civil penalties, acceptance of the criminal statute itself as a standard of care in a civil action is purely discretionary. See Comment and Illustrations, 2 Restatement Torts, 2d, § 288A, pp. 33–37.

Michigan cases have in effect followed this rule. For example, over a 65 year period, cases concerning the effect in a negligence action of violation of the statute requiring vehicles to keep to the right side of the road have almost consistently adopted a rebuttable presumption approach, even though the language of the statute is not written in terms of a presumption.  *  *  *

We think the test of the applicable law was well stated by our brother Justice Fitzgerald when he was a judge on the Court of Appeals. In Lucas v. Carson, 38 Mich.App. 552, 196 N.W.2d 819 (1972), he analyzed a case where, in spite of defendant's precautions, her vehicle "inexplicably slid into the rear of plaintiff's stopped car" where plaintiff was waiting at a traffic signal.  *  *  *

First, in analyzing whether the presumption of negligence attributed to a rear-end collision had been rebutted in the case before them, the Court of Appeals acknowledged that the usual grounds for rebuttal, sudden emergency, did not appear in this case. In effect accepting defendant's contention that the doctrine of sudden emergency was not the sole basis for rebutting a presumption of negligence, the Court held:

"The general rule appears to be that evidence required to rebut this presumption *as a matter of law* should be positive, unequivocal, strong, and credible. In the case at bar, defendant driver contended that she was at all times driving in a reasonable and prudent manner.  *  *  *  [T]here was sufficient evidence at least to generate a jury question regarding rebutting of the presumption."  *  *  *

This is the approach we follow today.  *  *  *

[An] attraction of this approach is that it is fair. "If there is sufficient excuse or justification, there is ordinarily no violation of a statute and the statutory standard is inapplicable." Satterlee v. Orange Glenn School Dist. of San Diego County, 29 Cal.2d 581, 594, 177 P.2d 279, 286 (1947) (dissenting in part). It would be unreasonable to adhere to an automatic rule of negligence "where observance would subject a person to danger which might be avoided by disregard of the general rule." Tedla v. Ellman, 280 N.Y. 124, 131–132, 19 N.E.2d 987, 991 (1939).

The approach is logical. Liability without fault is not truly negligence, and in the absence of a clear legislative mandate to so extend liability, the courts should be hesitant to do so on their own. Because these are, after all, criminal statutes, a court is limited in how far it may go in plucking a statute from its criminal milieu and inserting it into the civil arena. The rule of rebuttable presumption has arisen in part in response to this concern, and in part because of the reluctance to go to the other extreme and in effect, discard or disregard the legislative standard.  *  *  *

*B. Violation of Statute as Negligence Per Se.* While some Michigan cases seem to speak of negligence per se as a kind of strict liability, Holbert v. Staniak, 359 Mich. 283, 290, 102 N.W.2d 186 (1960), an examination indicates that there are a number of conditions that attempt to create a more reasonable approach than would result from an automatic application of a per se rule.

[Reference is made here to the court's construing the statute, determining its purpose and applying principles of proximate cause.]

Despite such limitations, the judge-made rule of negligence per se has still proved to be too inflexible and mechanical to satisfy thoughtful commentators and judges. It is forcefully argued that no matter how a court may attempt to confine the negligence per se doctrine, if defendant is liable despite the exercise of due care and the availability of a reasonable excuse, this is really strict liability, and not negligence. Prosser, The Law of Torts (4th ed.), § 36, p. 197. Since it is always possible that the Legislature's failure to deal specifically with the question of private rights was not accidental, and that there might have been no legislative intent to change the law of torts, such treatment of the statute may well be a gross perversion of the legislative will. It is troublesome, too, that "potentially ruinous civil liability" may follow from a "minor infraction of petty criminal regulations", [citation] or may, in a jurisdiction burdened by contributory negligence, serve to deprive an otherwise deserving plaintiff of a much-needed recovery. * * *

*C. Violation of Statute as Evidence of Negligence.* Just as the rebuttable presumption approach to statutory violations in a negligence context apparently arose, at least in part, from dissatisfaction with the result of a mechanical application of the per se rule, a parallel development in our state with respect to infractions of ordinances and of administrative regulations, has been that violations of these amount to only evidence of negligence. [Citations]

We have not, however, chosen to join that small minority which has decreed that violation of a statute is only evidence of negligence. In view of the fairness and ease with which the rebuttable presumption standard has been and can be administered, we believe the litigants are thereby well served and the Legislature is given appropriate respect.

*D. Application of Statutory Standard to This Case.* We have seen, therefore, that while some of our Michigan cases seem to present negligence per se as an unqualified rule, the fact of the matter is that there are a number of qualifications which make application of this rule not really a per se approach at all. Not only must the statutory purpose doctrine and the requirement of proximate cause be satisfied, but the alleged wrongdoer has an opportunity to come forward with evidence rebutting the presumption of negligence.

An accurate statement of our law is that when a court adopts a penal statute as the standard of care in an action for negligence, violation of that statute establishes a prima facie case of negligence, with the determination to be made by the finder of fact whether the party accused of violating the statute has established a legally sufficient excuse. If the finder of fact determines such an excuse exists, the appropriate standard of care then becomes that established by the common law. Such excuses shall include, but shall not be limited to, those suggested by the Second Restatement of Torts, § 288A, and shall be determined by the circumstances of each case.

In the case at bar, moreover, the statute itself provides a guideline for the jury, for a violation will not occur when it is impracticable to use the sidewalk or to walk on the left side of a highway. This is ordinarily a question for the finder of fact, [citation] and thus the statute itself provides not only a legislative standard of care which may be accepted by the court, but a legislatively mandated excuse as well. *  *  *

*  *  * [W]e find the jury was adequately instructed as to the effect of the violation of this particular statute on plaintiff's case. *  *  *

The Court of Appeals is reversed and the trial court is affirmed. Costs to plaintiff.

———————

1.  Section 288A of the Restatement, referred to in the principal case, reads as follows:

"(1) An excused violation of a legislative enactment or an administrative regulation is not negligence.

"(2) Unless the enactment or regulation is construed not to permit such excuse, its violation is excused when

"(a) the violation is reasonable because of the actor's incapacity;

"(b) he neither knows nor should know of the occasion for compliance;

"(c) he is unable after reasonable diligence or care to comply;

"(d) he is confronted by an emergency not due to his own misconduct;

"(e) compliance would involve a greater risk of harm to the actor or to others."

This list is "not intended to be exclusive."

2.  When a prosecution under a criminal statute is involved, the "soft spot" is normally the discretionary authority of the district attorney in deciding whether to prosecute. Within that discretion he can determine that the accused's conduct was sufficiently excusable that a prosecution would not be fair. There is no such "soft spot" in a civil action for negligence. The plaintiff has been injured and he wants compensation regardless of any excuse that the defendant might present. To prevent unjust results, the common law has come to recognize that excuses should be recognized in some instances.

3.  The principal case classifies the approaches to this problem into three groups: (1) negligence per se, (2) prima facie negligence and (3) some evidence of negligence. Most commentators would agree with this

classification. But there may be disagreement on the content of the first two groups. The Restatement espouses the negligence per se approach, but it also permits excuses as indicated in § 288A. The two concepts are regarded as fitting together in an accurate delineation of the per se approach. The second classification (prima facie negligence) would then apply to jurisdictions in which the issue goes to the jury even when there is no credible evidence of a recognized excuse, but merely testimony that the defendant acted with due care. It is in this situation alone that a distinction exists between the two classes. These differing classifications, of course, are merely a matter of semantics. What significance do they have on the content of an instruction to the jury?

4. In light of the Restatement, Second, and the principal case, how might the following situations be decided?

A. A statute provides that no vehicle shall be driven on the highway at night without a tail light. Without any fault or knowledge of defendant, his tail light goes out while he is driving at night, and as a result plaintiff is injured in a collision with him. Brotherton v. Day & Night Fuel Co. (1937) 192 Wash. 362, 73 P.2d 788. What if defendant discovered that the light was out, but continued to drive carefully to a near-by filling station? Taber v. Smith (Tex.Civ.App.1930) 26 S.W.2d 722.

B. A statute prohibits automobile drivers from passing at an intersection. Defendant approaches an intersection concealed from view and not marked by any warning sign, of whose existence he is ignorant, and as he reaches it attempts to pass. Hullander v. McIntyre (1960) 78 S.D. 453, 104 N.W.2d 40.

C. A child, too young to know or appreciate the statute, crosses a street in the middle of the block? Morley v. Rogers (1953) 122 Utah 540, 252 P.2d 231; Maker v. Wellin (1958) 214 Or. 332, 327 P.2d 793, 329 P.2d 1114. Suppose an adult does not know of the jay-walking statute.

D. Defendant drives on the left side of the road to avoid hitting a child who has darted out from the right. Burlie v. Stephens (1920) 113 Wash. 182, 193 P. 684; Sims v. Eleazar (1921) 116 S.C. 41, 106 S.E. 854. Would it be negligence *not* to violate the statute?

––––––––

## FREUND v. DeBUSE

Supreme Court of Oregon, 1972.
264 Or. 447, 506 P.2d 491.

DENECKE, Justice. The plaintiff alleged he was injured when the car he was driving was struck in the rear by defendant's pickup. The defendant testified the collision occurred because his brakes unexpectedly failed. The jury returned a verdict for the defendant and plaintiff appeals.

The plaintiff contends the trial court erred in failing to instruct the jury that the defendant was liable. The basis of plaintiff's motion was that the defendant was negligent per se because his brakes were not "adequate to control the movement of and to stop and hold such [his] vehicle" and his brakes were not "maintained in good working order," all in violation of ORS 483.444. The defendant's testimony was that after the collision he "tore apart" his wheel and found a broken brake drum which was the cause of the brake failure.

Just weeks ago in Barnum v. Williams, 264 Or. 71, 504 P.2d 122 (1972), we expressed the difficulty this court has had in the application of the negligence per se doctrine. The *Barnum* case involved an "operational" motor vehicle statute, driving on the "wrong side" of the road. We held "that if a party is in violation of a motor vehicle statute, such a party is negligent as a matter of law unless such party introduces evidence from which the trier of fact could find that the party was acting as a reasonably prudent person under the circumstances." [Citation] The issue here is whether this rule also should be applied to violations of motor vehicle equipment statutes. We hold it should.

Initially, the law of Oregon was that violation of a statute setting the standard required for motor vehicle equipment was negligence per se. We stated that it was negligence per se although the violator might have acted as a reasonably prudent person. Nettleton v. James, 212 Or. 375, 386, 319 P.2d 879 (1958). In the same case, however, we stated that if the violation of the equipment statute was because of a "latent defect" the operator might not be liable.

In McConnell v. Herron, 240 Or. 486, 493, 402 P.2d 726 (1965), in which the defendant had defective brakes, we departed from the strict negligence per se doctrine. We stated: " * * * We are now of the opinion that the motor vehicle code was not intended to eliminate the element of fault from the law of torts. * * *. Accordingly, we apply to equipment defects the same rule we have applied in the past to operational errors. Liability in both situations is based upon fault rather than upon a theory of absolute liability." 240 Or. at 491, 402 P.2d at 729.

We did not, however, "apply to equipment defects the same rule we have applied in the past to operational errors." Instead, we adopted a rule somewhere between the rule applicable to operational errors and our former rule for equipment statute violations. We stated a party would be excused from a violation of an equipment statute if he could prove "that his noncompliance was caused by circumstances beyond his control and that it was impossible, regardless of his degree of care, for him to comply with the statute." [Citation]

We were quickly called upon to apply the standard applied in McConnell v. Herron, supra to violations of both equipment and operational statutes. In Pozsgai v. Porter, 249 Or. 84, 86–88, 435 P.2d 818 (1968) we acknowledge that we were applying a different negligence per se rule for violations of equipment statutes than for violations of operational statutes. We admitted that "theoretically" there may be "no justification for the rule of *McConnell* which treats the violation of safety equipment statutes differently than the violation of operational statutes." [Citation]

In Ainsworth v. Deutschman, 251 Or. 596, 446 P.2d 187 (1968), we held that the statement of the rule in McConnell v. Herron, supra, for violations of the equipment statutes was incorrect. We adopted the suggested language in Pozsgai v. Porter, supra, and stated that violations of equipment statutes would not be negligence per se if such violations could not be avoided by the exercise of the highest degree of care, although it was not "impossible, regardless of the degree of care he might have exercised, for him to comply with the statute." [Citation]

There is no logical or empirical basis for treating violations of vehicle equipment statutes differently than vehicle operational statutes and our experience has taught us that attempts to preserve any distinction have resulted in confusion.

McConnell v. Herron, supra and Ainsworth v. Deutschman, supra, are overruled insofar as they hold that violations of vehicle equipment statutes are negligence per se unless the violator can establish that the violation occurred despite his exercise of a standard of care higher than that of a reasonably prudent person. We hold, as we did in Barnum v. Williams, supra, "that if a party is in violation of a motor vehicle [equipment] statute, such a party is negligent as a matter of law unless such party introduces evidence from which the trier of fact could find that the party was acting as a reasonably prudent person under the circumstances." [Citation]

The next question is whether the evidence introduced by the defendant is sufficient for a jury to find that the defendant acted as a reasonably prudent person despite his violation of the statute. We find that it is.

The vehicle was a 1955 pickup which defendant had purchased in 1968, about eight months prior to the collision. The jury could find that the defendant had no prior trouble with the brakes except that about three weeks before the collision he adjusted them. He testified that because of normal wear of the brake lining he had to push the brake pedal down too far to get braking. He corrected this by adjusting the pedal.

The defendant testified the broken brake drum caused the brake failure in this manner:

"A. * * * [Y]our brake drum is round with brake lining. They push out against the brake drum. And this brake drum cracked and spread out under the pressure of the application of the brakes, allowing the—excessive amount of fluid to enter the wheel cylinder. The piston that pushes the brake lining out, causing the brake pedal to go to the floor. * * *

"Q.   Where does all that fluid go when you push on your pedal?

"A.   You have a wheel cylinder drum.   It is a small cylinder on a wheel with a piston in it.   During normal braking, the brake lining will only push so far and you will only travel a short distance, but due to the broken drum, you travel the whole distance;  the cylinder absorbs all the fluid that was in the master cylinder."

We find this to be sufficient evidence to enable the jury to find that the defendant acted as a reasonably prudent person.   When there is no prior warning of any possible defect in the brakes a reasonable vehicle operator is not required to "tear apart" the wheel to inspect for a defect.

Affirmed.

McALLISTER, Justice (dissenting).   In my dissenting opinion in Barnum v. Williams, Or., 504 P.2d 122, 127 (1972) I pointed out that the majority had incorrectly interpreted our prior cases involving motor vehicle operational statutes.   In the present case the majority overrules our prior decisions involving safety equipment statutes.   In my opinion the two lines of cases, although applying different standards, were, prior to *Barnum,* entirely consistent.   For the reasons stated in my dissent in that case, I cannot join the majority in abandoning the rule of negligence per se.

Moreover, in my opinion, the defendant failed to meet his burden of proof that he could not even, by the exercise of the highest degree of care, discover the defect in the brake drum.

I dissent.

––––––––

1.   This case illustrates the difficulties one court has had in attempting to find the most suitable adjustment for applying a bad-brakes statute. Other states have experienced similar difficulties with the construction of this type of statute, and the interpretations range all the way from strict liability, making the defendant liable if his brakes fail to execute properly without regard to whether the condition was discoverable or not, Spalding v. Waxler (1965) 2 Ohio St.2d 1, 205 N.E.2d 890, 31 O.O.2d 1, to ordinary negligence, essentially making the statute ineffective in any respect, Phillips v. Britannia Hygienic Laundry Co. [1923] 1 K.B. 539.   Cf. Maloney v. Rath (1968) 69 Cal.2d 442, 71 Cal.Rptr. 897, 445 P.2d 513, allowing an excuse but holding that the duty to use care to maintain the brakes in compliance with the statute cannot be delegated even to a repairman.

2.   Certain types of statutes are commonly interpreted to make the defendant liable without regard to his negligence or excuse for the violation they include:

A.   Child labor acts, providing under criminal penalty that no minor under a minimum age shall be employed in certain occupations, as in Krutlies v. Bulls Head Coal Co. (1915) 249 Pa. 162, 94 A. 459;  Blanton v. Kellioka Coal Co. (1921) 192 Ky. 220, 232 S.W. 614.

B. Pure Food Acts that prohibit the commercial sale of adulterated food. Doherty v. S. S. Kresge Co. (1938) 227 Wis. 661, 278 N.W. 437; Bolitho v. Safeway Stores (1937) 109 Mont. 213, 95 P.2d 443.

C. The Federal Safety Appliance Act, requiring that railway cars used in interstate commerce be equipped with automatic couplers and other safety devices, in good operating condition. O'Donnell v. Elgin, J. & E. R. Co. (1949) 338 U.S. 384. Accord, St. Louis S. W. R. Co. v. Williams (5 Cir. 1968) 397 F.2d 147 (Boiler Inspection Act).

D. Various factory acts making specific requirements for the safety of employees. Koenig v. Patrick Const. Corp. (1948) 298 N.Y. 313, 83 N. E.2d 133; Continental Can Co. v. Horton (8 Cir. 1957) 250 F.2d 637.

E. "Safe place" statutes, requiring lights and other protection in tenement houses, or premises open to the public. Monsour v. Excelsior Tobacco Co. (Mo.App.1938) 115 S.W.2d 219; Smulczeski v. City Center of Music and Drama (1957) 3 N.Y.2d 498, 146 N.E.2d 769.

F. Statutes prohibiting the sale of firearms and other dangerous objects to minors. See Note (1960) 20 La.L.Rev. 796.

3. When strict liability is imposed because no excuse is permitted, it often is held that the legislative purpose cannot be given full effect unless the defenses of contributory negligence and assumption of risk are made unavailable to the defendant.

4. *Reasonable Care Per Se.* Suppose defendant shows that he complied with all regulatory statutes and administrative regulations. Should his conduct be deemed "reasonable care per se"? See Raymond v. Riegel Textile Corp. (1 Cir. 1973) 484 F.2d 1025 (Flammable Fabrics Act); Black v. Public Service Electric & Gas Co. (1970) 56 N.J. 63, 265 A.2d 129, 136 (evidence of care); Licha v. Northern Pacific R. Co. (1937) 201 Minn. 427, 276 N.W. 813; Wilson v. Piper Aircraft Corp. (1978) 282 Or. 61, 577 P.2d 1322. Should the answer depend on how completely the product or activity is regulated by government?

# APPENDIX E

More Long Essay Questions

1
QUESTION ONE
(ONE HOUR)

A, B, and C cut across the property of D on their way home after an evening at Tony's Tavern. The footpath across D's land, "Blackacre," frequently was used by patrons of Tony's as a shortcut from the drinking establishment to town where most of them lived. A, B, and C were feeling the effects of numerous rounds of ale quaffed during the course of the evening.

While on the footpath, they were beset by robbers X, Y, and Z. X announced, "Stand and deliver. Your money or your lives." Y struck A and B with a heavy stick, knocking both of them unconscious. Z relieved them of their valuables: wallets, rings, watches, and money.

As Y approached C, C leaped forward and wrestled the stick from Y's hand. Y turned to run, but C hit him over the head, killing him. X and Z, fearing for their lives, ran away, with C in hot pursuit.

Hearing a commotion, D came out of his house and saw C chasing X and Z with stick in hand. Presuming that C was attacking X and Z, he subdued C by confronting him with a loaded gun. Over C's vocal protests, D locked him in a closet until the sheriff could be summoned.

D did not bother to try to stop X and Z, assuming that in capturing C he had rescued them from danger. In fact, the two thieves took the occasion to continue their flight, cutting through the woods of Blackacre. Unfortunately for them, X ran off a bluff on the property, breaking both legs and an arm in the fall, while Z, taking a different route, fell into a concealed pit set out by D to capture bears and other wild animals that roamed Blackacre. Z received a painful injury to his posterior when he landed on a metal bear trap.

Meanwhile, A and B regained consciousness, and discovered Y's body. Thinking, perhaps, that they might be held responsible for Y's untimely departure from this terrestrial orb, they, too, began to run through the woods of Blackacre. Both fell into D's gravel quarry, which was not apparent to them because it was night.

The splashing in the quarry aroused D, who had secured C in the closet by this time. When D got to the quarry, he discovered A and B. Because A was closer to shore, D attempted to rescue A by holding out to him a long branch; this attempt was successful, and D was able to pull A to shore. Then, D told A that because B was his (A's) friend, he (A) could rescue him (B) while he (D) went home to wait for the sheriff. A, who was exhausted, did nothing, and B drowned.

In this whole pitiful affair, who is liable to whom for what in civil tort actions that may be brought?

2
QUESTION TWO
(ONE HOUR)

The Exxoff Oil Corporation sold improperly refined jet fuel to Untied Airlines. Untied stored the fuel at its gates at Lax Airport in El Lei, a city on the West Coast. Several of Untied's pilots complained to company brass that they were having trouble getting enough power for liftoff after refueling at Lax. The fleet of Untied jets was inspected, and all were found to be in good condition. Untied did not test the fuel in its storage tanks.

On the night of August 12, Fritz "Flyboy" Mondo and Delia Rownde went out for a wild night in El Lei. "Flyboy" and Delia were pilot and chief stewardess respectively on Untied Flight 13, departing from Lax for Honolulu at 7:55 a.m. Nursing terrible hangovers but otherwise sated from their night of excess, the two appeared at the airport in time to get Flight 13 underway.

With 295 passengers and a crew of ten (10), all normal preflight procedures and safety checks were undertaken, and the aircraft was cleared for departure. As part of the preparation for takeoff, Flight 13 had been refueled using the adulterated Exxoff jet fuel in Untied's storage tanks.

During the previous night, a heavy fog from the ocean just west of the airport had blanketed the city, combining with the normally prevailing air pollution to reduce visibility to a point just above that which would require closing the airport. Air traffic controllers could have increased the intervals between takeoffs as a safety measure, but they did not.

When cleared for takeoff, Captain "Flyboy" noticed as he increased his speed taxiing down the runway that the aircraft was not able to attain full power. Still, he believed he could get the plane off the ground. He did, but it promptly dropped back down, landing in the ocean about one mile beyond the runway it had so recently departed. "Flyboy's" comments, recorded on the plane's "little black box," cannot be reprinted here.

Delia, rather than direct the passengers to the emergency exits, ran screaming to the cockpit to see if "Flyboy" had survived. He had. The tail of the plane broke off on impact with the seats furthest aft, and sank like a rock along with the 70 passengers and two (2) crew members sitting in the seats. Most of the other passengers were injured on impact, but many of them were able to extricate themselves from their seats and escape from the cabin. One man with a heart condition was struck by a heart attack and died in his seat. Once in the water, some of the survivors were able to board inflatable life rafts; others clung to their buoyant seat backs; others attempted to tread water.

When Flight 13 went down, Fisch and O'Kelly were sailing in Fisch's new catamaran in the vicinity. The impact of the crash produced a huge wave, which overturned the catamaran. Fisch was able to swim, and made his way back to the capsized vessel; O'Kelly regrettably could not, and was lost at sea.

Rescue efforts were hampered by the fog; a rescue helicopter sent out by Lax Airport had to return to the airport after arriving at the scene, because visibility was so poor that the pilot thought it would endanger his crew to participate in the rescue effort. Eventually, some 114 survivors were pulled from the drink, including "Flyboy" and Delia, who had made their way together to one of the life rafts. The death toll was set at 195 (not including O'Kelly) after it was determined that four of those who perished were pregnant women. Three of the deceased were eaten by sharks who happened to be feeding in the area.

While the rescue effort was underway, an explosion rocked the sunken plane. This was explained when a note was found at the gate from which Flight 13 had departed at Lax Airport; the note read: "Death to American swine. I carry a bomb which will destroy Flight 13 at 8:25 a.m. You cannot stop me. I die for Allah, Colonel Khadafy, and the revolution. Abdul Chakakhan." Untied's records indicated that a passenger, A. Chakakhan, had boarded the ill-fated flight.

Discuss the issues raised by the facts, including liability of the potential defendants, theories upon which potential plaintiffs might proceed, and damages recoverable. You may assume that there are wrongful death and survival statutes. You do not need to discuss any defenses (e.g.--contributory negligence, assumption of risk).


PART I
Essay Question
(1 hour)

Wilson Badde was the mayor of Filthytown, a large northeastern city. Living in the city were members of FOAM (Filthytown Organization Against Movement), a radical group whose motto, "Filthy Is Beautiful," was lived out in their daily lives. Repeated efforts by the city to get FOAM to clean up its act were fruitless. FOAM members were cited numerous times for violations of health ordinances prohibiting leaving refuse on the premises, keeping livestock within the city limits, and refusing to permit city building and health inspectors into the house to look for other violations.

The city was able to obtain a court order condemning the FOAM house, but the residents refused to leave; in fact, they barricaded themselves inside with an arsenal of weapons which they used to threaten neighbors and passersby.

In response to this crisis, Mayor Badde called in the Filthytown Police S.W.A.T. team which cordoned the area and took positions facing the FOAM house. Fearing a bloodbath if S.W.A.T. stormed FOAM, Badde ordered a police helicopter to drop an explosive device on the FOAM house to open a hole in the roof through which tear gas could be lobbed. Instead of a low grade concussion explosive, a high explosive incendiary device was used, which ignited the wooden structure of the FOAM house.

The fire quickly spread from house to house; soon, the entire block was engulfed. The Filthytown Fire Department was called by Mayor Badde to fight the conflagration. To prevent the spread of the fire, Mayor Badde ordered three houses at the end of the block to be dynamited before the flames reached them. Because of this, the owners were unable to remove their belongings.

One of the fire trucks severed an electric power line. Tad Cobble, a TV news commentator covering the event, stepped on the power line and was electrocuted. Acne Market, across the street, was without power for 24 hours during which time all the frozen goods, meat, poultry and fish were ruined. Looters removed many canned goods from the market shelves.

The FOAM members in the house were inevitably consumed by the holocaust. Rex Skewer, a bystander, and Smokey deBarre, a fireman, ran into the house to attempt to rescue survivors; they were able to pull out one small child, although they saw a grown FOAM member trapped under a fallen timber pleading for help. Skewer and deBarre decided it was too risky to go back into the building. "I'm not risking my neck for some radical," remarked deBarre. Skewer collapsed of smoke inhalation and was taken to the hospital.

When the havoc was surveyed, twenty houses including the FOAM home and the three houses dynamited to prevent the spread of the fire were totally destroyed. Ten people died including nine FOAM residents and Cobble who was electrocuted. The Acne Market incurred losses of inventory. A number of firemen plus Skewer were treated for injuries. Little Rennie Quist, the child who was pulled from the FOAM house, continues to have nightmares of the event during which he courted death and witnessed the supreme agony of his mother burned to death by the flames.

What tort actions may be brought against whom in this fact pattern? What theories may be used, and what damages may be recovered? What defenses may the various defendants employ? Assume for purposes of this question that the state in which Filthytown is located has not adopted a comparative negligence statute, and that sovereign immunity has been abolished as to municipalities. Assume also that all city employees were acting within the scope of their employment responsibilities.

ESSAY QUESTION


Union Halide operated a plant that produced fertilizer near Watsamatta, Indiana, a small town on the outskirts of the Chicago metropolitan area. The plant was built in an area populated primarily by dairy farmers, although over the years encroaching suburbs in the form of residential communities and shopping centers had substantially altered the pastoral setting of Watsamatta and environs. By 1985, the town had expanded to the point that residential areas were directly across the Bopaul River from the plant, which had been built originally about five miles from the town.

In 1965, before the present growth of Watsamatta occurred, a number of the local dairy farmers had filed a nuisance action against Union Halide charging that it was dumping chemical waste into the Bopaul River causing damages to them in the form of harm to dairy cattle and grain as well as diminution in the value of their land. A settlement approved by the court was reached under which the plaintiffs in that action received a lump sum award as compensation for all past and future damages incurred as a result of Union Halide's activities.

Since 1965, a number of the farms have changed hands. The new owners fall into two groups: farmers who purchased their land from the previous owners, and suburbanites who purchased their homes from real estate developers who had bought out the original farmers. It is clear that none of the homeowners was informed of the prior suit or of Union Halide's continuing activities by the developers, although careful investigation on the part of potential buyers would have disclosed such facts. The farmer sellers all had communicated to their immediate purchasers that future suits against Union would not be barred because that is what their attorney in the first suit had said.

Many of the new property owners, upon learning of Union's polluting and their own damages, decided to file suit in the spring of 1985. They had gone to company officials to request that the dumping of chemicals cease or that the plant be closed, without success. They had gone to government officials at all levels who were all unwilling to get involved because of the economic benefit Union Halide provides to the region. The property owners believe that a civil suit is the only course of action left to them at this time.

On April 1, 1985, during the evening shift at the Union Halide plant, a leak in one of the chemical storage tanks resulted in the release of a cloud of toxic chemical gas into the atmosphere. The wind carried the cloud across the Bopaul River and over the farms and residential areas on the other side. The ensuing pestilence wreaked havoc on the countryside by destroying crops, killing livestock, and contaminating water. The toll in human life was 489, although countless individuals who did not die suffered injuries, some temporary, but others permanent. Fortunately, the toxic cloud dissipated before reaching the center of Watsamatta or Chicago beyond.

The accident occurred when a valve, which was supposed to control the release of chemical gasses into a purification chamber before releasing them into the atmosphere, malfunctioned. The valve was produced by the Valvo Corporation for Chemtank, Inc., the manufacturer of the chemical storage tank and purification system. The tank and system were built to specification specifically for the Union Halide Watsamatta plant, although similar systems had been produced and were operating without problem throughout the world. In fact, the Watsamatta plant had had no previous problems with the system.

A worker at the Union plant had not turned off the system when the pressure in the tank began to rise above the normal operating range for the system, but the valve malfunctioned at a level of pressure below that for which it had been tested. The test results had been communicated by Valvo to Chemtank and then to Union.

The day after the disaster, Marvin Bellicose arrived in Watsamatta from California where he practiced law, armed with a team of investigators, a legal secretary, and his press agent. Making representations that he was the greatest tort lawyer in the world, that he had won big verdicts in similar cases before, and that he would represent clients in an Indiana suit against Union Halide, Bellicose began the arduous task of lining up clients.

On April 10, the Watsamatta Tattler printed an expose of Bellicose and his practices. The Tattler purchased the story from a freelance journalist, Patrick O'Kelly, who had made a career of following Bellicose around the world writing stories about his flamboyant behavior and notorious cases. (Ironically, some time earlier O'Kelly had miraculously survived an airline disaster in which Bellicose had represented him and a number of other plaintiffs; unfortunately, O'Kelly lost the case because he was an unforeseeable plaintiff.

O'Kelly's story contained a number of incorrect statements in it, including the following: that Bellicose shared his room at the Watsamatta Hilton with his secretary, and that his contingent fees were higher than those of local attorneys. The article also intimated that Bellicose was not qualified to practice law in Indiana; in fact, although he was licensed in California, he probably could retain local counsel and/or appear pro hac vice in this case. Because of O'Kelly's reputation as a Bellicose authority, the Tattler did not check any of the facts in the story for accuracy, but printed it verbatim.

As a result of the Tattler story, Bellicose suffered great public humiliation, particularly since the story was subsequently picked up by the wire services and reported nationally. Even more

significantly, a number of the clients he had garnered for the
Union Halide suit sought other counsel, and he was able to
recruit no new clients for the lawsuit thereafter despite
continued efforts. Bellicose believed that the story had affected
his ability to attract and retain other clients as well.

You are a local attorney in Watsamatta. You have witnessed
all these events, and are frankly interested in some of the
action(s). Assess the various tort actions that might be pursued
as a result of the injuries that have been incurred by the
potential plaintiffs described in this fact pattern. Indicate, if
you can, the likelihood of success of these actions; if you
can't, indicate the facts you would need to know in order to make
such a determination.

Part I
Essays

1.
(45 minutes)

Super Sav is a grocery store in a decaying urban
neighborhood. Super Sav owns a lot next door to the building in
which the store itself is located on which parking for the cars
of customers is provided. In order to assure the safety of its
patrons, Super Sav constructed a six-foot chain-link fence around
the lot and installed floodlights. A loading dock and trash
dumpster are located on the lot.

Because neighbors behind the store had complained about the
glare of the lights, the noise of trucks unloading late at night,
and the smell of trash, the store's management had taken bulbs
out of the lights along the back fence, and moved the dumpster
from the back of the lot to the front. In moving the dumpster,
the trash company had broken the fence so that there was a 3' x
5' opening in the corner. Super Sav had been given a check for
$500 to repair the fence and signed a release absolving the trash
company from any further liability.

On the night of June 6, Katy Turpentine was shopping at
Super Sav after parking her car in the back row of the parking
lot. By the time she finished shopping, the lot was nearly empty
and no other customers were in the lot; nor were there any
security guards in the area. As she reached her car, she
experienced the touch of cold steel in the small of her back.
What she felt was a small handgun, popularly known as a Saturday
Night Special, manufactured by Lethal, Inc., held firmaly in the
hand of Wlad "The Impaler" Jaundice, a local contract killer who
had fallen on hard times since botching his last hit. Because it
was Saturday night, Turpentine knew she was in trouble. Wlad
grabbed her purse, shot her in the arm, jumped into Turpentine's
car and drove off.

As Wlad was making his getaway, he approached a manufacturing plant operated by duPoisont Chemical Co. A fog produced by emissions at the plant obscured Wlad's vision of the highway ahead. Because of the poor visibility, he could not see a van belonging to Dean's Furniture Rentals stopped in the road. Wlad hit the brakes but could not avoid slamming into the rear of Dean's truck, injuring both himself and the truck driver, Hal Kelp. In addition, both Wlad and Kelp developed a severe rash from chemicals in the fog.

A story about the entire incident, which appeared in The Tattler, the local newspaper, was noticed by D & B Financial Analysts. D & B reported the following in a newsletter circulated for a subscription fee to approximately 50 commercial lenders in the area:

### SUPER SAV FACES PROBLEMS

Super Sav Market on Main Street has been plagued by security problems, such as the one described in the June 7 Tattler (copy enclosed), and fearful customers appear to be staying away in droves. If Super Sav is unable to address these problems, the store may be forced to close its doors after 70 years in the business.

In fact, this mugging was the first incident of its kind and Super Sav records indicated that the adverse publicity had not hurt business. However, as a result of the D & B report, Super Sav was unable to obtain credit for funds to complete improvements to the parking lot and the store.

Discuss the possible tort actions presented in this fact pattern.

Alley

2.
(45 minutes)

Bill Badluck learned that a local gardening club was offering a prize of $200.00 to the community member with the nicest front lawn. Bill decided to enter the competition. He went to the local gardening supply shop ("Guady's"). He told Cal Clerk, an employee of the shop, that he was a novice at lawn care and asked her help in selecting appropriate tools, including an electric hedge trimmer. Cal suggested "Hedgers 100," manufactured by Hedgers, Inc. [For purposes of this exam, the electric hedge trimmer looked and worked exactly like a manual hedge trimmer, except that an electric current flowed into the tool through a long extension cord causing the blades to cross and cut.] There was an ON/OFF switch on one handle that controlled the flow of electricity. The operator needed only to guide the clippers. The clippers came in a box on which it was printed: "These electric hedge trimmers are easy to use and safe for beginning gardeners." Inside the box was a 6-page instruction booklet, which included the following statements:

Page 1    NEVER PUT HANDS OR FINGERS NEAR BLADES unless machine is disengaged.

Page 4    This tool is not a toy. Children should not be permitted to play with it.

Page 6    Guide clippers over hedges slowly, to prevent leaves from catching in the blades and jamming machine.

The "Hedgers 100" model was priced at $50.00. Bill looked at several larger hedge trimmers but rejected them as being too expensive. When Bill arrived home, he took the clippers out of the box and put the instructions away, unread.

Bill's neighbor Norris brought over a bag of fertilizer that he had purchased seven years before from Guady's, but had never used and gave it to Bill. The fertilizer, manufactured by Smelly Stuff, Inc., had the following label affixed to it:

This fertilizer contains chemicals and, thus, like all chemicals, should be treated with care. Always wear gloves when handling fertilizer as it may cause a reaction on skin exposed to it. The liability of Smelly Stuff for any loss due to product's use is limited to a refund of the purchase price.

Bill did not own gloves and decided not to purchase any.

Bill recruited his 13-year-old son Pete to trim the hedges while he spread fertilizer in the garden. All went well for the first 1/2 hour. However, a piece of shrubbery got stuck between the blades and caused the hedge trimmer to jam when Pete began to go faster. Pete reached in between the blades and dislodged the piece of hedge. The clippers immediately began to move and cut off part of Pete's finger. When Bill saw Pete was bleeding, he covered his face with his hands in anguish. He inadvertently inhaled some of the fertilizer that was on his hands, which caused extensive damage to his respiratory system. Bill developed serious respiratory problems, Pete lost a finger, the hedge trimmer jammed permanently, and Bill lost his opportunity to compete in the competition.

The Badlucks came to see you and asked you to represent them. In the course of pre-trial discovery, you have learned the following facts:

1.   On the larger and more expensive models of electric hedge trimmers manufactured by Hedgers, Inc., Hedgers has installed a device that causes the machine to return to the OFF position automatically whenever the blade jammed. Thus, in order to start the hedge clippers operating again, the operator must manually move the switch to the ON position again. Hedgers did not include the device on its "100" size as this model tends to jam quite frequently and this device would have to be replaced after every few uses at a cost of $25.00 per replacement.

2.   Smelly Stuff, Inc. has never received any notice that any consumer but Bill suffered a respiratory problem due to exposure to the fertilizer.

Against whom will you advise your clients to seek recovery? On what basis? For what losses will you seek recovery? What defenses do you anticipate the defendant(s) will raise? Evaluate your chances for success.

# APPENDIX F

More Short Answer Questions

## Sample Short Answer
## Exam Questions

Ten-year-old Bobby Scott was driving his daddy's snowmobile over the river and through the woods to pick up grandmother and bring her back for Thanksgiving dinner. He gets to grandmother's, and picks her up, but when he arrives home grandmother is nowhere to be found. The next day grandmother is found frozen in a snowbank. Discuss Bobby's potential tort liability.

Charles witnessed Diana run over Margaret with a car. Diana's operation of the vehicle appeared to be negligent. Charles ran to help Margaret. While assisting Margaret, Charles was struck by a car negligently driven by Andrew. In the confusion of the accident, a package Charles had set down when he went to the aid of Margaret was lost. May Charles recover from Diana for his injuries? For the loss of his package? From Andrew for either? If Charles recovers a judgment of $10,000 from Diana, and the jury determines that Diana and Andrew were equally responsible for Charles's loss, how much, if anything, may Diana recover from Andrew? If Andrew, at the accident scene, wrote Charles a check for $10,000.00, and Charles signed a note saying, "I, Charles, release Andrew for any future liability for my injuries. I do not release Diana. /s/Charles," will Charles still be able to recover from Diana? Is Diana relieved of liability if an insurance policy owned by Charles pays Charles $10,000.00 for his injuries? What if Charles and Diana are married? What if Charles and Andrew are brothers? What ever happened to Margaret? Explain your answers.

Mrs. Hapless and daughter Harriet were getting into their car when Roger Reckless drove his auto down the street at a high speed. Reckless avoided hitting Mrs. Hapless only because he turned sharply to the left and into a tree. Mrs. Hapless had her back to Reckless's automobile so she did not realize that he missed striking her by inches. However, she did see him crash into the roadside rotted tree owned by Gary Grumpy. The impact caused the tree to fall in the direction of Harriet. Mr. Hapless, who was still back at the house, heard Mrs. Hapless call out: "Harriet, the tree is going to hit you." Then he heard the sound of the tree contacting the ground. Mr. Hapless suffered a heart attack as a result. Mrs. Hapless fainted. Harriet Hapless escaped all physical injury, because she quickly ran out of the tree's path. However, she began biting her nails after this incident. Discuss the liability of the various parties to each other.

Roger Reckless immediately returned to the scene (see question 4) to give aid. Roger had a certificate stating that he was qualified to administer CPR. The certificate had expired, but Roger began to administer to Mr. Hapless anyway despite a state law that prohibited anyone from administering CPR without a valid certificate. Roger, who had been drinking beer all morning, at

first began to administer artificial resuscitation into Mr.
Hapless's ear, but soon realized his error and corrected his
conduct. Unfortunately, Mr. Hapless died. Bob Bumbling, a doctor,
was walking down the street when he saw Mrs. Hapless unconscious
on the sidewalk. He ran up to the home of Gary Grumpy and knocked
on the door. When Mr. Grumpy answered, Bumbling asked Grumpy to
please call an ambulance. Grumpy promised to do so, but as soon
as he shut the door, he returned to the football game he was
watching. Another neighbor did call an ambulance. Bumbling
continued his walk. Discuss the liability of the various parties
to each other.

4

SHORT ANSWER QUESTIONS

(ONE HOUR)

CAVEAT: DO NOT USE MORE THAN ONE BLUE BOOK PAGE SINGLE-SPACED OR
TWO BLUE BOOK PAGES DOUBLE-SPACED PER SHORT ANSWER!!!!

1.    D approaches A, with whom he has argued, and threatens him
with a gun, shouting loudly, "I'll kill you, you b------, if it's
the last thing I do!" D begins blasting, and A ducks for cover.
C, a child walking by, is struck by a bullet from D's gun, and
falls to the ground. B, the mother of C, witnesses the event and
experiences extreme emotional distress. A testifies that when D
began to shoot at him, D could see both B and C, but opened fire
anyway. May any or all of A, B, and C recover damages on the
basis of intentional tort theory?

2.    D, driving his automobile, negligently runs down P, breaking
his leg. While P is lying in the road, X drives by and also
strikes P, breaking his arm. When P arrives at the hospital, X-
rays determine that he has several cracked ribs, but it is not
clear which of the accidents caused the injury to the ribs,
although it is undisputed that one of them did. To what extent
are D and X liable to P?

3.    P was a passenger on D's ship, the "Palsgraf." The ship
leaves port, apparently in seaworthy condition, for a day cruise
in good weather conditions. The ship disappears without a trace.
Assuming that there is a survival statute, may P's survivors
succeed in an action against D? On what grounds?

4.    Who said the following:

    a.    "The risk reasonably to be perceived defines the duty
to be obeyed and the risk imports relation; it is risk to another
or to others within the range of apprehension."

    b.    "Due care is a duty imposed on each one of us to
protect society from unnecessary danger, not to protect A., B.,
or C. alone. . . . Unreasonable risk being taken, its
consequences are not confined to those who might probably be
hurt."

c. "[D]uty is a function of three variables: (1) The probability [P] that [the event will occur]; (2) The gravity of the resulting harm [L]; (3) The burden of adequate precautions [B] . . . in algebraic terms: liability depends on whether B is less than L multiplied by P."

How would each decide the following case? A is struck by D's negligently operated automobile. A is thrown at an odd angle through the air, and his body strikes the support for a scaffolding, causing it to collapse. P, a house painter working on the scaffolding, collapses with it, and is injured. P sues D.

5. P buys a television set at D's store. D's servant negligently leaves open the door on the loading dock. P, seeking directions to pick up his set, is told by X, another customer on his way out, "Turn left at the door to the loading dock." Actually, X meant to tell P to turn right. P, following X's directions, turns left, and falls through the door of the loading dock to the concrete below, cracking his skull. Will D be relieved of liability in a suit brought against him by P, because of X's instructions? Why or why not?

6. D is in the business of repossessing automobiles. He is sent to repossess a car at 425 Cardozo Court. He finds a car fitting the description of the auto to be repossessed across the street from 425. He takes the car, and discovers one hour later that it belongs to P, who lives at 426 Cardozo Court, across the street from 425. D returns the car. What action, if any, does P have against D? Will P prevail? Why or why not?

7. D is a manufacturer of automobiles. The 1984 Leymon, one of its products, contains a defective hood latch that comes loose at speeds in excess of 65 mph in one out of 20,000 cars. When this happens, the hood will fly up, obscuring the driver's ability to see. The defect was not discovered until 200,000 Leymons were sold and on the road. It would cost $50 per automobile to recall and replace the latches, but D takes no action to do so. P is injured while riding in X's new Leymon when the latch comes loose, the hood flies up, and X loses control of the car and hits a telephone pole. P's damages are estimated by his attorneys to be $300,000. May P recover from D? Why or why not?

8. D, who is a lawyer, enters into a fee agreement with P to represent P in a personal injury matter. The agreement contains the following clause: "P agrees that D shall take such steps as necessary to effectuate settlement of this matter." After negotiations with the other party, D recommends to P acceptance of a settlement offer of $10,000, which P accepts. Later, at a party, P tells X, another lawyer, about the case. X says, "I can't believe it; that case should never have been settled. A first year law student could have gotten a minimum of $50,000 in a jury trial." P checks with other lawyers, all of whom agree that the case should have gone to trial. Does P have any recourse against D? On what theory? Will he prevail?

9.   In the cases In re Polemis, Wagon Mound 1, and Wagon Mound 2, the British courts wrestled with the question of reasonably forseeable risks and consequences in cases where the damage that results may be different from the damage reasonably to be anticipated. What are the policy considerations underlying the rules that evolved from these cases? Do you agree with the position of the British courts? Why and why not?

10.   D, who is fourteen years old, mows lawns during the summer to earn money. He operates a riding tractor lawn mower in his work. One day, while mowing P's yard, D observes Wanda Kissya (a girl in D's class at school) walking by in a scanty and revealing outfit. Temporarily distracted, D fails to notice P, Jr., P's toddler son, in the path of the mower. Sparing the details, suffice it to say that P, Jr. is mowed and mulched. Is D responsible for P, Jr.'s death? What if P had been negligent in allowing P, Jr. out of the house while D was mowing?

11.   D invites P to come up to her place for a nightcap. P agrees. After one beer, P is still thirsty, and D directs him to the kitchen to get another beer. P gets the beer from the refrigerator and, while opening it, leans his hand against an exposed pipe. The pipe turns out to be an uninsulated hot water pipe, which D had been meaning to cover up, but had never gotten around to doing. P's hand is severely burned. Is D liable to P? What rationale?

SHORT ANSWER QUESTION
QUESTION THREE
( 20 minutes )

Marjorie Schoolgirl was driving without a valid driver's license at a speed of 39 miles per hour in a zone that had a legal limit of 35 miles per hour. Suddenly, Haddie Mayes darted out from between two cars parked on the right side of the street. She was struck by Marjorie's vehicle and severely injured. What would be the result if Haddie sued Marjorie for her injuries?

SHORT ANSWER QUESTION
QUESTION ONE

A city ordinance states: "It shall be a violation of the law for any person to use city property without the permission of the city." D and several friends used a parcel of land belonging to the city as a park without permission. P fell and was injured while walking in the park. P sued D, citing violation of the statute as the basis of civil liability. Will a court hold D liable, and why?

Part II
Short Answers
(Answer 3 out of 4)

1.
(15 minutes)

One of your clients, Dr. Hatchett, has come to see you for advice. His practice is limited to OB-GYN patients, and has been very successful. Unfortunately, he just received a notice from his malpractice insurance carrier increasing his annual premiums from $15,000.00 to $50,000.00. The letter from the company pointed out that although he had never been sued, doctors in his specialty faced a 70 percent chance of being sued for malpractice during their careers. Dr. Hatchett is outraged that his premiums should be so high in spite of his own unblemished record. He is considering canceling his insurance, and taking his chances. He is also interested in the recent articles about legislation that would modify the tort recovery system by limiting pain and suffering and punitive damage awards, forcing arbitration, placing a cap on attorney's fees, and providing for periodic payments of damage awards for the life of the victim. He would like you to advise him what he should do about the malpractice insurance, and about the impact of these alternative compensation systems on his practice, and his legal rights.

2.
(15 minutes)

The neighborhood children always teased Buster Brown's pet bull terrier. Over the July 4 holiday, they kept throwing firecrackers over the fence into the yard where the dog was kept. The terrified animal bolted through the gate, breaking it down, and rushed across the street where it seriously mauled little Brian Dailey who had not been throwing firecrackers (only) because he was attending a party for his aunt. Brown also kept a number of hogs on the premises, and these animals followed through the breach and stampeded Esta Clock's daisies, petunias, and other flora. Meanwhile, little Tommy Greed (who also was not one of the children throwing firecrackers) wandered into the yard, fell into the pond Brown had made to water his hogs, and drowned.

What tort actions may be brought? On what basis will plaintiffs argue for recovery? What defense might be presented by defendants?

3.
(15 minutes)

Larry Liar brought a silver teapot to an auction being conducted to raise money for a local charity [proceeds were to be split between charity and seller]. Liar told the auctioneer that the teapot had been crafted by Paul Revere, a famous eighteenth century silversmith. Indeed, although the teapot was heavily tarnished, the word "Revere" was visible. The teapot was set on display with other items for inspection by prospective bidders. At auction time, the auctioneer described the pot as "a genuine Revere." Ima Sucker, a collector of Paul Revere crafted silver, immediately recognized that the bidders and auctioneer did not appreciate the value of such a piece. He was the successful bidder, having offered $75.00, but he knew that it was worth at least twice that amount. Sucker was especially pleased as he now had a complete Revere tea service and the value of the entire set was $1,000.00 more than the value of the individual pieces. When Sucker began to polish the pot at home, he discovered that the name "Charlie" proceeded the word Revere. Research disclosed that Charlie Revere was a twentieth century insurance salesman for whom silversmithing was a hobby. The teapot's only value was its silver content of $50.00.

Does Sucker have any legal recourse against Liar? For what? Do you anticipate any problems?

4.
(15 minutes)

A Roman Catholic nun, Sister Candida, was depicted on a greeting card produced by California Dreamers, Inc., and sold throughout the United States. The card bore a black and white photograph of Sister Candida seated in a chair, with a caption, "It's all right if you kiss me." Inside the card, the caption added, "So long as you don't get in the habit."

California Dreamers had obtained the photograph when it purchased the portfolio of a deceased photographer, and assumed that this photo was of a model in nun's clothing. At no time did Sister Candida consent to publication of her picture.

When Sister Candida learned about the card from her niece in Iowa, she was extremely upset and sought the advice of an attorney. She considers the depiction to impute to her a vile and suggestive remark, and the words on the card to constitute filthy, seamy, and degrading verse.

Sister Candida comes to you for advice. She would like to know whether the publication of this card is actionable and whether she might succeed in a suit against California Dreamers, Inc. What is your advice?

[Questions 3 and 4 deal with problem B below]

### - B -

Annie B. Still brought her three-year-old daughter Vanna to the home of Ira Insurer when she came by to drop off her insurance premiums. Isador Insurer, the twelve-year-old son of Ira, was mowing the lawn using his father's lawn tractor. When Annie went inside, at Ira's invitation, for a cup of coffee, she left Vanna on the front steps. Vanna soon wandered onto the lawn, sat down and began to play. Unfortunately, Isador did not notice Vanna playing in the grass and in the course of mowing the lawn, he ran over her foot and seriously injured it.

3.  (15 minutes)   Discuss the potential liability of Ira for the injuries sustained by Vanna.

4.  (15 minutes)   Discuss the potential liability of Isador for the injuries sustained by Vanna.

[Questions 5, 6, and 7 deal with problem C below]

### - C -

M. B. McManymen owned a restaurant called the "MacAttack." Because she was one of the best customers of Fisch's Fish Market, Dave Fisch, the owner, allowed her into the area normally reserved for employees to inspect the fish. One day, while looking at fish, McManymen slipped and fell on a banana peel that was on the floor and fractured her left arm. This injury put an end to McManymen's aspirations of becoming a concert violinist. Several years later, McManymen was in an automobile accident. Because of the weakened condition of her left arm, it broke (although had the arm not been weakened by the prior fracture, it would not have broken).

5.  (15 minutes)   Discuss whether McManymen can recover from Fisch for negligence and, if so, for what injuries.

6.  (15 minutes)   Would your answer regarding Fisch's liability change if Fisch had told his employees, prior to McManymen's fall, that it was a violation of company policy to bring food onto the work floor?

7.  (15 minutes)   How would your answer regarding the extent of liability be changed if McManymen were (seven) 7 months pregnant at the time of the fall and the following day gave birth to a stillborn baby?

[Questions 8 and 9 deal with problem D below]

- D -

On April Fool's Day, Jack Jokes put on a bandit's mask, took the starter's pistol that he used when he officiated at track meets (loaded with blanks and incapable of firing bullets), and set out to trick his friends who were playing poker at the home of Garfield D. Katt. Jack burst into the kitchen, while pointing the pistol, and ordered the gamblers to put up their hands and hand over their money. Garfield, believing the robbery to be genuine, was so frightened that he fainted, fell, and died due to the concussion he sustained in the fall. Jack was secretly glad as he had never liked Garfield. Pattie Melt suspected the robber's identity and that the robbery was a practical joke, but was uncertain, so she cooperated. Jack took Pattie's money and that night wrote a note to Pattie telling her about the joke, that he had the money, and that it would be returned promptly.

8.   (15 minutes)   Discuss Jack's liability, if any, for Garfield's losses.

9.   (15 minutes)   Discuss Jack's liability, if any, for Pattie's losses.


[Questions 10, 11, 12 and 13 deal with problem E below]

- E -

Paul S. Graff was attacked by a gang of young hoodlums (who were members of a gang called Daley's Dogs) as he walked down the street. One of the assailants struck him with a tire iron, while two others held him. A fourth took Graff's wallet; the leader, Brian Daley, kept watch while the muggings took place. Graff, badly bruised but conscious, went to the Mother of Mercy Hospital to be checked out. Mark Thyme, the resident on duty, bandaged Graff's head and sent him home. Although Graff complained of some dizziness, Dr. Thyme did not conduct any special tests or order Graff to remain in the hospital for observation. The next day, Graff got up and, feeling better, went out to play touch football. During the game, while playing quarterback, Graff was tackled by his friend Willy "Icebox" Parry, who forgot that they were playing touch. Graff collapsed, and died the next day, although before he died he signed the following note: "In consideration of $10,000 paid to me, I release Icebox Parry from liability for my injuries in the football game. /s/Paul S. Graff." An autopsy disclosed that an artery in Graff's brain was congenitally weak; the artery was weakened further in the beating; it ruptured following the football injury, causing Graff's death.

10. (15 minutes)   May Graff's estate recover in tort against some or all of the gang members? On what theories? What defenses, if any, are available?

11. (15 minutes)   May Graff's estate recover in tort against Dr. Thyme? On what theories? What defenses, if any, are available?

12. (15 minutes)   May Graff's estate recover in tort against Parry? On what theories? What defenses, if any, are available?

13. (15 minutes)   Graff sued and obtained a judgment against Brian Daley's gang and Dr. Mark Thyme in the amount of $300,000. The jury found that the gang was 30 percent responsible, Dr. Thyme 30 percent responsible, Parry 30 percent responsible, and Graff 10 percent responsible. Dr. Thyme had liability insurance; Graff carried his own accident insurance, which will pay up to $200,000. The gang members were destitute, impecunious, and otherwise judgment-proof. Parry was independently wealthy. In a comparative negligence jurisdiction, who will be required to contribute to satisfy the judgment and what will each contribution be? What if the jurisdiction has not adopted comparative negligence? Explain your answers.

# Index

Courses, 19–22
civil procedure,
20–21
constitutional law, 21
contracts, 20
criminal law, 21
legal writing, 22
professional responsi
bility, 21–22
property, 20
selection of,
144–145. *See also*
Course selections.
torts, 19–20
Course selections,
144–145
bar review approach,
144
best method, 145
pragmatic considera
tions, 144
substantive basis, 144
Cramming, 77
Criminal law, 21
Culture of law school,
28–32
breaks, 30–31
competition, 31–32
rules and procedures,
28–30
socializing, 30–31
Curriculum, 19–22

**D**
Daily list, 124
Day school, 10
Diet, 133
Disposition of case, 49
Dissenting opinions, 49
Diverse students,
139–141
diversity students,
140
physically challenged
students, 141
second career stu
dents, 140–141
women, 139–140
Diversity students, 140
Drugs, 135–136
Due process concept,
29–30

**E**
Edwards, Ted, 130
Electronic databases, 75
Emanuel's (outlines),
65
Emotional involvement,
26–27
*Erie Railroad v.*
*Tompkins*, 21
Essay examinations,
80–81
more questions,
236–247
sample question,
81–83
Ethnic students, 140
Evening school, 10
Examinations
anxiety, 104–105
beforehand prepara
tion, 87
essay, 80–83,
236–247
evaluations, 112,
116–117
final, 17–19
instructions, reading
of, 87
IRAC, 95–97
kinds, 80–86
logic, 97–99. *See also*
Logic.
multiple-choice,
84–86
nature of, 86
ongoing study, role
of, 77–78
organization for,
88–95
practice questions
and answers, 80,
105–119
question, reading of,
87–88
"red herrings," 96
review for, 78–80.
*See also* Review for
exams.
short answer, 83–84,
248–257
stress, 77, 104–105.
*See also* Stress.

taking, 77–120
time management,
102–104. *See also*
Time management.
writing, 99–102. *See*
*also* Writing exami
nations.
Exercise, 133

**F**
Facts of case, 48
Falling behind, 18
Federal Rules of Civil
Procedure, 20
Final examinations,
17–19
first semester, 17
Financial aid, 126–127
Financial Aid Office,
127
Financial planning, 126
First classes, 12, 14
First year, after the,
142–151
Foreign study, 149–150
*Foster v. Preston Mill*
*Co.*, 200–202
Franklin, Marc,
175–176
*Freund v. DeBuse*,
231–235
Full-time students, 122,
127–128

**G**
*Garratt v. Dailey*,
34–42, 50, 59–60,
65
Gibson, T. J., 134–135
Gilbert Law Summaries
on Torts, 175–176
Gilbert's (outlines), 65
*Golden v. Amory*,
203–204
Grades, posting of, 18

**H**
Harvard Law School,
11
Help
assignments, 24–25
stress, 134–135